THE PENDENT SEMI-CIRCLE SKYPHOS

THE PENDENT SEMI-CIRCLE SKYPHOS

A study of its development and chronology and an
examination of it as evidence for
Euboean activity at Al Mina.

ROSALINDE KEARSLEY

Ellen Macnama

BULLETIN SUPPLEMENT 44
1989

University of London
Institute of Classical Studies

Published and distributed by
INSTITUTE OF CLASSICAL STUDIES
31–34 Gordon Square, London WC1H 0PY

S.B.N. 900587 58 X
I.S.S.N. 0076-0749

CONTENTS

ACKNOWLEDGEMENTS

This study was submitted in partial fulfilment of the requirements for the MA Honours degree at the University of Sydney in November 1979. I am greatly indebted to my supervisor, Dr J.-P. Descoeudres, both for his guidance during the major part of my research and also for his continued interest and assistance in the preparation of this manuscript. During the absence of Dr Descoeudres overseas during 1979, Associate Professor J.R. Green supervised the final preparation of the thesis and I am very grateful for this help and encouragement and in a more general sense for the benefit of his experience with the material from the excavations at Zagora.

I should also like to acknowledge my debt to the late Mr V.R.d'A. Desborough, who made available material from Lefkandi which was then unpublished and who gave generously of his time to discuss other relevant matters during my visit to Oxford in December 1976.

Thanks are due to many others also for their assistance in a variety of ways: Professor P. Amandry, Miss A. Andreiomenou, Dr M. Ballance, Dr P. Bikai, Dr A. Birchall, Professor J. Boardman, Dr R.T. Braidwood, Professor H.-G. Buchholz, Professor A. Cambitoglou, Dr H.W. Catling, Dr G. Chourmousiadis, Professor J.N. Coldstream, Mr B.F. Cook, Professor Paul Coubin, Mrs L. Gee, Professor A.J. Graham, Associate Professor B.F. Harris, Miss C. Harward, Professor J.B. Hennessy, Dr A.W. Johnston, Professor E.A. Judge, Miss M. Karras, Dr C. Krause, Professor D. Levi, Dr L. Marfoe, the late Dr A.W. McNicoll, Dr C. Mee, Dr P.R.S. Moorey, Mr E. Pentazos, Dr B. Philippaki, Mr M.R. Popham, the late Mrs I.K. Raubitschek, Mr D. Ridgway, Mrs K. Rhomiopoulou, Mrs E. Sakellarake, Mr K. Sheedy, Professor A.M. Snodgrass, Dr P. Themelis, Dr A. von Bothmer, Professor C.C. Vermeule, Dr G. Voza, Dr S. Wolff, Professor N. Yalouris, Mrs Ph. Zaphieropoulou. I wish also to express my special thanks to members of staff at the British School at Athens whose help during my visits in 1977 and 1978 facilitated my research on the pendent semicircle skyphos.

Pottery from Al Mina is published by kind permission of the Trustees of the British Museum, the Visitors of the Ashmolean Museum, Oxford, and the Managing Committee of the Museum of Classical Archaeology, Cambridge. Acknowledgement is also due to the Managing Committee of the British School at Athens for permission to publish pottery from Teke and other material in the Collection of the British School at Athens, to the Director of the Zagora Excavations and the Council of the Athens Archaeological Society for permission to include pottery from the Sydney University excavations at Zagora, and to the Fogg Museum, Harvard University, for permission to publish inv. 1953.116 from Cyprus.

Finally, I especially want to express my gratitude to my husband, Dr W. Kearsley, who made time to write the computer programme for the numerical analysis, and to Mr J.M. Murphy and Miss Margaret Packer of the Institute of Classical Studies for their helpfulness in dealing so patiently with difficulties created by our long-distance negotiations during the course of production, and to Miss Patricia Connolly for her hard work in typing the text itself.

November 1983
Macquarie University, Sydney

LIST OF FIGURES AND MAPS

Figures 6, 7, 10, 16–19, 24–30, 42 and 43 are reduced by 30%; figures 34–39 by 20%; figure 21(a-b) is 1:3; figures 40(c) and 41(a) are 1:1.5. The remaining drawings are to scale.

The profile drawings are by the author except for the following, for which grateful acknowledgement is made: Dr J.-P. Descoeudres - Figs. 3d; 11a-e; 12; 13; 14; 26; 40b, d; 41b; Associate Professor J.R. Green - Fig. 32a-c; Professor J.N. Coldstream - Fig. 21a, b.

Fig. 40(c) is drawn after W.A. Heurtley, "A Note on Fragments of Two Thessalian Protogeometric Vases found at Tell Abu Hawam", *QDAP* 4 (1934-1935) pl. LXXXVIII. Fig. 41(a) is drawn after R. Saidah, "Objets grecs d' époque géométrique découverts récemment sur le littoral libanais (à Khaldé près de Beyrouth)", *AAS* 21 (1971) Fig. a.

LIST OF PLATES

8 (a) Sydney Nicholson Museum 73.03 (*244*)

   (b) Thessaloniki 4714 Kalamaria (*85*)

   (c) Mykonos 755 Delos 16 (*54*)

   (d) Mykonos 752 Delos 6 (*44*)

9 (a) Oxford 1954.271/12 Al Mina (*14a*)

   (b) Oxford 1954.271/13 Al Mina (*14b*)

   (c) Oxford 1954.271/7 Al Mina: lekanis

   (d) Athens, British School, Lefkandi no no. (*165*)

The photographs are by the author except for Pl. 1(b) which is after D. Levi, "La Necropoli geometrica di Kardiani a Tinos", *ASAtene* 8-9 (1925-1926), fig. 28, and Pl. 8(a) which was made available by Professor A. Cambitoglou, Curator of the Nicholson Museum, Sydney.

LIST OF TABLES AND DIAGRAMS

ABBREVIATIONS

AA	Archäologischer Anzeiger
AAA	Archaiologika Analekta ex Athenon
AASOR	Annual of the American Schools of Oriental Research
ADeltChr	Archaiologikon Deltion. Meros B. Chronika
AE	Archaiologike Ephemeris
AJ	The Antiquaries Journal
AJA	American Journal of Archaeology
AmAnt	American Antiquity
ASAtene	Annuario della Scuola Archaeologica di Atene
AntK	Antike Kunst
ArchRep	Archaeological Reports
BABesch	Bulletin Antieke Beschaving
BASOR	Bulletin of the American Schools of Oriental Research
BCH	Bulletin de Correspondence Hellénique
BICS	Bulletin of the Institute of Classical Studies, University of London
BMB	Bulletin du Musée de Beyrouth
BSA	Annual of the British School at Athens
CAH	Cambridge Ancient History
CVA	Corpus Vasorum Antiquorum
Délos XV	C. Dugas and C. Rhomaios, *Exploration Archéologique de Délos* Vol. XV (Paris 1934).
Eretria V	J.-P. Descoeudres, "Die vorklassische Keramik aus dem Gebiet des Westtors" in *Eretria V* (Bern 1976) 13-58.
Eretria VI	J.-P. Descoeudres, "Euboeans in Australia: Some Observations on the Imitations of Corinthian Kotylai made in Eretria and found in Al Mina" in *Eretria VI* (Bern 1978) 7-19.
Ergon	To Ergon tes Archaiologikes Hetaireias
GGAPC	E. Gjerstad, *Greek Geometric and Archaic Pottery Found in Cyprus* (Stockholm 1977).
GGP	J.N. Coldstream, *Greek Geometric Pottery* (London 1968)
IEJ	Israel Exploration Journal
IstMitt	Istanbuler Mitteilungen

JHS	Journal of Hellenic Studies
Kition IV	J.N. Coldstream, "The Greek Geometric and Plain Archaic Imports", in *Excavations at Kition IV. The Non-Cypriote Pottery* (Nicosia 1981) 17-22.
Lefkandi I	M.R. Popham and L.H. Sackett (eds), *Lefkandi I*, Text and Plates, (London 1979, 1980).
Lefkandi 1968	M.R. Popham and L.H. Sackett, *Excavations at Lefkandi, Euboea, 1964-66*: a preliminary report (London 1968).
Marmariani	W.A. Heurtley and T.C. Skeat, "The Tholos Tombs of Marmáriane", *BSA* 31 (1930-31) 1-55.
NSc	Notizie degli Scavi
PGP	V.R. Desborough, *Greek Protogeometric Pottery* (Oxford 1952).
PGRT	N.M. Verdelis, *Ho Protogeometrikos Rhythmos tes Thessalias* (Athens 1958)
PPS	Proceedings of the Prehistoric Society
QDAP	Quarterly of the Department of Antiquities, Palestine
RBibl	Revue Biblique
RDAC	Report of the Department of Antiquities, Cyprus
SCE	Swedish Cyprus Expedition
Sukas I	P.J. Riis, *Sukas I. The North East sanctuary and the first settling of Greeks in Syria and Palestine* (Copenhagen 1970)
Sukas II	G. Ploug, *Sukas II. The Aegean, Corinthian and Eastern Greek Pottery and Terracottas* (Copenhagen 1973)
Vergina I	M. Andronikos, *Vergina I. To Nekrotapheion ton Tumbon* (Athens 1969)

MUSEUMS

Athens NM	National Museum, Athens
Boston	Museum of Fine Arts, Boston
Cambridge	Museum of Classical Archaeology, Cambridge
Copenhagen NM	National Museum, Copenhagen
London	British Museum, London
New York	Metropolitan Museum of Art, New York
Nicosia	The Cyprus Museum, Nicosia
Or. Inst.	Oriental Institute, Chicago
Oxford	Ashmolean Museum, Oxford

CHAPTER 1

INTRODUCTION

Al Mina lies at the mouth of the Orontes River on one of the few natural
harbours of the North Syrian coastline, from which there was also ready
access to the inland. Because its position allowed trade with the many
Aramaean cities scattered across the Amuq plain, and also with the
Assyrian empire further to the east, the site has increased greatly our
understanding of the revival of contacts between Greece and the world
of the Near East after the end of the Dark Ages. Excavated before the
Second World War, Al Mina even today constitutes our chief source of
information on Greek settlement in the East Mediterranean during the
Geometric period, although in recent years other sites of apparently
similar nature have been discovered.[1] It is through the medium of
such settlements that the exchanges which led to the appearance of
oriental motifs in Greek art of the eighth and seventh centuries must
have taken place and it is possible also that it was here that the Greeks
first assimilated the North Semitic alphabet before adapting it to their
own purposes.[2]

    The large amount of Greek pottery from Al Mina allows the ident-
ification of those city-states involved in the trade and indicates the
varying degree of their participation during the history of the site.
The pottery is also an indirect source of absolute dates for Greek
chronology, because of its association with North Syrian and Cypriot
wares found in historically datable contexts elsewhere in the Near East.
Al Mina's importance in both these respects has often been stressed
since Sir Leonard Woolley excavated the site in the 1930s.

    It is unfortunate therefore that publication of the material is still
limited. Apart from Woolley's own articles, which are of a preliminary
nature, only small selections of the Greek, Syrian and Cypriot pottery
have been made available.[3] As a result there has been considerable
discussion in recent years over the way in which the history of the site
should be reconstructed.[4] For example, at the time of excavation,
Woolley defined three main periods by reference to the architectural
changes. The two earliest levels (X-IX) were grouped closely together;

levels VIII and VII were seen as successive phases of the second period; and VI-V were linked in the same way.[5]   Since then, however, Woolley's view of the stratigraphy has often been ignored in favour of two-period division, with the break coming after level VII.[6]

These differences are due to disagreement with Woolley's absolute chronology for the early levels in favour of a higher chronology based on dates for the associated local pottery.[7]   This tendency to rely on the Near Eastern material for chronological purposes was felt necessary because the identification of much of the Greek pottery from the early levels was for a long time uncertain, and its chronological relationship to the Attic or Corinthian series unclear.   However, since the initial publication of the Greek pottery by Martin Robertson,[8] the increased knowledge of individual East Greek and Cycladic fabrics has not only enabled more precise classification of the origin of much of the pottery, but also produced a more reliable chronological framework from the purely Greek point of view.[9]

But even now there remain some problems of fabric identification, especially in the case of the fragments of the pendent semicircle skyphos.[10] Generally interpreted as being the earliest pottery at the site, [11] the psc skyphos fragments are of particular relevance for the date of its foundation and for identification of the Greek city-states involved at that time.   This is especially so as virtually all the rest of the pottery from levels IX and VIII is of Late Geometric style, and those who accept 825 for the foundation of Al Mina (according to the Near Eastern dating) rely on the pendent semicircle skyphos fragments and the very small amount of other pottery that may date before 750 to fill the gap between the late ninth century and the date of the bulk of the material.[12] The origin and chronology of the psc skyphos is therefore of particular importance for Al Mina, and the re-examination of the class as a whole is an essential preliminary step to solving the confusion which surrounds those skyphoi found in the Near East.[13]

In 1952 Desborough published the first systematic study of the pendent semicircle skyphos.[14]   The material available at the time was subdivided into three wide-ranging groups: Type A, with a low slightly outcurving lip; Type B, with a high more-or-less overhanging lip; and Type C, with a lip that is swept back in a concave curve.   These groups were considered to be classified in order of development, since Desborough believed that the low-footed skyphos evolved from the Attic Protogeometric skyphos, and that Type A was the closest of the three groups to this prototype.   The link with Attic Protogeometric on the one hand, and the distribution of the psc skyphoi on the other, suggested a further two-fold conclusion to Desborough:

    a.   that the shape, together with its characteristic decoration, should have appeared about the time of the end of Attic Proto-geometric or very soon afterwards; and

    b.   that the initial development of the skyphos took place in the Northern Cycladic area.

Desborough viewed the central geographical position of the Northern Cyclades as a cultural bridge by which the pendent semicircle skyphos spread north not only to Thessaly but also to Skyros and Macedonia. (Because of uncertainty about the local pottery sequence in these districts, however, he was unable to suggest a date for this latter event.)

The existence of Type C, consisting mainly of skyphoi from the Northern Cyclades and the East Mediterranean, was placed predominantly in the first half of the eighth century, since it appeared that those found in the East (which Desborough believed to be imports from the Northern Cyclades) could not be earlier than the end of the ninth century. Although in 1952 Desborough felt that a lower limit of *ca.*750 for the group was implied by the absence of the skyphos from the Western Greek colonies founded during the second half of the eighth century, fragments discovered in Near Eastern contexts of about 700 later led him to extend the lower range of this Type.[15]

Writing 16 years after Desborough, Coldstream put forward several new proposals.[16] He raised the date for the beginning of the Type C lip to 850 BC, but maintained 750 as a definite lower limit. In this way Type C was allotted a lifetime of a whole century, while Types A and B together were given 50 years. In addition, Coldstream suggested that the Type C lip was usually associated with a shallow body, in contrast to Types A and B in which a deep bowl was more frequently found. Thus he introduced the concept of a change in body profile as a chronological factor, in addition to the acknowledged changes in lip type. And he linked this with the move from a pronounced foot to an almost flat base, combining both these features with some stylistic analysis of the decoration to identify certain skyphoi as degenerate and late within the class as a whole.

But in his publication of pottery from the Euboean site of Lefkandi, Desborough reiterated his initial opinion that the shape and size of the lip was of overwhelming importance in classifying pendent semicircle skyphoi, specifically rejecting the view that variations in the body or the foot could provide valuable typological information.[17] Meanwhile the chronological implication of the absence of the pendent semicircle skyphos from the Greek colonies in the West had been stressed particularly in 1957 by Boardman in the context of a more general study of Euboea and Euboean pottery.[18] He suggested also that the entire life of the class must be limited to a period of approximately half a century, from 800-750, although he felt a few examples might belong slightly earlier.

Boardman's chief concern with the pendent semicircle skyphos, however, lay in the possibility that examples found in the Near East may have originated in Euboea and thus reflect the island's overseas activity in the first half of the eighth century. Not long afterwards, excavations at Lefkandi, Eretria and Pithecusae produced abundant evidence to support his emphasis on Euboean involvement in foreign trade during the eighth century.[19] Indeed the site of Lefkandi has proved the key site for analysis of the pendent semicircle skyphos class. The British School excavations have demonstrated conclusively that it was a major manufacturer of this class over a very long period.[20] Nevertheless no direct connection has yet been proved between the pendent semicircle skyphoi discovered in Euboea and those from Al Mina or from the Near East generally.[21] It is surprising therefore that the largely speculative character of Boardman's arguments has been almost forgotten and that the problems surrounding both the origin and the chronology of the pendent semicircle skyphos are frequently presumed to have been solved by the more general knowledge of Euboean activities supplied by Lefkandi and Eretria.

In fact, far from solving the problems, the recent information has added a new dimension. For example, it has been pointed out that there are difficulties in the assumption that the pendent semicircle skyphoi at Al Mina are Euboean and date to the first half of the eighth century if Euboean activity in the West during the same period is felt to be reflected almost exclusively not by the pendent semicircle skyphos but by the chevron skyphos.[22] A further problem lies in the fact that while pendent semicircle skyphoi in the East Mediterranean occur in Late Geometric contexts,[23] it appears that Lefkandi and Eretria were scarcely producing the skyphos at that time.[24]

Questions such as these determined the direction of this study. Although the original plan had been to study the geometric pottery of Al Mina in order to explore further its connections with the various Greek city-states, and particularly with Euboea, it was clear after a survey of the literature that the most intractable problems were connected closely with the pendent semicircle skyphos. Only when the origin and chronology of this skyphos were better understood could any substantial progress be made towards a more accurate appreciation of the history of Al Mina in the eighth century. This study attempts to trace the evolution of the pendent semicircle skyphos as a shape, and to plot its distribution in space. The catalogue which forms Chapter 2 includes all documented occurrences of pendent semicircle skyphoi known at the time of writing. The material is arranged alphabetically by site, and reference to catalogue entries is made in the text by an italic number following the name of a skyphos, for example, Se"Seklo *200*. The distribution map (Figure 33, p. 72) contains all sites in the catalogue, with the addition of one site where a fragment which may possibly be from a pendent semicircle skyphos has been found. Because it is impossible to be sure if it actually is a skyphos, however, it is not included in the catalogue. (Reference to publication of this fragment is given in brackets following its entry in the accompanying key to the map.)

As far as possible, the material in the catalogue was personally inspected.[25] All measurements are in centimetres, and brackets around a measurement indicate that it has been scaled off from a photograph or drawing. Where possible, the fabric and paint colour of skyphoi and fragments are classified according to the *Revised Soil Color Chart.*[26]

CHAPTER 2

C A T A L O G U E

The catalogue which follows is arranged in alphabetical order according
to site, with these exceptions:

(a) when the provenance of a skyphos is known only in general terms,
     the catalogue entry has been made under the name of the region
     or district, for example, Cyprus *33,* Thessaly *223;*

(b) skyphoi of which the provenance is completely unknown are grouped
     at the very end of the catalogue;

(c) there is some ambiguity about the provenance of the 16 items listed
     under Delos. These skyphoi were among the material moved to
     Rheneia when Delos was purified in the fifth century BC and al-
     though actually excavated on Rheneia, since their origin and the
     circumstances of the removal of the material are reliably known,
     it seemed preferable to include them under Delos rather than Rheneia.
     On the other hand, the six Rheneia skyphoi are from local graves
     and there is no reason to suppose that their history was at all
     unusual;

(d) occasionally, especially in the case of material from an island site,
     the entry appears in the catalogue under the name of the island
     rather than that of the individual site, for example, Ikaria *82.*

(e) The standard decorative scheme for both sides of the pendent
     semicircle skyphos is: Exterior: paint on the lip, handles, lower
     body and foot. Reserved zone between the handles containing two
     sets of pendent semicircles. Interior: painted, frequently with a
     reserved band on the lip and sometimes with a reserved dot on the
     floor. Any variations are noted specifically in the catalogue.

While it is true that the catalogue aims to be a complete list of pendent
semicircle skyphoi, some wall fragments known to the author have been
excluded deliberately. These are from sites such as Al mina and Tell
Tayinat from which other and more informative material has been found

and the wall fragments added nothing new (these fragments have, however, been used in the analysis of fabric presented in Chapter 3). On the other hand, wall fragments are included from sites which would not otherwise be represented in the catalogue (for example, Tabbat al Hammam). Since the overall distribution of the pendent semicircle skyphos is of some importance in itself, it was felt that these sites should be listed in spite of the limited nature of the evidence.

The amount of detail supplied for each item varies considerably, reflecting the availability of information. In the case of published skyphoi there is sometimes no more than a report that pendent semicircle skyphos fragments have been found at a site, while on other occasions more detail is given. The same situation applies to some unpublished skyphoi. Whatever information is available has been included.

As far as possible I have tried to be consistent in the spelling of Greek place names. However, some inconsistencies have intentionally been retained where there are well-established forms. In general the spelling conforms with that found in Coldstream's *GGP* and *Geometric Greece* (Chapter 1, nn.3, 10).

To make the catalogue more accessible for general purposes, a list of sites grouped according to broad geographical areas follows:

ATTICA

Athens

CENTRAL GREECE

Delphi
Kalapodhi
Orchomenos
Vranesi Copaidos

CRETE

Gortyn
Knossos
Phaistos
Teke

CYCLADES

Antiparos
Delos
Donousa
Kardiani
Naxos
Paros
Rheneia
Tenos
Zagora

CYPRUS

Amathous
Cyprus
Kazaphani
Kition
Kouklia
Palekythro
Salamis
Soli

EAST GREECE

Antissa
Cos
Didyma
Emporio
Iasos
Ikaria
Larisa
Methymna
Phocaea
Sardis
Smyrna
Troy
Vati

EUBOEA

Chalcis
Eretria
Kerinthos
Lefkandi

NEAR EAST

Al Mina
Askalon
Hama
Ibn Hani
Khaldeh
Mersin
Nineveh
Ras el Bassit
Sarepta
Tabbat al Hammam
Tell Abu Hawam
Tell Halaf
Tell Judaidah
Tell Sukas
Tell Tayinat
Tyre

NORTH AEGEAN

Skyros
Thasos

MACEDONIA

Chauchitsa
Kalamaria
Karabournaki
Saratse
Vergina

THESSALY

Arg. Tirnavou
Iolcos
Kapakli
Larisa
Marmariani
Nea Ionia
Phthiotic Thebes
Pteleon
Sesklo
Thessaly

WEST MEDITERRANEAN

Veii
Villasmundo

AL MINA

Not all the sherds from Al Mina have a context. When it is known, it is through the indication painted on each fragment by the excavation team. Only ten of the 18 fragments in the catalogue are so marked, and of the wall and shoulder fragments not listed in the catalogue two of the six have a context. One (Oxford 1954.271/17) is marked level IX and the other (1954.271/9), level VIII. See too, *PGP*, 181-5; *GGP*, 157, 310-312; *Sukas I* 142-52.

1.   **London** 1955.4-22.2, rim fr.   *Fig 40(a)*

   Ht 4.4; **w** 5.5; **diam lip** (reconstructed) 13; **th** 0.3-0.4. Pinkish brown clay (5YR 7/4) with small white inclusions and a few flecks of mica. Brownish slip (7.5YR 7/5). Paint outside mainly brown-black (5YR 2/1) with dark brown arcs (5YR 4/2), streaky. Inside, brownish red (2.5YR 5/6). **Lip**, not offset, ht 1.5. **Ext:** seven arcs of one set. Blobs of paint have been dropped on the surface. **Int:** painted except for reserved line on lip. **Context:** level IX.

   Robertson (Chapter 1 n.3) 3, Fig. 1a; Descoeudres/Kearsley (Chapter 1 n.3) 49 n.135, Fig. 44.

2.   **London** 1955.4-22.3, rim fr.   *Fig 1(a)*

   Ht 4.0; **w** 7.8; **diam lip** (reconstructed) 12; **th** 0.2-0.3. Pinkish brown clay (5YR 7/4) with small white inclusions and a few flecks of mica. Brownish, pale orange slip (7.5YR 7/5). Brownish red paint (2.5YR 5/6) on both outside and inside. **Lip**, offset, ht 1.3. **Ext:** two sets of seven semicircles, intersecting.[1] **Int:** painted except for thin reserved line on lip. **Context:** unknown.

   Robertson (Chapter 1 n.3) 3, Fig. 1b; *PGP* pl.26,2 below: *Sukas I* 147, Fig. 48f.

3.   **London** 1955.4-22.4, rim fr.   *Fig 41(c)*

   Ht 3.0; **w** 5.9; **diam lip** (reconstructed) 12; **th** 0.4-0.3. Pinkish brown clay (5YR 7/4) with small white inclusions. Brownish slip (7.5YR 7/4). Paint outside is dark brown (5YR 3/2) on the lip and brownish red (2.5YR 5/8) on the arcs, streaky. Inside, dull reddish brown paint (2.5YR 4/4). **Lip**, offset, ht 1.3. **Ext:** two sets of seven semicircles, intersecting. **Int:** painted except for wide reserved line on lip. **Context:** levels IX-VIII.

   Robertson (Chapter 1 n.3) 3, Fig. 1c; *PGP* pl.26,3; *Sukas I* 147, Fig. 48g.

4.   **London** 1955.4-22.5, rim fr.   *Fig 1(b)*

   Ht 4.7; **w** 11.5; **diam lip** (reconstructed) 13; **th** 0.4.   Pale orange clay (7.5YR 7/6) with a few dark inclusions and some mica.   Light brown slip (7.5YR 6/4).   Brown-black paint (5YR 3/1) on both outside and inside.   **Lip**, offset, ht 1.5. **Ext**: two sets of six semicircles, intersecting. **Int**: painted except for thin reserved line on lip. **Context**: unknown.

   Robertson (Chapter 1 n.3) 3, Fig. 1d.

5.   **London** 1955.4-22.8, shoulder fr.   *Fig 1(c)*

   Ht 4.4; **w** 4.4; **th** 0.4-0.3.   Pinkish brown clay (5YR 7/4) with small white inclusions and a few flecks of mica.   Brownish slip (7.5YR 7/4).   Bright reddish brown paint (5YR 4/6) on both outside and inside. **Lip**, offset, preserved ht 1.6. **Ext**: six arcs of one set. **Int**: painted except for reserved band on lip. **Context**: unknown.

   Robertson (Chapter 1 n.3) 3, Fig. 1g.

6.   **London** 1955.4-22.9   *Fig 1(d)*

   Ht (complete) 5.9; **w** 9; **diam lip** (reconstructed) 13; **th** 0.4-0.3. Pinkish brown clay (5YR 7/4) with one or two flecks of mica.   Light yellow-orange (7.5YR 8/4) slip.   Paint outside mainly dull reddish brown (5YR 4/3) with arcs lighter (5YR 5/4); inside, streaky dark brown (5YR 3/2).   **Lip**, not offset, ht 1.0.   Almost flat base. **Ext**: five arcs of one set. **Int**: painted except for thin reserved line on lip. **Context**: unknown.

   Robertson (Chapter 1 n.3) 3, Fig, 1h; *PGP* pl.26,1; *Sukas 1* 147, Fig. 48a; Descoeudres/Kearsley (Chapter 1 n.3) 51 n.141, Fig. 50.

7.   **London** 1955.4-22.10, base fr.   *Fig 1(e)*

   Ht 5.9; **w** 12; **diam base** 6.1; **th** 0.3-5.   Pale orange clay (7.5YR 7/6) with some small white and dark inclusions and a little mica.   Light brown slip (7.5YR 6/4).   Mainly dark brown paint (5YR 4/2) on both outside and inside.   Almost flat base. **Ext**: two sets, probably of six semicircles, intersecting. **Int**: painted streaky. **Context**: unknown.

   Robertson (Chapter 1 n.3) 3, Fig. 1j.

8.   **London** 1955.4-22.11, rim fr.   *Fig 41(d)*

   Ht 4.0; **w** 3.5; **diam lip** (reconstructed) 11; **th** 0.3-4.   Pinkish brown clay (5YR 7/4) with a few white inclusions.   Surface, brownish pale orange (7.5YR 7/5).   Mainly brownish-black paint (5YR 2/1) on both outside and inside; arcs reddish brown (5YR 5/7).   **Lip**, offset, ht 1.1 **Ext**: five arcs of one set and two of the other, intersecting. **Int**: painted except for narrow reserved band on lip. **Context**: levels IX-VIII.

   Robertson (Chapter 1 n.3) 3, Fig. 1k; *PGP* pl.26,2 above; *Sukas I* 147, Fig. 48d; Descoeudres/Kearsley (Chapter 1 n.3) 49 n.135, Fig.48.

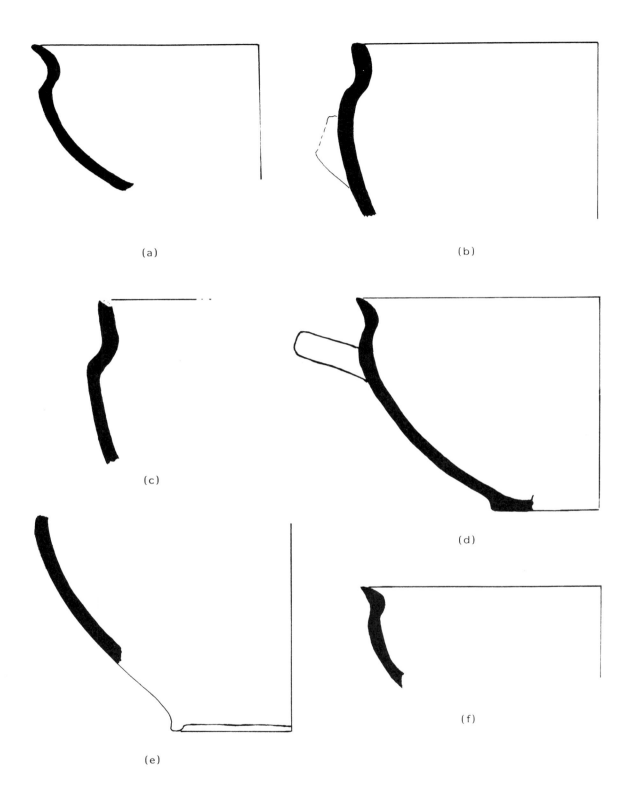

Fig. 1 Al Mina (a) London 1955.4-22.3 (*2*); (b) London 1955.4-22.5 (*4*);
(c) London 1955.4-22.8 (*5*); (d) London 1955.4-22.9 (*6*);
(e) London 1955.4-22.10 (*7*); (f) Oxford 1954.271/10 (*10*).

9.   Oxford 1954.271/1, rim fr.   *Fig 41(e)*

Ht 2.4; w 3.4; **diam lip** (reconstructed) 14; **th** 0.3. Dark pinkish brown clay (5YR 6/3) with small white inclusions. Light brown slip (7.5YR 6/4). Black paint on both outside and inside. **Lip**, offset, ht 1.0. **Ext**: four arcs of one set. **Int**: painted except for reserved band on edge of lip. **Context**: levels IX–VIII.

Popham *at al.* (Chapter 1 n.3) 152, Fig. 1,10; pl.14,10.

10.   Oxford 1954.271/10, rim fr.   *Fig 1(f)*

Ht 2.8; w 3.2; **diam lip** (reconstructed) 13; **th** 0.3. Light pinkish brown clay (5YR 7/3) with a few dark inclusions. Dark yellow-beige slip (10YR 8/4). Mainly reddish brown to bright reddish brown paint (5YR 5-4/8) on the outside and the inside. **Lip**, not offset, ht 1.0. **Ext**: six arcs of one set. **Int**: painted except for reserved band on edge of lip. **Context**: unknown.

Descoeudres/Kearsley (Chapter 1 n.3) 51 n.141, Fig. 51.

11.   Oxford 1954.271/4, rim fr.   *Fig 2(a)*

Ht 3.1; w 6.5; **diam lip** (reconstructed) 12; **th** 0.3. Greyish brown clay (5YR 6/2) with light brown slip (7.5YR 6/4). Mainly brownish black paint (5YR 2/1) on both inside and outside. Arcs, light reddish brown paint (5YR 5/4). **Lip**, offset, ht 1.3. **Ext**: five arcs of one set. **Int**: painted except for a reserved band on the edge of the lip, very streaky. **Context**: unknown.

Popham *et al.* (Chapter 1 n.3) 152, Fig. 1,1; pl.14,1.

12.   Oxford 1954.271/5, rim fr.   *Fig 41(f)*

Ht 2.5; w 4; **diam lip** (reconstructed) 12; **th** 0.3. Pinkish brown clay (5YR 7/4) with brownish slip (7.5YR 7/4). Brownish black paint (5YR 2/1) on both inside and outside, with some arcs reddish brown (5YR 5/6). **Lip**, offset, ht 1.2. **Ext**: four arcs of one set and two of the other, intersecting. **Int**: painted except for thin reserved band on edge of lip, streaky. **Context**: level VIII.

Popham *et al.* (Chapter 1 n.3) 152, Fig. 1,3; pl.14,3; Descoeudres/ Kearsley (Chapter 1 n.3) 49 n.135, Fig. 49; Gjerstad (Chapter 1 n.3) 116.

13(a).   Oxford 1954.271/2, rim fr.   *Fig 2(b)*

Ht 2.2; w 4.2; **diam lip** (reconstructed) 13; **th** 0.3. Light pinkish brown clay (5YR 7/3) with small dark and white inclusions. Pinkish brown slip (5YR 7/4). Dark brown paint (5YR 3/2) on both inside and outside. **Lip**, offset, ht 1.0. **Ext**: part of one set of seven semicircles. **Int**: painted except for reserved band on lip. **Context**: levels IX–VIII.

Popham *et al.* (Chapter 1 n.3) 152, Fig. 1,4; pl.14,4.

13(b). Oxford 1954.271/3, rim fr. [2]   *Fig 2(c)*

Ht 1.6; **w** 3.2; **diam lip** (reconstructed) 13; **th** 0.3. Pinkish brown clay (5YR 7/4) with small white inclusions. Light brown slip (7.5YR 6/4). Brownish black paint (5YR 2/1) on both inside and outside. Lip, offset, ht 1.0. **Ext**: three arcs of one set, streaky. **Int**: painted except for reserved band on edge of lip. **Context**: levels IX–VIII.

Popham *et al.* (Chapter 1 n.3) 152, Fig. 1,9; pl.14,9;

14(a). Oxford 1954.271/12, rim fr. [3]   *Fig 2(d), Pl.9(a)*

Ht 3.7; **w** 3.7; **diam lip** (reconstructed) 11; **th** 0.3. Pale pink clay (2.5YR 7/3) with cream yellow slip (7.5YR 8/3). Mainly brownish black paint (5YR 3/1) on both inside and outside. **Lip**, offset, ht 1.5. **Ext**: five arcs of one set and seven of the other, intersecting. **Int**: painted except for a reserved band on the edge of the lip. **Context**: level VIII.

Popham *et al.* (Chapter 1 n.3) 152, Fig.1,6–7; pl.14,6; Gjerstad (Chapter 1 n.3) 116.

14(b). Oxford 1954.271/13, rim fr.   *Fig 2(e), Pl.9(b)*

Ht c.3.6; **w** 4; **diam lip**?; **th** 0.3. Dark pink clay (2.5YR 6/3) with cream yellow slip (7.5YR 8/3). Brownish black paint (5YR 3/1) on both inside and outside. **Lip**, offset, ht 1.5. **Ext**: part of one set of seven semicircles, very smeared. A small section of the framing stroke on the right. **Int**: painted except for reserved band on edge of lip. **Context**: level VIII.

Popham *et al.* (Chapter 1 n.3) 152, Fig. 1,6–7; pl.14,7.

15.   Oxford 1954.271/6, rim fr.   *Fig 41(g)*

Ht 4.5; **w** 4.5; **diam lip** (reconstructed) 12; **th** 0.3–4. Pinkish brown clay (5YR 7/4) with brownish slip (7.5YR 7/4). Brownish red paint (2.5YR 5/6) on both inside and outside. **Lip**, offset, ht 1.0. **Ext**: part of one set of seven semicircles and the glaze below. **Int**: painted except for reserved band on edge of lip. **Context**: levels IX–VIII.

Popham *et al.* (Chapter 1 n.3) 152, Fig. 1,5; pl.14,5; Descoeudres/ Kearsley (Chapter 1 n.3) 49 n.135, Fig. 46.

16.   Oxford 1954.271/16, rim fr.   *Fig 2(f)*

Ht 2.7; **w** 4.7; **diam lip** (reconstructed) 15; **th** 0.3. Pinkish orange clay (2.5YR 7/6) with small white inclusions. Light beige slip (10YR 7/3). Dark brown (5YR 4/2) to reddish brown (5YR 5/6) paint on the outside and yellowish brown (10YR 5/6) on the inside. **Lip**, not offset, ht 1.5. **Ext**: five arcs of one set. **Int**: painted except for reserved band on edge of lip. **Context**: unknown.

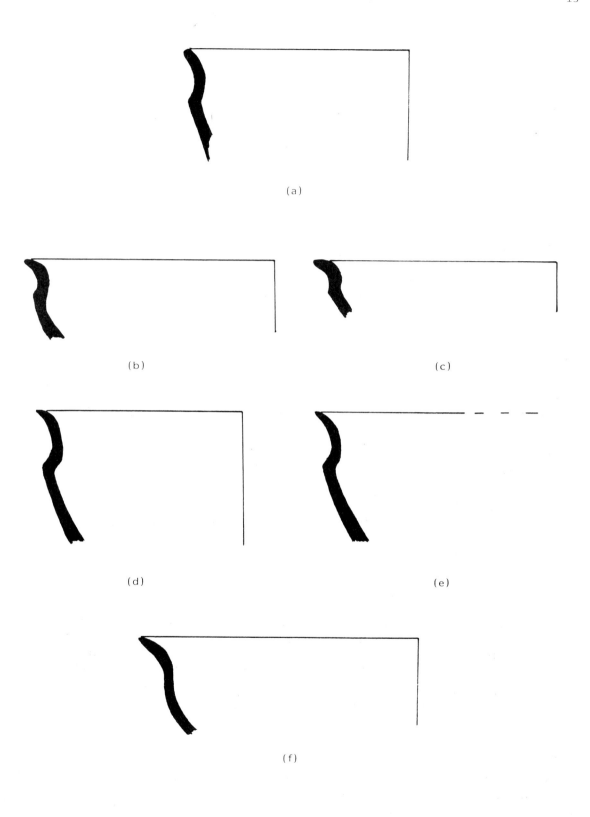

Fig. 2   Al Mina   (a) Oxford 1954.271/4 (*11*);   (b) Oxford 1954.271/2 (*13a*);
(c) Oxford 1954.271/3 (*13b*);   (d) Oxford 1954.271/12 (*14a*);
(e) Oxford 1954.271/13 (*14b*);   (f) Oxford 1954.271/16 (*16*).

Popham *et al.* (Chapter 1 n.3) 152, Fig. 1,2; pl.14,2; Descoeudres/ Kearsley (Chapter 1 n.3) 51 n.143.

(For rim fragment, Oxford 1954.271/7, see pl.9(c) and Chapter 7 n.39 below.)

AMATHOUS

17/1.　　Limassol, Amathous no number.

Ht 9.6; **diam lip** 14.5; **diam base** (6.0). **Lip**, offset, ht (1.5); **foot**, ht (0.6). **Ext**: two sets of ten semicircles, intersecting. **Int**: painted except for reserved band on lip and dot on floor. **Context**: tomb 334, containing pottery of Cypro-Geometric III and Cypro-Archaic I. Also an Attic or Atticising skyphos of the Middle Geometric I period (850-800).

V. Karageorghis, "Chronique des fouilles à Chypre en 1981", *BCH* 106 (1982) 692-4, Fig. 26. (The title is reversed with Fig. 25).

17/2.　　Limassol, Amathous 77.1261.27, rim fragment with part of the handle.

Fine clay of rather orange appearance, with inclusions. Black paint. **Ext**: only one set of ten semicircles preserved. **Context**: Area A, tomb NW.194.I - mixed deposit of Late Geometric to Roman date.

P. Aupert, "Rapport sur les travaux de la mission de l'école française à Amathonte en 1977", *BCH* 102 (1978) 956-959, Fig. 33. Descoeudres/Kearsley (Chapter 1 n.3) 49 n.134.

In this tomb, four other fragments of pendent semicircle skyphoi were found: 77.1261.23 and 77.1261.42, both with complete profile and handle; 77.1261.29, rim and handle fragment; 77.1257.52, rim only. The paint varies from black to brown or reddish brown (Aupert, *BCH* 102 [1978] 958).

18.　　Limassol, Amathous no number.

Ht 9.0; **diam lip** 14.0. **Lip** swept back with a concave profile. Substantial ring foot. **Ext**: two sets of nine semicircles, intersecting. **Int**: painted except for reserved band on lip. **Context**: tomb 321 containing material from Cypro-Geometric III to Cypro-Archaic I (800-600).

V. Karageorghis, "Chronique des fouilles à Chypre en 1980", *BCH* 105 (1981) 1019 Fig. 123.

19.　　Limassol, Amathous no number.

Ht 14.5, **diam lip** 21.5. Fabric, Cypriot Bichrome III. **Lip**, offset; conical **foot**. **Ext**: two sets of eleven semicircles, not intersecting. Reserved band on lip and reserved bands on lower body. **Context**: as *18*.

V. Karageorghis, *BCH* 105 (1981) 1019 Fig. 124.

ANTIPAROS

20.   **Paros** (?), rim fr.

       Ht 6.0; **w** 3.5. Reddish brown, fairly fine clay with fine mica. Light brown paint. **Lip,** offset, ht (2.0). **Ext:** nine arcs of one set. **Int:** painted. **Context:** unstratified.

       G. Bakalakis, "Aus den Grotten in Antiparos und Paros", *AA* 84 (1969) 130 Fig. 4:1 and 131 Fig. 5:1.

ANTISSA

21.   Several fragments with concentric circles or semicircles, at least two of which probably belong to pendent semicircle skyphoi. From inside and below a structure of the tenth-eighth centuries.

       W. Lamb, "Antissa", *BSA* 32 (1931-1932) 45, 47, Fig. 9a,c.

ARGYROPOULI TIRNAVOU

22.   **Volos K3022** (Arg.Tirn. 1964, tholos III)   *Fig 35(b), Pl.3(b)*

       Ht 9.7; **diam lip** 15.1; **diam base** 6.2; **th** 0.5. Pinkish brown clay (5YR 7/4), very hard. Brownish orange slip (5YR 6/6). Black paint on both inside and outside. **Lip,** offset, ht 1.8; **foot,** ht 0.5. **Ext:** two sets of 12 semicircles, intersecting. **Int:** painted except for broad reserved band on lip. **Context:** according to the museum inventory, from the tholos tomb.

ASINE

See Catalogue Appendix (p.191).

ASKALON

23.   A pendent semicircle skyphos fragment from Askalon is reported by R.W. Hamilton, "Excavations at Tell Abu Hawam", *QDAP* 4 (1934-5) 24, and said to be of identical ware to the fragment at Tell Abu Hawam.

       PGP 181; *Sukas I* 142 n.569.

ATHENS

24.   Two rim fragments were found in an undated context in the Kerameikos at Athens and are published in W. Kraiker and K. Kübler, *Die Nekropolen des 12 bis 10 Jahrhunderts, Kerameikos I* (Berlin 1939) 124 n.1, pl 38. See *PGP* 169, 189, where Desborough reported that he was unable to find these two sherds some years later.

CHALCIS

25.   **Athens, British School, rim fr.** [4]   *Fig 3(a)*

Ht 1.5; w 2.2; **diam lip** (reconstructed) ca.10; **th** 0.3-4. Light pinkish brown clay (5YR 8/3) with a few dark inclusions. Brownish red paint (2.5YR 5/6) on the outside and dull reddish brown (2.5YR 4/4) on the inside. **Lip, offset, ht 1.0. Ext:** four arcs of one set. **Int:** painted except for reserved band on edge of lip. **Context:** unknown.

Boardman (Chapter 1 n.3 1957) 2 pl.1(a), 1; Popham *et al.* (Chapter 1, n.3) 152 n.5. Three wall fragments are also illustrated in Boardman, pl.1(a), 2, 4, 5.

26.   **Athens, British School, rim fr.**   *Fig 3(b)*

Ht 4.3; w 4.5; **diam lip** (reconstructed) 15; **th** 0.4. Cream yellow clay (7.5YR 8/3). Light (10R 5/6) to very dark (10R 3/4) red paint on the outside, and bright orange red (10R 5/8) on the inside. **Lip, offset,** ht 2.0. **Ext:** five arcs of one set. **Int:** painted on edge of lip and below. In between, three thin bands and four wide reserved strips. **Context:** unknown.

27.   **Athens, British School, rim fr.**   *Fig 3(c)*

Ht 3.0; **w** 2.7; **diam lip** ?; **th** 0.3-4. Yellow orange clay (7.5YR 8/6) with some mica and small white inclusions. Black paint on both inside and outside. **Lip, not offset, ht 1.2. Ext:** six arcs of one set. **Int:** painted. **Context:** unknown.

28.   **Chalcis, no number, rim fr.**

Ht 3.4; **w** 4.2; **diam lip** (reconstructed) 18; **th** 0.3. Light red clay (2.5YR 6/7), very well-levigated and hard-fired. Light brown (6-7.5YR 6/5-6) surface. Brownish red (10R 4/4) to dark brown (10R 3/1) paint. **Lip, offset, ht** (1.3). **Ext:** ten arcs of one set. **Int:** painted except for reserved line on top of lip. **Context:** a well containing material mainly of the second half of the seventh century but with some Late Geometric, Classical and Hellenistic sherds also. (A few fragments were published in A. Andreiomenou, "Chalkis", *ADeltChr* 16 [1960] pl.132.)

29.   **Chalcis, no number, rim fr.**   *Fig 3(d)*

Ht 5.1; w 7.5; **diam lip** (reconstructed) ca.15; **th** 0.4. Clay and paint as above. **Lip, not offset, ht** ca.2.3. **Ext:** part of one set of seven semicircles and, on the right-hand side of the arcs, part of a cross-hatched lozenge. Towards the bottom of the lip, a thin reserved band. **Int:** painted except for reserved line on top of lip. **Context:** unstratified.

A. Andreiomenou "Chalkis" *ADeltChr* 16 (1960) pl.132γ.

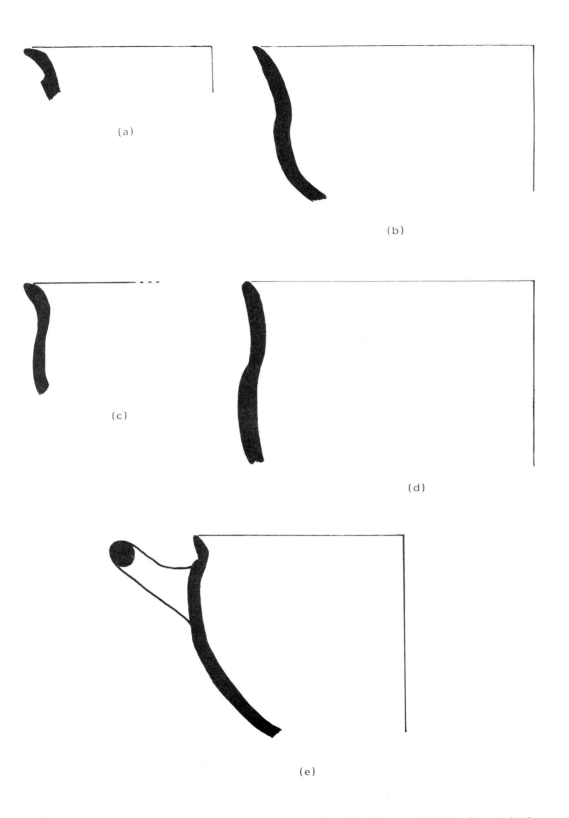

Fig. 3 Chalcis   (a) Athens, British School (*25*);   (b) Athens, British School (*26*);
(c) Athens, British School (*27*);   (d) Chalcis no no. (*29*);
(e) Chalcis 1385 (*30*).

30.   Chalcis 1385, rim fr. [5]   *Fig 3(e)*

Ht (complete) 6.7; **diam lip** (reconstructed) 11.5; **diam base** (3.5);
th 0.3.   Light yellow orange (2.5YR 8/4) clay, well levigated with a few
specks of mica.   Brownish (7.5YR 7/4) surface.   Black paint on both
inside and outside. **Lip,** offset, ht 0.9. **Foot** ht (0.4). **Ext:** two sets
of seven semicircles, intersecting. **Int:** painted except for thin reserved
band on edge of lip. **Context:** unstratified.

A. Andreiomenou, "Nea Lampsakos", *ADeltChr* 16 (1960) 150;
Andreiomenou "Ereunai kai Tychaia Heuremata en te Polei kai te Eparchia,
Chalkidos" *ADeltChr* 27 (1972) 182 pl.66 α. *GGP* 152-4.

See also Catalogue Appendix (p.192).

CHAUCHITSA

31.   **Thessaloniki** 4647.   *Fig 34(c), Pl.2(a-b)*

Ht 10.0; **diam lip** 13.5-12.5; **diam base** 5.7; **th** 0.3. Orange clay
(5YR 7/6), very micaceous and rather soft.   The paint ranges from
purplish brown (2.5YR 4/2) to brown (5YR 6/4) and brownish red (2.5YR
5/6) on both inside and outside. **Lip,** not offset, but slight ridge at
shoulder, ht 2.3. **Foot** ht 0.5. **Ext:** two sets of seven semicircles, just
intersecting, on one side only.   Handle zone on other side is empty.
The paint on the lower part of the skyphos is very faded, but seems to
be put on in two broad bands with reserved strip between. **Int:** painted.
Context: tomb, date of associated local pottery uncertain.   But see
Coldstream (Chapter 1, n.10) 106 n.66.

S. Casson, "Excavations in Macedonia II", *BSA* 26 (1923-24, 1924-
25) 10, Fig. 3; *PGP* 190-191.

CLAZOMENAE

See Catalogue Appendix (p.192).

COS

32.   An unpublished skyphos was seen by Desborough in the Cos
Museum.   According to him (*PGP* 185-6) it is similar in shape to Cyprus
33 and dates to the early ninth century.   Coldstream identifies this
skyphos as a Cycladic import from Seraglio Grave 27 and dates it to
local MG I, second half of the ninth century (*GGP* 267).   (For general
discussion of the Seraglio cemetery, see Desborough, *The Greek Dark
Ages* [London 1972] 172-178.)

See also Catalogue Appendix (p.192).

CYPRUS

33.   **Boston 72.76.**   *Fig 39(b)*

Ht 8.9-9.1; **diam lip** 13.5-14.0; **diam base** 5.6; **th** 0.4. Light yellow orange clay (7.5YR 3/4), hard-fired. Pinkish beige slip (7.5YR 7/3). Mainly black paint, except for the arcs which are reddish brown (5YR 5/6). **Lip**, offset, ht 1.1. **Foot** ht 0.9. **Ext:** two sets of seven semicircles, intersecting. **Int:** painted except for reserved circle in centre (diam 1-1.5) and reserved line on lip. **Context:** unknown.

A. Fairbanks, *Catalogue of Greek and Etruscan Vases. I, Museum of Fine Arts* (Boston 1928) pl.XVI 225; *PGP* 181-5; H.W. Catling, "A Pendent Semicircle Skyphos from Cyprus and a Cypriot Imitation", *RDAC* (1973) 181 no. 9; *GGAPC* 24 n. 22; pl.I,14.

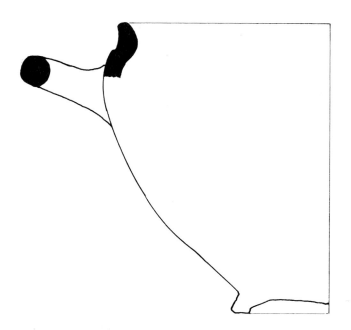

Fig. 4 Cyprus. Cambridge (Mass.), Fogg 1953.116 (*34*)

34.   **Cambridge (Mass.), Fogg 1953.116.**   *Fig 4*

Ht 8.0; **diam lip** 11.7-12.2; **diam base** 5.3; **th** 0.4. Pinkish orange clay (2.5YR 7/6), hard-fired. Pale orange slip (7.5YR 7/4-6). Black to brownish red (2.5YR 5/6) on both outside and inside. **Lip**, offset, ht 0.8. **Foot** ht 0.6. **Ext:** two sets of nine semicircles, intersecting. **Int:** painted except for reserved band on lip and small circle in centre (diam 2-2.5). **Context:** unknown.

G.M.A. Hanfmann, "On some Eastern Greek wares found at Tarsus", in S. Weinberg (ed.), *Studies Presented to Hetty Goldman* (New York 1956) 179 Fig. 16; Catling *RDAC* (1973) 181 no. 13; *GGAPC* 24 n.22.

35. New York 74.51.589.[6]

Ht 8.5; diam lip (12.8); diam base (5.7). Paint is dark brown except for the arcs which are reddish brown. **Lip**, offset, ht (1.0); **foot** ht (0.8). **Ext**: two sets of ten semicircles, intersecting. **Int**: painted except for reserved band on lip. **Context**: unknown.

J.L. Myres, *Handbook of the Cesnola Collection of Antiquities from Cyprus. The Metropolitan Museum of Art* (New York 1914) 289 no. 1710; G.M.A. Richter, *The Metropolitan Museum of Art. Handbook of the Greek collection* (Cambridge Mass. 1953) pl.16f; *PGP* 181-185; Catling, *RDAC* (1973) 180 no. 7; *GGAPC* 24 n.22, pl.I,10.

36. New York 74.51.592.

Ht 7.6; diam lip (12.5); diam base (4.6). Hard, light-coloured clay. Reddish paint all over except for a few patches of black. **Lip**, offset, ht (0.8); **foot** ht (0.8). **Ext**: two sets of seven semicircles, intersecting. **Int**: painted, except for reserved line on lip. **Context**: unknown.

J.L. Myres, *Handbook* 289 no. 1711; *PGP* 181-5; Catling *RDAC* (1973) 181 no. 8; *GGAPC* 24 n.22, pl.I,11.

37. Stanford University, (Palo Alto, California) 799 (3677). [7]

Ht 8.2; diam lip 13.8; diam base (6.3). Pink-red clay. Brownish paint except for the arcs which are orange-brown. **Lip**, offset, ht (1.0); **foot** ht (0.8). **Ext**: two sets of ten semicircles, intersecting. **Int**: painted except for narrow band on lip. **Context**: possibly from either Alambra or Dali.

L.P. di Cesnola, *Descriptive Atlas of the Cesnola Collection of Cypriote Antiquities,* Vol II (New York 1894) pl.CXLVI no.1085; Catling, *RDAC* (1973) 181 no. 10.

38. Nicosia 1979/XII-8/1.

Ht 9.5; diam lip 16.0. **Lip**, offset, short and flaring. Substantial ring **foot**. **Ext**: two sets of 13 semicircles, intersecting. **Context**: unknown.

V. Karageorghis, "Chronique des fouilles à Chypre en 1979. 1. Musée de Chypre (Nicosie)", *BCH* 104 (1980) 763 Fig. 7; K. Nicolaou, "Archaeology in Cyprus, 1976-80", *ArchRep* (1980-81) 59.

39. Formerly Wellcome Foundation R1936/1108 (now University of Newcastle-upon-Tyne 686).[8]

Lip offset and swept back. Substantial ring **foot**. **Ext**: two sets of nine semicircles, intersecting. **Context**: unknown.

40.   **Nicosia C74.**

Lip offset and swept back.   Substantial ring **foot**. **Ext**: two sets of nine semicircles, intersecting. **Context**: unknown.

Dunbabin (Chapter 1 n.6) 72 Appendix A; Catling *RDAC* (1973) 181 no. 12; *GGAPC* 24 n.22; pl.II,1.

41.   **Nicosia B711**

Lip offset, short and flaring. **Ext**: two sets, probably of 12 semicircles, intersecting.

PGP 181, pl.25,C; Catling *RDAC* (1973) 181 no. 11; *GGAPC* 24 n.22, pl.I,13.

See also Catalogue Appendix (p.192).

DELOS

As stated in the preface to the catalogue, the 16 items listed here are some of that material removed from Delos and buried on Rheneia by the Athenians in the fifth century BC when Delos was purified. Although all the skyphoi are extensively restored with complete profiles, in some cases there appears to be nothing preserved on which the shape or size of the foot could have been based.   Such skyphoi are here classified only as rim fragment. *PGP* 153-5, 186-9.

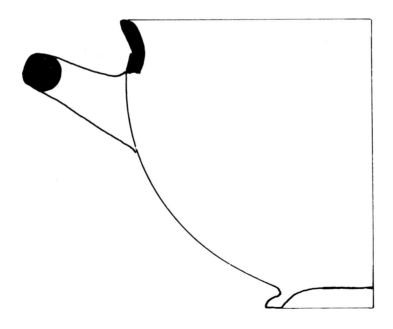

Fig. 5 Delos 4. Mykonos 733 (42)

42.   **Mykonos** 733.   *Fig 5*

Ht 7.9; **diam lip** 13.4; **diam base** 5.8; **th** 0.4. Yellow orange clay (7.5YR 8/6) with orange slip (5YR 7/6). Mainly black paint with patches of brownish red (2.5YR 5/8). **Lip**, offset, ht 1.2; **foot** ht 0.6. **Ext**: two sets of seven semicircles, not intersecting. **Int**: painted except for reserved band on lip. **Context**: Delos purification trench, Rheneia. Mixed burials.

Délos XV pl. XXVI, no. 4.

43.   **Mykonos** 736.

Ht 7.5; **diam lip** 10.5; **diam base** 5.5; **th** 0.4. Yellow orange clay (7.5YR 8/6) with yellowish brown slip (7.5YR 6/6-8). Mainly black paint. **Lip**, offset, ht 1.2; **foot** ht 0.7. **Ext**: two sets of eight semicircles, intersecting. **Context**: as last.

Délos XV pl. XXVI, no. 5.

44.   **Mykonos** 752.   *Fig 6, Pl.8(d)*

Ht 7.8; **diam lip** 12.5; **diam base** 5.5; **th** 0.4. Yellow orange clay (7.5YR 8/6) with brownish orange slip (5YR 6/6). Black paint with brownish-red arcs (2.5YR 5/6). **Lip**, offset, ht 1.0; **foot** ht 0.7. **Ext**: two sets of nine semicircles, intersecting. **Int**: painted, except for reserved band on lip. **Context**: as *42*.

Délos XV pl.XXVI, no. 6.

45.   **Mykonos** 753.   *Fig 39(d)*

Ht 7.5; **diam lip** 12.6; **diam base** 5.0; **th** 0.3. Yellow orange clay (7.5YR 8/6) with light brown slip (7.5YR 6/4). Mainly black paint. **Lip**, offset, ht 0.8; **foot** ht 0.6. **Ext**: two sets of ten semicircles, intersecting. **Int**: painted except for reserved band on lip. **Context**: as *42*.

Délos XV pl.XXVI, no. 7.

46.   **Mykonos** 756.   *Fig 38(c)*

Ht 8.4; **diam lip** 13.0; **diam base** 5.3; **th** 0.4. Pale orange clay (7.5YR 7/6) with a very few traces of slip. Mainly black paint with patches of brownish orange (5YR 6/6). **Lip**, offset, ht 1.1; **foot** ht 0.7. **Ext**: two sets of ten semicircles, intersecting. **Int**: painted except for reserved band on lip and reserved circle in centre. **Context**: as *42*.

Délos XV pl.XXVI, no. 8; Descoeudres/Kearsley (Chapter 1, n.3) 44 n.120, Fig. 41.

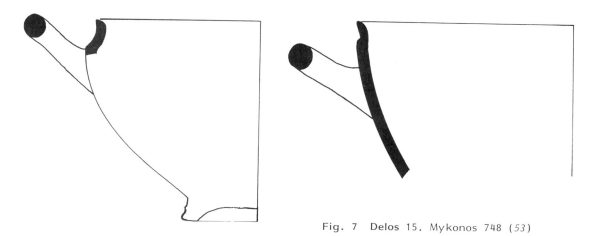

Fig. 7 Delos 15. Mykonos 748 (*53*)

Fig. 6 Delos 6. Mykonos 752 (*44*)

47.   **Mykonos** 867, rim fr.

Diam lip (reconstructed) 13.2. Yellow orange clay (7.5YR 8/6)
with light dull brown slip (7.5YR 6/3). Black paint. **Lip**, offset,
ht 1.2. **Ext**: two sets of seven semicircles, intersecting. **Context**: as *42*.

Délos XV pl. XXVI, no. 9.

48.   **Mykonos** 959.   *Fig 38(d)*

Ht 7.3; **diam lip** 13.0; **diam base** 5.1; **th** 0.3. Light yellow
orange clay (7.5YR 8/4), hard-fired with small white inclusions. Brownish
slip (7.5YR 7/4). Mainly black paint, but some dull reddish brown
(2.5YR 4/4-6). **Lip**, offset, ht 0.8; **foot** ht 0.6. **Ext**: two sets of eight
semicircles, intersecting. **Int**: painted except for reserved band on lip.
Context: as *42*.

Délos XV pl. XXVI, no. 10.

49.   **Mykonos** 737.

Ht 7.5; **diam lip** 13.5; **diam base** 5.5; **th** 0.4. Light yellow
orange clay (7.5YR 8/4) with brown slip (5YR 6/3). Mainly black paint.
Lip, offset, ht 0.9; **foot** ht 0.6. **Ext**: two sets of ten semicircles, intersecting. **Int**: traces of paint. **Context**: as *42*.

Délos XV pl. XXVI, no. 11.

50.   **Mykonos** 734, rim fr.

     Diam lip (reconstructed) 13.0; **th** 0.4. Yellow orange clay (7.5YR 8-7/6). Mainly black paint. **Lip,** offset, ht 1.2. **Ext:** two sets of twelve semicircles, intersecting. **Int:** painted except for reserved band on lip. **Context:** as *42.*

Délos XV pl. XXVI, no. 12.

51.   **Mykonos** 739, rim fr.

     Diam lip (reconstructed) 12.1; **th** 0.4. Pinkish orange clay (2.5YR 7/6). Mainly black paint, brownish red (2.5YR 5/8) in patches. **Lip,** offset, ht 1.4. **Ext:** two sets of eight semicircles, intersecting. **Int:** painted except for reserved band on lip. **Context:** as *42.*

Délos XV pl. XXVI, no. 13.

52.   **Mykonos** 742, rim fr.

     Diam lip (reconstructed) 13.3. Cream-yellow clay (7.5YR 8/3) with yellowish brown slip (7.5YR 6/6). Mainly black paint, brownish red in patches (2.5YR 5/8). **Lip,** offset, ht 1.2. **Ext:** six arcs from each of two sets, intersecting. **Context:** as *42.*

Délos XV pl. XXVI, no. 14.

53.   **Mykonos** 748. rim fr.   *Fig 7*

     Diam lip (reconstructed) 16.4; **th** 0.4. Pinkish brown clay (5YR 7/4) with a few discoloured traces of slip. Black paint. **Lip,** offset, ht 0.8. **Ext:** two sets of nine semicircles, intersecting. **Int:** painted except for reserved band on lip. **Context:** as *42.*

Délos XV pl. XXVI, no. 15.

54.   **Mykonos** 755.   *Fig 38(a), Pl.8(c)*

     Ht 9.8; **diam lip** 16.5-17.2; **diam base** 6.5; **th** 0.5. Light yellow orange clay (7.5YR 8/4) with light brown slip (7.5YR 6/4). Black paint with reddish brown (5YR 4/6) arcs. **Lip,** offset, ht 1.2; **foot** ht 0.9. **Ext:** two sets of ten semicircles, intersecting. **Int:** painted. **Context:** as *42.*

Délos XV pl. XXVI, no. 16.

55.   **Mykonos** 1416, rim fr.

     Diam lip (reconstructed) 13.2; **th** 0.4. Yellow orange clay (7.5YR 8/6) with brownish slip (7.5YR 7/4). Black paint. **Lip,** offset, ht 1.1. **Ext:** three arcs of one set. **Int:** painted. **Context:** as *42.*

Délos XV pl. XXVI, no. 17.

56.　**Mykonos** 754, rim fr.　　　　　　　　　　　　*Fig 8*

　　Diam lip (reconstructed) 16.0; **th** 0.4-0.5.　Light yellow orange clay (7.5YR 8/4) with a few specks of mica and light dull brown slip (7.5YR 6/3).　Black paint.　**Lip**, offset, ht 1.9.　**Ext**: two sets of five semicircles, not intersecting.　**Int**: painted.　**Context**: as *42*.

　　Délos XV pl. XXVI, no. 18.

57.　**Mykonos** 745.　　　　　　　　　　　　　　*Fig 9*

　　Ht 10.5; **diam lip** 16.6; **diam base** 5.9; **th** 0.5.　Light yellow orange clay (7.5YR 8/4) with brownish orange slip (5YR 6/6).　Mainly black paint, bright reddish brown (5YR 4/6) on the arcs.　**Lip**, offset, ht 1.9; **foot** ht 0.5.　**Ext**: two sets of eight semicircles, intersecting.　**Int**: painted, except for reserved band on lip.　**Context**: as *42*.

　　Délos XV pl. XXVI, no. 19.

　　Several other fragments have been found actually on Delos.　Some are from settlement material: See F. Poulsen and C. Dugas, "Vases archaiques de Délos", *BCH* 35 (1911) 360, Figs. 16, 17, from west of the Artemision; H. Gallet de Santerre and J. Tréheux, "Rapport sur le dépôt égéen et géométrique de l'Artémision à Délos", *BCH* 71-72 (1947-48) 245 (republished in H. Gallet de Santerre, *Délos primitive et archaique* [Paris 1958] 213 n.3, pl.29).

DELPHI

58.　**Delphi** 5909.　　　　　　　　　　　　*Fig 34(a), Pl.1(c)*

　　Ht 12.0; **diam lip** 15.7-16.4; **diam base** 6.5; **th** 0.4.　Light dull brown clay (7.5YR 6/3) with dull brown slip (7.5YR 5/3).　Brownish-black paint (5YR 3/1), turning to brownish orange (5YR 6/6) in patches.　**Lip**, not offset but a slight ridge at point where lip joins body, ht 2.0; **foot** ht 0.4.　**Ext**: two sets of seven semicircles, not intersecting and containing in the centre an hour-glass motif.　**Int**: painted except for reserved band on lip.　**Context**: mixed, settlement NE of the Temple of Apollo (*PGP* 190-2, 199-200).

　　Descoeudres/Kearsley (Chapter 1 n.3) 44 n.117, Fig. 38.

59.　**Delphi** 1957, rim fr.　　　　　　　　　　　*Fig 10(a)*

　　Ht 3.4; **w** 5.7; **diam lip** (reconstructed) 15.0; **th** 0.4.　Pinkish brown clay (5YR 7/4) with brown orange slip (5YR 6/6) and some white inclusions.　Dark reddish brown paint (2.5YR 4/6) on exterior and dull pink (10R 6/4) on the inside.　**Lip**, offset, ht 1.2.　**Ext**: eight arcs of one set.　**Int**: painted.　**Context**: settlement, unstratified.

　　L. Lerat, "Fouilles à Delphes, à l'est du grand sanctuaire", *BCH* 85 (1961) 355, Fig. 40.

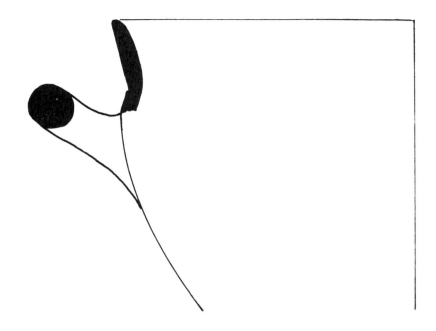

Fig. 8   Delos 18. Mykonos 754 (*56*)

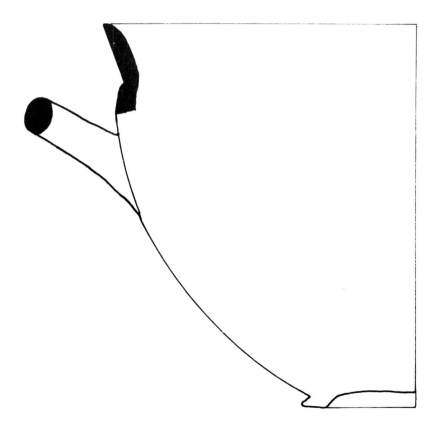

Fig. 9   Delos 19. Mykonos 745 (*57*)

60.   **Delphi** no number, rim fr.   *Fig 10(b)*

Ht 5.0; **w** 5.5; **diam lip** (reconstructed) 15.0; **th** 0.3-4. Cream-yellow clay (7.5YR 8/3) with dark pinkish brown slip (5YR 6/3) and some white inclusions. Black paint. **Lip**, offset, ht 1.9. **Ext**: 11 arcs of one set. **Int**: painted except for reserved band on lip. **Context**: unknown.

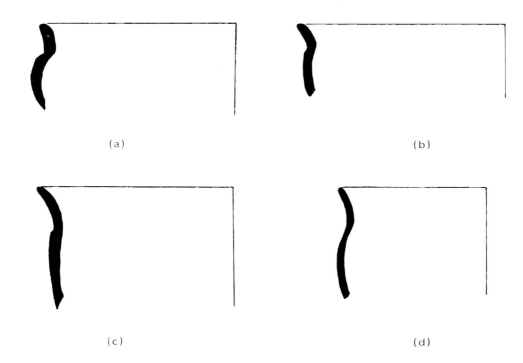

(a)   (b)

(c)   (d)

Fig. 10 Delphi. (a) Delphi 1957 (*59*); (b) Delphi no no. (*60*);
(c) Delphi no no. (*61*); (d) Delphi no no. (*63*).

61.   **Delphi** no number, rim fr.   *Fig 10(c)*

Ht 3.0; **w** 3.7; **diam lip** (reconstructed) 16.0; **th** 0.4. Orange clay (5YR 7/6) with brown slip (5YR 6/4). Mainly black paint, with dark brown arcs (5YR 4/2) outside; inside, dull reddish brown (2.5YR 4/4). **Lip**, offset, ht 1.0. **Ext**: ten arcs of one set. **Int**: painted except for reserved band on edge of lip. **Context**: unknown.

62.   **Delphi** no number, rim fr.

Ht 6.6; **w** 8.0; **diam lip** 16.0; **th** 0.5. Light pinkish brown clay (5YR 7/3) with black core, rather soft fabric. Small white inclusions. Black paint on both inside and outside. **Lip**, offset, ht 1.0. **Ext**: only one set of nine semicircles preserved. **Int**: painted except for reserved band on lip. **Context**: unknown.

63.   **Delphi** no number, rim fr.   *Fig 10(d)*

Ht 4.5; **w** 5.0; **diam lip** ?; **th** 0.3.   Yellow orange clay (7.5YR 8/6) with grey core and white inclusions. Brownish orange slip (5YR 6/6). **Lip**, no offset, ht 1.4. **Ext**: eight arcs of one set. **Int**: painted, except for reserved band on edge of lip. **Context**: unknown.

64.   **Delphi** no number. A rim fragment with one set of six intersecting semicircles from the excavation of deposits around the east and west facades of the Temple of Apollo in 1892-1901. P. Perdrizet, *Fouilles de Delphes*. V (Paris 1908) 17 Fig. 74; *PGP* 190.

In the storeroom at Delphi were four other rim fragments which duplicated the above in shape, together with five shoulder fragments and seven wall fragments. *64* could not be found.

DIDYMA

65.   A rim fragment is published in K. Tuchelt, "Didyma 1969/70", *Ist.Mitt* 21 (1971) 59, pl.3, no.9.

DONOUSA

66.   A skyphos, **ht.** 14.5; **diam lip** 19.5-20.0. Details of decoration are not clear from the photograph, but there are at least ten semicircles in each set and no intersection. **Context**: next to a wall adjoining a geometric structure.

Ph.Zapheiropoulou, "Apo ton Geometrikon Synoikismon tes Donouses", *AAA* 6 (1973) 256-259, Fig.3; J.-P. Michaud, "Chronique des fouilles en Grece en 1973", *BCH* 98 (1974) 695, Fig. 272; Zapheiropoulou, "Donousa", *ADeltChr* 28 (1973) 544-547, pl.508b.

EMPORIO

67.   **Chios**, Emporio 157, rim fr.

Diam lip c. 20.0. Pink clay with self slip. Brown, streaky paint. **Lip**, offset, ht 2.2. **Ext**: two sets of six semicircles, intersecting. **Context**: associated with material of late eighth century or early seventh.

J. Boardman, *Excavations in Chios, 1952-1955, Greek Emporio* (London 1967) 118, Fig. 72 and pl. 30.

ERETRIA

68.   Eretria FK E/8 B640, rim fr. [9]   *Fig 11(a)*

Ht 3.2; w 3.6; diam lip (reconstructed) 12.0; th 0.3. Light red clay (3.5YR 6/6) with reddish-yellow surface (6.5YR 6/6). No slip or mica. Red paint. **Lip**, offset, ht 1.4. **Ext**: four arcs of one set. **Context**: Temple of Apollo. Late Geometric I-II deposit.

69.   Eretria FK E/8 B650, rim fr.   *Fig 11(b)*

Ht 3.9; w 4.6; **diam lip** (reconstructed) 11.0; **th** 0.3. Brownish-pink clay (7.5YR 5-7/5) with yellow-brown surface (9YR 7/4-6). No slip or mica. **Lip**, offset, ht 1.2. **Ext**: seven arcs of one set. Streaky paint. **Context**: as last.

Descoeudres/Kearsley (Chapter 1 n.3) 49 n.135, Fig. 47.

70.   Eretria FK E/8 B639, rim fr.   *Fig 40(b)*

Ht 3.3; w 3.6; **diam lip** (reconstructed) 12.0; **th** 0.2-3. Reddish-yellow clay (5YR 6/6) with polished light-brown surface (7.5YR 6-7/5). No slip or mica. Black paint. **Lip**, not offset, ht 1.2. **Ext**: six arcs of one set. **Context**: as *68*.

Descoeudres/Kearsley (Chapter 1 n.3) 49 n.135, Fig. 45.

71.   Eretria no number, rim fr.   *Fig 11(c)*

Ht 2.9; w 3.8; **diam lip** (reconstructed) 10.0; **th** 0.2-3. Fabric as *70*. **Lip**, offset, ht 1.3. **Ext**: three arcs of one set. **Context**: bothros of Late Geometric date.

72.   Eretria no number – Eretria Agora excavation 1979, rim fr. *Fig 11(d)*

Ht 5.5; w 4.2; **diam lip** (reconstructed) 10.0; **th** 0.2. Fabric as *69*. **Lip**, not offset, 1.0. **Ext**: two sets of five semicircles, not inter-secting. **Context**: Late Geometric.

According to Dr J.-P. Descoeudres there are three further frag-ments of similar shape to *72:* one from the Agora area and two others from the Temple of Apollo. All were found in Late Geo-metric contexts.

73.   Eretria FK 1643.19, rim fr. [10]   *Fig 41(b)*

Ht 3.3; w 3.3; **diam lip** ?; **th** 0.2-3. Hard-fired clay with light grey core (7.5YR 7/0) and a few coarse white inclusions. Black to brownish red paint (2.5YR 4-5/6). **Lip**, offset, ht 0.9. **Ext**: only part of one set of six semicircles preserved. **Int**: painted. **Context**: bothros containing material of late seventh and early sixth centuries.

Descoeudres/Kearsley (Chapter 1 n.3) 51 n. 137.

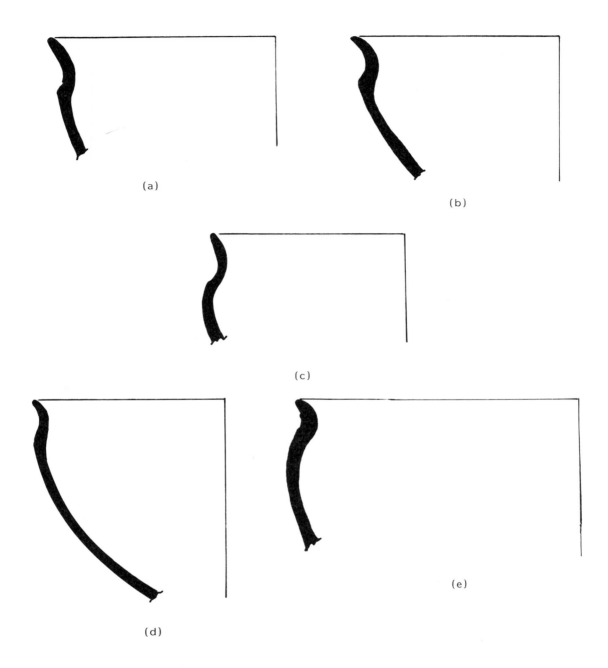

Fig. 11 Eretria. (a) Eretria FK E/8 B640 (*68*); (b) Eretria FK E/8 B650 (*69*); (c) Eretria no no. (*71*); (d) Eretria no no. (*72*); (e) Eretria FK 3038.1 (*74*).

74.   **Eretria** FK 3038.1, rim fr.   *Fig 11(e)*

Ht 4.1; **w** 7.0; **diam lip** (reconstructed) 15.0; **th** 0.4. Dark pinkish clay (4YR 6/1-3), hard-fired, with a light brown slip (9YR 6/4). Greyish green paint (5Y 4/1). **Lip**, offset, ht 0.9. There is a small protruberance half-way up the exterior of the lip. **Ext**: five arcs of one set and part of the painted stripe on the right-hand side. **Int**: painted, except for reserved band on rim. **Context**: associated with material of the seventh-sixth centuries and later.

Other fragments (with uninformative contexts) are also known from Eretria:

(a) *PGP* 189 - probably that published in (b) below.

(b) J. Boardman, "Pottery from Eretria", *BSA* 47 (1952) pl.1a, 18.

(c) P. Themelis, "Eretria", *AAA* 3 (1970) 314, Fig. 1.

GORTYN

75.   Herakleion 11.518, rim fr.

Well-levigated pink clay with slip. Black paint. **Ext**: only one set, probably of seven semicircles, preserved. **Int**: painted, except for reserved band on lip. **Context**: mixed deposit (Late Minoan III, Protogeometric and Geometric) in the area of the Protoarchaic altar.

G. Rizza and V. Santa Maria Scrinari, *Il santuario sull'acropoli di Gortina* I (Rome 1968) 140 no. 252 Fig. 236:7.

There are also two shoulder fragments: 141 no. 274, Fig. 239:6 and no. 275, Fig. 239:7, which may be from a pendent semicircle skyphos. Fig. 239:7 [no. 275] is said to be from a kalathos, but from the photograph it appears to be from the same vase as Fig. 239:6 which is not so identified.

HAMA
(*PGP* 181-185; *GGP* 311)

76.   Aleppo, Hama 7B23.

Ht (7.0); **diam lip** (11.0); **diam base** (4.4). Clay varies from clear brownish or yellowish-red, to grey-brownish. Very little mica, but a lot of fine white particles. Mainly black paint, brownish in parts. **Lip**, offset, ht (1.2); **foot** ht (0.8). **Ext**: two sets of six semicircles, intersecting. **Context**: Citadel, destruction level of 720 BC.

E. Fugmann, *Hama II,* 1 (Copenhagen 1958) 232; *Sukas I* 144, 148-152, Fig. 51a.

77.   Copenhagen NM, Hama L941.[11]   *Fig 12*

Ht 7.4; **diam lip** 11.0; **diam base** 3.6.   Clay and paint as above.
Lip, offset, ht 1.0; **foot** ht 0.7. **Ext**: two sets of seven semicircles,
intersecting. **Context**: citadel, probably destruction level of 720 BC.

Fugmann, *Hama II, 1* 261-2; *Sukas I* 148-153, Fig. 51b.

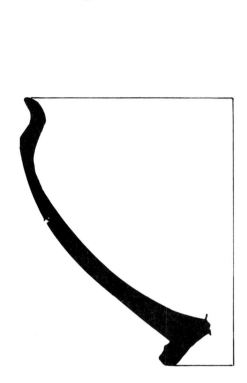

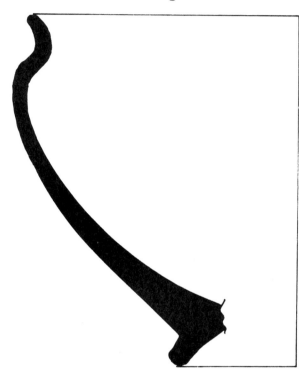

Fig. 12 **Hama**. Copenhagen NM,   Fig. 13 **Hama**. Copenhagen NM, Hama 6A290 (*78*).
Hama L941 (*77*).

78.   **Copenhagen NM, Hama** 6A290.   *Fig 13*

Ht 9.7; **diam lip** 14.2; **diam base** 6.2.   Clay and paint as above.
Lip, offset, ht 1.1; **foot** ht 0.7. **Ext**: two sets of eight semicircles,
intersecting. **Context**: tomb, dated 800-720.

P.J. Riis, *Hama II, 3* (Copenhagen 1948) 113, Fig. 134A;
Sukas I 148-153, Fig. 51c.

79.   **Copenhagen NM, Hama** 8A189, rim fr.   *Fig 14*

Ht 5.2; **diam lip** 11.0. Clay and paint as above. **Lip**, offset, ht 1.0.
Ext: two sets of seven semicircles, intersecting. **Int**: painted except for
a thin reserved band on the edge. **Context**: tomb, dated late ninth - 800 BC.

P.J. Riis, *Hama II, 3* 113, Fig. 134B; *Sukas I* 148-153, Fig. 51d.

See also Catalogue Appendix (p.194).

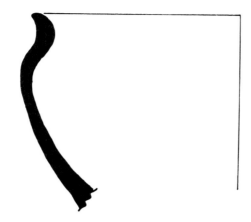

Fig. 14 **Hama**. Copenhagen NM, Hama 8A189 (*79*).

IASOS

80.   A rim fragment is published in D. Levi, "Le campagne 1962-1964 a Iasos", *ASAtene* 43-44 (1965-1966) 417, Fig. 26.

IBN HANI

81.   Two fragments: one rim with four arcs of one set, and a wall fragment with five arcs of one set. **Context**: unstratified, among Iron Age pottery of the 8th to the beginning of the 6th century.

A. Bounni *et al.*, "Rapport préliminaire sur la deuxième campagne de fouilles (1976) à Ibn Hani (Syrie)", *Syria* 55 (1978) 284, Fig. 29,1 and 6.

IKARIA

82.   One shoulder fragment from the site of Kambos is published.

H.-G. Buchholz, *Methymna* (Mainz 1975) 90, Fig. 25(b).

IOLCOS

(See also Kapakli and Nea Ionia)

83.   A rim fragment is published in D.R. Theocharis, "Iolkos, whence sailed the Argonauts" *Archaeology* 11 (1958) 18.

KALAMARIA

84.   **Thessaloniki** 5710   *Fig 15*

Ht 12.3; **diam lip** 18.0–18.5; **diam base** 6.5.   Orange clay (5YR 7/6), hard–fired and well–levigated.   Some dark inclusions.   Mainly brownish orange paint (5YR 6/6).   **Lip,** offset, ht 1.0; **foot** ht 0.5. **Ext:** two sets of ten semicircles, intersecting. **Int:** painted. **Context:** unknown.

W.A. Heurtley, *Prehistoric Macedonia* (Cambridge 1939) 238, no. 497; *PGP* 190–192.

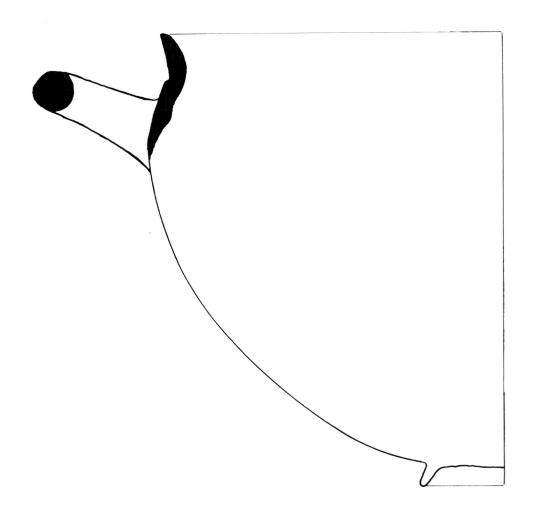

Fig. 15 **Kalamaria.** Thessaloniki 5710 (*84*).

85.   **Thessaloniki** 4714 (Ⅱ 634).   *Fig 39(a), Pl.8(b)*

Ht 10.5;   diam lip 15.5-17.2; **diam base** 5.9; **th** 0.4-5.   Light brown (7.5YR 6/4), hard-fired.   Mainly brownish red paint (2.5YR 5/6), but black in patches.   **Lip**, offset, ht 1.1; **foot** ht 0.3 (it appears that some of the foot has crumbled away).   **Ext:** one set of six semicircles and one set of seven together on the same side.   On the other, at least where the paint can still be seen clearly, two sets of seven semicircles. Intersection on both sides.   The paint is applied very carelessly. **Int:** painted. **Context:** unknown.

KALAPODHI

86.   One large rim fragment and nine other shoulder and wall frag-ments have been published from the sanctuary.   The excavators describe the shape as being between the high-lipped version from the Xeropolis-Lefkandi Pit Fill and the low-lipped version from the Levelling material. The fragments were found in the earliest Geometric levels and in terms of Attic chronology should be dated about the transition from Early Geometric to Middle Geometric I.

R.C.S. Felsch *et al.,* "Apollon und Artemis oder Artemis und Apollon?   Bericht von den Grabungen im neu entdeckten Heiligtum bei Kalapodi 1973-1977", *AA* 95 (1980) 48 Figs. 15, 17.

KAPAKLI (IOLCOS)[12]

(*PGP* 189-90)

87.   **Volos** K1354.   *Fig 36(c), Pl.4(a)*

Ht 9.9; diam lip 14.8-15.4; **diam base** 6.0; **th** 0.5.   Pale orange clay (7.5YR 7/6), hard-fired, with a brownish orange slip (5YR 6/6). Mainly brownish red paint (2.5YR 5/8).   **Lip**, offset, ht 1.7; **foot** ht 0.5. **Ext:** two sets of nine semicircles, intersecting. **Int:** painted, except for reserved band on edge of lip. **Context:** multiple burials covering tenth-eighth centuries.

PGRT pl.9, 56.

88.   **Volos** K1355.   *Fig 16, Pl.4(b)*

Ht 9.9-10.3; **diam lip** 15.8-17.2; **diam base** 6.4; **th** 0.4.   Bright yellow orange-orange clay (7.5YR 7-8/8) with brownish orange slip (5YR 6/6).   Mainly dark brown streaky paint (5YR 3/2) but brownish red arcs (2.5YR 5/8).   **Lip**, offset, ht 1.8; **foot** ht 0.6. **Ext:** two sets of nine semicircles, intersecting. **Int:** painted except for reserved band on lip. **Context:** as last.

PGRT pl.9, 57.

89.   Volos K1356   *Fig 35(a), Pl.5(a)*

   Ht 11.5-10.8; **diam lip** 15.6-16.0; **diam base** 6.7; **th** 0.4-5.
Yellow beige clay (10YR 8/3), rather soft and micaceous. Dark brown
paint (5YR 3/2). **Lip**, offset, ht 1.5; **foot** ht 0.5. **Ext**: two sets of
nine semicircles, not intersecting. **Int**: painted. **Context**: as *87*.

   PGRT 28, Fig. 19 and pl.9, 58.

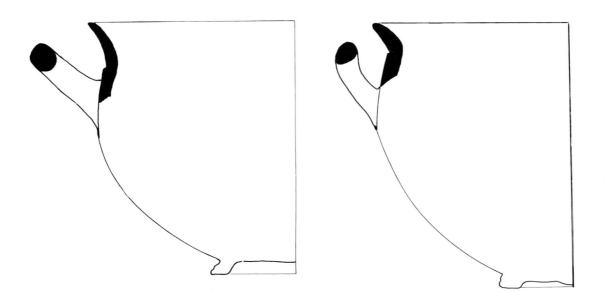

Fig. 16 Kapakli 57. Volos K1355 (*88*).   **Fig. 17 Kapakli** 59. Volos K1357 (*90*).

90.   Volos K1357   *Fig 17, Pl.6(a)*

   Ht 10.1-10.6; **diam lip** 15.0-15.5; **diam base** 5.7; **th** 0.5.   Yellow
beige clay (10YR 8/3), rather soft and micaceous.   Black paint.
Lip, offset, ht 1.2; **foot** ht 0.6. **Ext**: two sets of eight semicircles,
intersecting on only one side of the vase. **Int**: painted. **Context**: as *87*.

   PGRT pl.9, 59; Descoeudres/Kearsley (Chapter 1 n.3) 44 n. 119,
Fig 40.

91.   Volos K1358   *Fig 37(a), Pl.5(d)*

   Ht 11.0; **diam lip** 15.6-16.0; **diam base** 5.8; **th** 0.5.   Bright
yellow orange - orange clay (7.5YR 8-7/8), rather soft and very micaceous.
Paint ranges from dull reddish brown (5YR 4/3) to brownish red (2.5YR
5/8). **Lip**, offset, ht 1.3; **foot** ht 0.6. **Ext**: two set of nine semicircles,
not intersecting. **Context**: as *87*.

   PGRT 28, 60.

92.   **Volos** K1359   *Fig 18, Pl.6(b)*

       Ht 10.6-11.5; **diam lip** 16.4; **diam base** 5.0; **th** 0.5. Yellow beige clay (10YR 8/3), soft and micaceous. Black paint. **Lip,** offset, ht 1.2; **foot** ht 0.7. **Ext:** two sets of nine semicircles, not intersecting. **Int:** painted, except for reserved band on lip. **Context:** as *87*.

       PGRT 28, 61.

93.   **Volos** K1360   *Fig 19, Pl.7(d)*

       Ht 7.5; **diam lip** 11.8-12.2; **diam base** 6.0; **th** 0.3. Pale orange clay (7.5YR 7/6), hard-fired with a pale orange-yellowish brown slip (7.5YR 6-7/6). Black paint. **Lip,** offset, ht 1.4; flat **base. Ext:** two sets of seven semicircles, intersecting. Very carelessly painted. **Int:** painted, except for reserved band on edge of rim. **Context:** as *87*.

       PGRT 28, 63, Fig. 20.

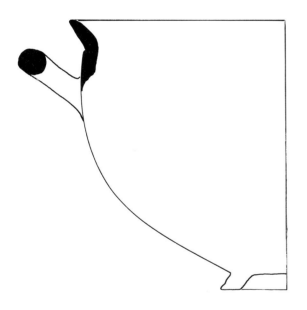

Fig. 18 **Kapakli 61.** Volos K1359 (*92*).   Fig. 19 **Kapakli 63.** Volos K1360 (*93*).

KARABOURNAKI

94.   A photograph of a large rim fragment has been published by K.A. Rhomaios in *Epitumbion Chr. Tsountas* (Athens 1941) 369, Fig. 5. Desborough mentions other sherds of similar skyphoi (*PGP* 190-2).

KARDIANI

95.　　**Tenos** B79.　　　　　　　　　　　　　　*Fig 20, Pl.3(a)*

　　　Ht 9.3; **diam lip** 12.6; **diam base** 5.4; **th** 0.3.　Fine, rather soft clay.　Light yellow orange (7.5YR 8/4) with a slightly darker slip. Micaceous.　Black paint, often streaky.　**Lip**, offset, ht 1.7; **foot** ht 0.7. Ext: two sets of seven semicircles, intersecting. Int: painted, except for reserved band on lip and small reserved circle in centre.
Context: unknown.

　　　GGP 153, pl.32e (under the number A1458); Coldstream (Chapter 1 n. 10) 38, Fig 8b; Descoeudres/Kearsley (Chapter 1 n.3) 44 n. 118, Fig. 39.

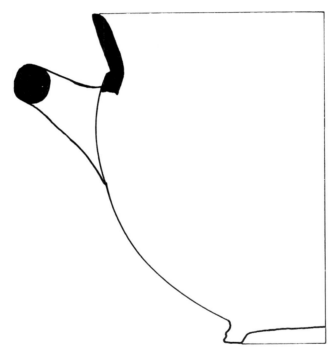

Fig. 20　Kardiani. Tenos B79 (*95*).

96.　　**Tenos, Kardiani Tomb III**, 3.[13]　　　　　*Pl.1(b)*

　　　Ht 11.0; **diam lip** 14.0; **diam base** 5.5.　Lip, a slight ridge where it joins the body, ht 1.6; **foot** ht 1.0. Ext: two sets, probably of eight semicircles, intersecting.　From the photograph, there appears to be a reserved band in the paint below the semicircle decoration. Int: painted.
Context: tomb, probably to be dated within the ninth century.

　　　D. Levi, "La Necropoli geometrica di Kardiani a Tinos", *ASAtene* 8-9 (1925-1926) 226, Fig. 28. *PGP* 159-60, 186-9.

KAZAPHANI

97.   One skyphos (Nicosia 1933/XI-29/1) referred to by Desborough in *PGP* 181, and illustrated on pl.25, C, left; Catling, *RDAC* (1973) 180 no. 6; *GGAPC* 24 no. 10; pl.I, 12.

KERINTHOS

98.   Two shoulder fragments are in a box labelled "Kerinthos" in the sherd room at the British School in Athens. They are both of light yellow-orange clay (7.5YR 8/4). One has no mica, but the other does have a little. One of these fragments may be that referred to by Boardman (Chapter 1 n.3 1957) 2 n. 8.

KHALDEH

99.   **National Museum, Damascus**   *Fig 41(a)*

    Ht (6.3); **diam lip** (12.0); **diam base** (5.4). **Lip**, offset, ht (1.2); **foot** almost flat. **Ext**: two sets of seven semicircles, intersecting. **Context**: tomb, dated late ninth-late eighth centuries on the basis of local pottery.

    R. Saidah, "Objets grecs d'époque géométrique découverts récemment sur le littoral libanais (à Khaldé près de Beyrouth)", *AAS* 21 (1971) 197, Fig. a; Descoeudres/Kearsley (Chapter 1 n.3) 48 n. 133.

KITION

100.   **Nicosia, Kition** 800, rim and handle fr.

    Ht (Reconstructed) *ca*.12.1; **diam lip** *ca*.17.1. Orange-brown clay, large and small white grits. Surface polished roughly. Semi-lustrous red paint. **Lip**, offset, tall and flaring. **Ext**: two sets of ten semicircles, not intersecting. Three reserved bands below the semi-circles and lower body reserved. **Int**: painted, except for reserved band on lip. **Context**: Temenos A. Kition 1967, Area II; end of 9th century (*GGAPC* 61); Euboean Subprotogeometric I or II, *ca*.900-850 BC (*Kition IV* 17-18).

    GGAPC 61 no. 3; pl.I, 3; *Kition IV* 17-18 no. 2, pls.XVI,2 and XVIII,1; V. Karageorghis, "Cyprus", *CAH* III Pt.1, 529; Descoeudres/ Kearsley (Chapter 1 n.3) 44 n. 122.

40

101.   Nicosia, Kition 4062, rim fr.

Ht 6.2; **diam lip** (reconstructed) 10.0.   Deep orange clay.   Red paint.   Short **lip**, swept back from the body with no carination. **Ext**: two sets of six semicircles, intersecting. **Int**: painted except for reserved band on lip. **Context**: Kition 1975, Area II, Temple 5, floor 3. End of ninth century (*GGAPC* 61-2).   Euboean Subprotogeometric III, *ca.*850-800 (*Kition IV* 18).

GGAPC 61-2 no. 4; pl.I, 4; *Kition IV* 18 no. 3; pls. XVI,3 and XVIII,5; Descoeudres/Kearsley (Chapter 1 n.3) 46 n. 123.

The lower part of a Subprotogeometric "Cycladic" skyphos is also published from Kition (inv. 3036): *GGAPC* 62, no. 5; *Kition IV* 18, no. 4.   Coldstream (*Kition IV* 20) believes this to be part of a full-circle skyphos rather than a pendent semicircle skyphos but either is possible.

KNOSSOS

102.   Herakleion. [14]

Ht 12.5.   Buff clay.   Red paint.   Tall **lip** with ridge at the join of lip and body; low **foot**. **Ext**: two sets of eight semicircles, not intersecting. **Context**: tomb with multiple burials of the Sub-Mycenaean/ Protogeometric periods to the seventh century.

H.G.G. Payne, "Early Greek Vases from Knossos", *BSA* 29 (1927-1928) 261 no. 147, pl.VI, 12; *PGP* 185-6.

There is also a rim sherd from the palace (M. Hartley, "Early Greek Vases from Crete", *BSA* 31 (1930-31) 80, Fig.20 no. 22).

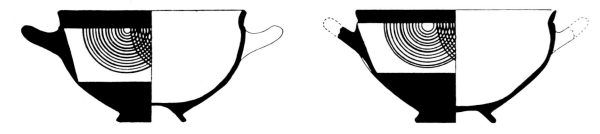

Fig. 21(a) Teke. Tomb G 123 (*103*).   Fig. 21(b) Teke. Tomb G 124 (*104*).

103.   Herakleion, Teke Tomb G no. 123. [15]   *Fig 21(a)*

Ht 9.2; **diam lip** 15.0; **diam base** (5.6).   Fine orange-brown clay, lustrous red-black paint.   Lip, offset, ht 1.2. High ring **foot**. **Ext**: two sets of 14 semicircles, intersecting. **Int**: reserved band on lip and reserved dot on floor. **Context**: tomb containing many cremations with pottery of mainly Cretan Early Geometric date, but some vases just going down to local Middle Geometric. For absolute chronology, *GGP* 241-4: end of ninth to early eighth century. Euboean Subprotogeometric III.

Unpublished, but for a preliminary report of the excavation, see H.W. Catling, "The Knossos area, 1974-76", *ArchRep* (1976-77) 11 ff.

104.   **Herakleion, Teke** Tomb G no. 124.   *Fig 21(b)*

Ht 9.3; **diam lip** 15.9; **diam base** (6.3). Soft orange-brown clay, red paint. Offset, lip, ht (0.9). **Ext:** two sets of 14 semicircles, intersecting. **Int:** as *103*.

Fragments of four more similar skyphoi were found in this tomb.

See also Catalogue Appendix (p.193).

KOUKLIA

105.   **Nicosia, Kouklia** 99.

Ht 7.0; **diam lip** 12.3; **diam base** (5.0). Pink clay with a light brown slip. Streaky paint. **Lip**, offset, ht (1.2); almost flat **base**. **Ext:** two sets of seven semicircles, intersecting. **Int:** painted, except for reserved line on lip. **Context:** tomb, *ca.* 700 BC.

V. Karageorghis, "Chronique des fouilles à Chypre en 1961", *BCH* 86 (1962) 388, Fig. 83a,b; Karageorghis, "Une tombe de guerrier à Palaepaphos", *BCH* 87 (1963) 267, Fig. 3; Karageorghis and L. Kahil, "Témoignages eubéens à Chypre et chypriotes à Eretrie", *AntK* 10 (1967) 133-5, pl.37, 2; *GGP* 157; J.N. Coldstream, "Cypro-Aegean exchanges in the 9th and 8th Centuries BC", *Praktika tou Protou Diethnous Kyprologikou Synedriou A* (Nicosia 1972) 19; Catling, *RDAC* (1973) 180 no. 5; *GGAPC* 24 no. 9, pl. 1, 9; Descoeudres/Kearsley (Chapter 1 n.3) 48 no. 133.

LARISA (THESSALY)

106.   **Volos K1352.**   *Fig 22, Pl.4(d)*

Ht 9.6-10.2; **diam lip** 14.4-17.9; **diam base** 5.5; **th** 0.4. Pale orange-yellowish brown clay (7.5YR 6-7/6), hard-fired, with brownish orange slip (5YR 6/6). Black paint, very faded. **Lip**, offset, ht 1.7; **foot** ht 0.7. **Ext:** two sets of ten semicircles, intersecting. **Int:** painted. **Context:** uncertain.

PGRT 27, Fig. 18.[16] *PGP* 189-90.

42

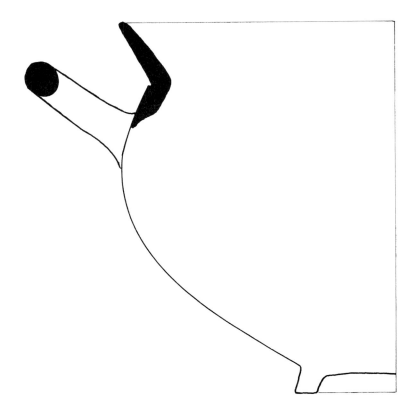

Fig. 22 **Larisa.** Volos K1352 (*106*).

LARISA (AEOLIS)

107.   One rim fragment found in a disturbed context: J. Boehlau and
K. Schefold, *Larisa am Hermos* III (Berlin 1942) pl.57, 4; *PGP* 190-192.

LEFKANDI

The Lefkandi excavation report is in two volumes: Plates (1979)
and Text (1980).   Page references below are to the Text only.

The chronological phases listed below are those given in *Lefkandi I,*
Appendix A, Tables 4 and 5 for the cemeteries and Xeropolis. The dates
assigned to these on page xiii are as follows:

Early Protogeometric - Late Protogeometric: *ca.*1050 - 900 (=LPG)

Subprotogeometric I: 900 - 875 (=SPG)

Subprotogeometric II: 875 - 850

Subprotogeometric III: 850 - 750

A.   CEMETERIES:[17] (i)   SKOUBRIS (=S)

108.   Eretria, Lefkandi S.T33:1.

Ht (12.5); diam lip (16.5); **diam base** (6.1). Local fabric.
Lip, offset, ht (2.2); **foot** ht (0.9). Ext: two sets of 14 semicircles,
intersecting. Int: painted, except for reserved band on lip and central
dot on floor. **Context:** tomb 33 (SPG II).

Lefkandi I 121, pll.102 and 265B (wrongly labelled S.T59A,4);
Desborough (Chapter 2 *32*) 198; Coldstream (Chapter 1 n. 10) 39, Fig. 9g.

109.   Eretria, Lefkandi S.T33:2.

Ht (9.4); diam lip (12.4); **diam base** (4.4). Local fabric. **Lip,** offset,
ht (1.6); **foot** ht (0.6). Ext: two sets of ten semicircles, intersecting.
Int: painted, except for reserved band on lip and central dot on floor.
Context: as last.

Lefkandi I 121, pl.102; Coldstream (Chapter 1 n. 10) 39, Fig. 9f.

110.   Eretria, Lefkandi S.T45:3

Ht (6.9); diam lip (10.4); **diam base** (4.8). Local fabric. **Lip,** offset,
ht (1.0); **foot** ht (0.6). Ext: two sets of ten semicircles, intersecting.
Int: painted, except for reserved band on lip and central dot on floor.
Context: tomb 45 (SPG II).

Lefkandi I 125, pl.105.

111.   Eretria, Lefkandi S.T56:3.

Ht (9.6); diam lip (14.3); **diam base** (6.0). Clay, slip and paint are
those of the local wheel-made ware. **Lip,** offset, ht (1.5); **foot** ht (0.6).
Ext: two sets of 16 semicircles, intersecting. Reserved on the lower
part of the foot. Int: painted, except for reserved band on lip.
Context: tomb 56 (SPG I).

Lefkandi I 128-9, pl.107.

112.   Eretria 8495, Lefkandi S.T59:2.   *Fig 23(a)*

Ht 6.7; diam lip 11.3-10.8; **diam base** 4.2; **th** 0.3. Local fabric.
Orange clay (5YR 7/6) with some small specks of mica. A pinkish
brown slip (5YR 7/4). Light red paint (10R 5/6). **Lip,** offset, ht 1.3.
foot ht 0.8. Ext: two sets of ten semicircles, intersecting. Int: painted,
except for band on lip and reserved dot on bottom. **Context:** tomb 59
(SPG III).

Lefkandi I 129-130; pll.108 and 265a; Sackett/Popham (Chapter
1 n. 19) 16; Coldstream (Chapter 1 n. 10) 63, Fig. 18j; Boardman
(Chapter 1 n. 6) 41, Fig. 13.

44

113.   Eretria, Lefkandi S.T59A:3

Ht (7.1); diam lip (10.0); diam base (4.5). Local pink to buff clay with pale buff slip. Mostly brown paint. Lip, offset, ht (1.2); foot ht (0.6).Ext: two sets of nine semicircles, intersecting. Int: painted, except for reserved band on lip and reserved dot on floor. Context: tomb 59A (SPG III).

Lefkandi I 129–130, pl.109.

114.   Eretria, Lefkandi S.T59A:4

Ht (10.0); diam lip (14.8); diam base (5.5). Fabric as *113*. Lip, offset, ht(1.2); foot ht (0.6). Ext: two sets of 14 semicircles, intersecting. Int: painted, except for reserved band on lip and reserved dot on floor. Context: as last.

Lefkandi I 129–130; pl.109. (Pl.265b is labelled S.T59A,4 but is in fact S.T33,1.) Sackett and Popham (Chapter 1 n. 19) 16; Coldstream (Chapter 1 n. 10) 63, Fig. 18h.

115.   Eretria, rim fr.

Diam lip 13.5.   Lip, offset, ht (1.8). Ext: only one set of ten semicircles preserved. Int: painted, except for reserved band on lip. Context: gully fill, mostly SPG I–II.

Lefkandi I 266, pll.273, 828 and 283, 8.

(ii)   PALIA PERIVOLIA (=P)

116.   Eretria, Lefkandi P.T2:1.

Ht (15.6); diam lip (17.5); diam base (6.3). Standard local fabric. Lip, offset, ht (2.0); foot ht (1.1). Ext: two sets of 14 semicircles, not intersecting.   Reserved on lower half of foot. Int: painted, except for reserved band on lip and central dot on floor. Context: tomb 2 (SPG. Undated).

Lefkandi I 141, 302; pl.125.

117.   Eretria, Lefkandi P.T3:14.

Ht (9.6); diam lip (12.8); diam base (5.5). Standard local fabric with usual range of variations in slip and paint. Lip, offset, ht (1.8); foot ht (0.5). Ext: two sets of seven semicircles, not intersecting and with hour-glass in centre. Int: painted, except for reserved band on lip. Context: tomb 3 (LPG, bordering on SPG I).

Lefkandi I 141–2, 300 n. 130; pll. 128 and 259e.

118.   Eretria, Lefkandi P.T21:10.

Ht (5.7); diam lip (8.8); diam base (4.2). Standard local fabric.
Lip, not offset, ht (0.7); foot ht (0.4). Ext: two sets of five semicircles,
intersecting on one side only. Int: painted, except for reserved band on
lip. Context: tomb 21 (SPG II).

Lefkandi I 148-9, pl.136.

119.   Eretria, Lefkandi P.T27:2.

Diam lip 27.0. Local fabric. Lip, not offset, ht (1.6). Ext: only
one set of eight semicircles preserved. Below the semicircles are two
reserved bands. Int: painted, except for reserved band on lip.
Context: tomb 27 (SPG I).

Lefkandi I 153-4, pl.143.

120.   Eretria, Lefkandi P.T39B:5.

Ht (7.2); diam lip (10.3); diam base (4.7). Standard local fabric.
Lip, not offset, ht (0.9); foot ht (0.4). Ext: two sets of nine semicircles,
intersecting. Int: painted, except for band on lip and reserved circle
on bottom. Context: tomb 39B (SPG I).

Lefkandi I 156-7, pl.146.

121.   Eretria, Lefkandi P. Pyre 31:1.

Diam lip (16.0). Clay and paint burnt to grey. Lip, offset, ht (2.8).
Ext: one set of seven semicircles, not intersecting. Int: painted, except
for reserved band on lip. Context: pyre 31 (SPG I? Undated).

Lefkandi I 165, 302; pl.154.

122.   Eretria, Lefkandi P. North Channel, rim fr.

Lip, not offset. Context: lower fill (LPG).

Lefkandi I 271; 299 n. 128, pl.276, 969.

123/1. Eretria, Lefkandi P. North Channel, rim fr.

Lip, offset. Context: upper fill (LPG - SPG III).

Lefkandi I 270, pl.275, 939.

(iii) TOUMBA (=T)

123/2. Eretria, Lefkandi T.T42:6.

Ht 7.0. Local fabric. Offset **lip;** ring **foot. Ext:** two sets of 11 semicircles, intersecting. **Int:** painted, except for reserved band on lip and dot on floor. **Context:** tomb 42 (SPG I).

M.R. Popham *et al.,* "Further Excavation of the Toumba Cemetery at Lefkandi, 1981", *BSA* 77 (1982) 223-224, 245, pll. 23:6 and 28(d).

123/3. Eretria, Lefkandi T. Pyre 13:13, rim fr.

Ht 11.2; **diam lip** 15.0. Burnt fabric. Offset **lip. Ext:** two sets of 12 semicircles, intersecting. **Int:** painted, except for reserved band on lip. **Context:** pyre 13 (SPG I-II).

Popham *et al., BSA* (1982) 227-8, 247, pl.25D.

A shoulder fragment, 1162, was found associated with Tomb 7. Probably of LPG date. *Lefkandi I* 277, pl.281A.

B. XEROPOLIS: AREA 2. (i) Moulds Deposit

Lefkandi I 27-31. All local fabric. **Context:** LPG. (Profiles of pl.13, 22 and 24 are not given on pl.30. Worthy of attention are the reserved bands below the semicircles on pl.13, 22.)

124. Eretria, rim fr.

Diam lip 20.0. Lip, not offset (*ca.*1.5). **Ext:** five arcs of one set.
Lefkandi I 28-29, pll.13:23, 30:7.

125. Eretria, rim fr.

Diam lip 16. Lip, offset, ht (1.3). **Ext:** ten arcs of one set.
Lefkandi I pll.13, 25 and 30,8.

126. Eretria, rim fr.

Diam lip 18. **Lip,** not offset, ht (1.8). **Ext:** part of one set preserved. Decoration very faded.
Lefkandi I pll.13, 21 and 30.9.

127. Eretria, rim fr.

Diam lip 12. Lip, offset, ht (1.3). **Ext:** nine arcs of one set.
Lefkandi I pll.13, 26 and 30,10.

128.   Eretria, rim fr.

Diam lip 14. Lip, offset, ht (1.5). Ext: two sets of ten semicircles, intersecting.

Lefkandi I pll.13, 20 and 30,11.

129.   Eretria

Ht (11.4); diam lip (15.6?); diam base (6.5). Lip, offset, ht (2.0); foot ht (0.3); Ext: two sets of six semicircles, not intersecting. Half hour-glass in the centre of the semicircles. Int: painted, except for reserved band on lip.

Lefkandi I pll.13, 19 and 30,12.

(ii) Pit fill

Lefkandi I 31-36. Local fabric. **Context**: SPG I-II. (Four of the following fragments, pl.31:4, 8-10, are not illustrated on pl.15. On the other hand there is no profile given on pl.31 of pl.15:109, 114-5, 119-121, 123.)

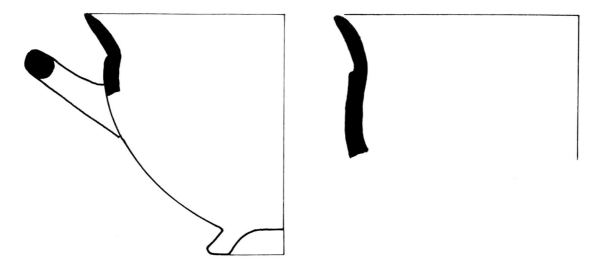

Fig. 23 Lefkandi. (a) Skoubris T59:2 (*112*); (b) Athens, British School (*165*).

130.   Eretria, rim fr.

Ht ?; diam lip (21.5). Lip, offset, ht (1.6); foot ht (0.8). Ext: two sets of 12 semicircles, not intersecting. Lower part of the foot reserved. Int: painted, except for reserved band on lip.

Lefkandi I pl.31,4.

48

131.   Eretria, rim fr.

Diam lip 15. **Lip,** offset, ht (1.5). **Ext:** two set of 12 semicircles, not intersecting. **Int:** painted, except for reserved band on lip.

Lefkandi I pll.15, 122 and 31,5.

132.   Eretria, rim fr.

Diam lip (18.0). **Lip,** offset, ht (1.8). **Ext:** two sets of nine semicircles. intersecting. **Int:** painted, except for reserved band on lip.

Lefkandi I pll.15, 110 and 31,6.

133.   Eretria, rim fr.

Diam lip 15. **Lip,** offset, ht (1.5). **Ext:** two sets of 13 semicircles, intersecting. **Int:** painted, except for reserved band on lip.

Lefkandi I pll.15, 108 and 31,7.

134.   Eretria, rim fr.

Diam lip 15. **Lip,** offset, ht (2.0). **Ext:** ?; **Int:** painted, except for reserved band on lip.

Lefkandi I pl.31,8.

135.   Eretria, rim fr.

Diam lip 20. **Lip,** offset, ht (2.0). **Ext:** ?; **Int:** painted, except for reserved band on lip.

Lefkandi I pl.31,9.

136.   Eretria, rim fr.

Diam lip 14. **Lip,** offset, ht (1.2). **Ext:** ten arcs of one set and nine of the other, intersecting. **Int:** painted, except for reserved band on lip.

Lefkandi I pl.31,10.

(iii) **Levelling material**

Lefkandi I 36-42. Local fabric. **Context:** SPG III. (Pl.33:4-28 are not illustrated on pl.18; while there are no profiles on pl.33 of pl.18:261-275; 278-285; 287-296).

137.   Eretria, rim fr.

Diam lip (13.0). **Lip**, offset, ht (1.0). **Ext**: two sets of 12 semicircles, intersecting. **Int**: painted, except for reserved band on lip.

Lefkandi I pll.18, 276 and 33,1.[18]

138.   Eretria, rim fr.

Diam lip 13.0. **Lip**, offset, ht (0.8). **Ext**: two sets of 12 semicircles. intersecting. **Int**: painted, except for reserved band on lip.

Lefkandi I pll.18, 277 and 33,2.

139.   Eretria, rim fr.

Diam lip 14. **Lip**, offset, ht (0.9). **Ext**: ten arcs of one set. **Int**: painted.

Lefkandi I pll.18, 286 and 33,3.

140.   Eretria, rim fr.

Diam lip 14. **Lip**, not offset, ht (0.6). **Ext**: two sets of seven semicircles, not intersecting. **Int**: painted, except for reserved band on lip.

Lefkandi I pl.33,4.

141.   Eretria, rim fr.

Diam lip 18. **Lip**, not offset, ht (0.6). **Ext**: only one set of ten semicircles preserved. **Int**: painted.

Lefkandi I pl.33,5.

142.   Eretria, rim fr.

Diam lip 14. **Lip**, offset, ht (1.8).

Lefkandi I pl.33,6.

143.   Eretria, rim fr.

Diam lip 13. **Lip**, offset, ht (0.9).

Lefkandi I pl.33,7.

144.   Eretria, rim fr.

Diam lip 12. **Lip**, offset, ht (1.2).

Lefkandi I pl.33,8.

145. Eretria, rim fr.
Diam lip 17. **Lip**, offset, ht (0.9).
Lefkandi I pl.33,9.

146. Eretria, rim fr.
Diam lip 11. **Lip**, offset, ht (0.9).
Lefkandi I pl.33,10.

147. Eretria, rim fr.
Diam lip 18. **Lip**, offset, ht (0.9).
Lefkandi I pl.33,11.

148. Eretria, rim fr.
Diam lip 11. **Lip**, offset, ht (0.9).
Lefkandi I pl.33,12.

149. Eretria, rim fr.
Diam lip 16. **Lip**, offset, ht (0.9).
Lefkandi I pl.33,13.

150. Eretria, rim fr.
Diam lip 16. **Lip**, offset, ht (1.2).
Lefkandi I pl.33,14.

151. Eretria, rim fr.
Diam lip 12. **Lip**, offset, ht (1.2).
Lefkandi I pl.33,15.

152. Eretria, rim fr.
Diam lip ?. **Lip**, offset, ht (0.9).
Lefkandi I pl.33,16.

153. Eretria, rim fr.
Diam lip 15. **Lip**, offset, ht (1.5).
Lefkandi I pl.33,17.

154.   Eretria, rim fr.
        Diam lip 12. Lip, offset, ht (0.9).
        Lefkandi I pl.33,18.

155.   Eretria, rim fr.
        Diam lip 12. Lip, offset, ht (1.2).
        Lefkandi I pl.33,19.

156.   Eretria, rim fr.
        Diam lip 14. Lip, offset, ht (0.9).
        Lefkandi I pl.33,20.

157.   Eretria, rim fr.
        Diam lip 14. Lip, offset, ht (1.2).
        Lefkandi I pl.33,21.

158.   Eretria, rim fr.
        Diam lip 12. Lip, offset, ht (0.9).
        Lefkandi I pl.33,22.

159.   Eretria, rim fr.
        Diam lip 12. Lip, offset, ht (0.9).
        Lefkandi I pl.33,23.

160.   Eretria, rim fr.
        Diam lip 10. Lip, offset, ht (0.9).
        Lefkandi I pl.33,24.

161.   Eretria, rim fr.
        Diam lip 14. Lip, offset, ht (1.2)
        Lefkandi I pl.33,25.

162.   Eretria, rim fr.
        Diam lip 12. Lip, offset, ht (0.9).
        Lefkandi I pl.33,26.

163.   Eretria, rim fr.

Diam lip 13. Lip, offset, ht (1.0).

Lefkandi I pl.33,27.

164.   Eretria, rim fr.

Diam lip 12. Lip, offset, ht (1.0).

Lefkandi I pl.33,28.

There are photographs of other pendent semicircle skyphos fragments on pll.22:A.472-3, E,F; 23:507-515; 24:560-566, 603-4; 25:653-9; 273:827 829-834; 277:1025; 278:B. See also *Lefkandi 1968* Fig. 59 and Popham *et al.* (Chapter 1 n. 3) pl.14,b.

165.   **Athens, British School, rim fr.**[19]   *Fig 23(b), Pl.9(d)*

Ht 3.9; w 4.0; diam lip (reconstructed) 13.0; th 0.4-5. Dark pinkish brown (5YR 6/3) to light yellow orange clay (7.5YR 7/2). Black paint. **Lip,** offset, ht 1.8. **Ext:** seven arcs of one set. **Int:** painted, except for reserved band on lip. **Context:** Xeropolis, unstratified.

See also Catalogue Appendix (p.193).

MARMARIANI
(*PGP* 135-142; 189-190)

166.   **Athens NM, Marmariani 115.**   *Fig 37(d), Pl.7(b)* .

Ht 8.9; diam lip 12.3-13.3; diam base 5.2; **th** 0.4. Pale orange clay (7.5YR 7/6), hard-fired and very micaceous with a few white and dark-coloured inclusions. Mainly black paint, but bright reddish brown arcs (5YR 4/8). **Lip,** not offset, ht 1.0; **foot** ht 0.6. **Ext:** two sets of 11 semicircles, intersecting. **Int:** painted. **Context:** multiple burial extending from the Sub-Mycenaean period to first half of the eighth century. From tomb V.

W.A. Heurtley and T.C. Skeat, "The Tholos Tombs of Marmáriane", *BSA* 31 (1930-1931) 28, Fig. 12.

167.   **Athens NM, Marmariani 116.**   *Fig 37(c), Pl.7(a)*

Ht 10.1; diam lip 14.5-15.1; diam base 5.8; **th** 0.3. Brownish clay (7.5YR 7/4), rather coarse and soft and very micaceous. White inclusions. Brownish red paint (2.5YR 5/6). **Lip,** not offset, but a slight ridge in places, ht 1.3; **foot** ht 0.6. **Ext:** two sets of eight semi-circles, intersecting on one side only. **Int:** painted. **Context:** as last but tomb unknown.

Marmariani 28, pl.VII.

168.   Athens NM, Marmariani 117.

Ht 9.0.   Buff clay with pinkish paint. **Ext**: two sets of nine semicircles, intersecting. **Int**: painted. **Context**: as *166*.

Marmariani 28, pl.VII.   (This skyphos could not be found when I visited the Museum in February 1977.)

169.   Athens NM, Marmariani 118.   *Fig 24, Pl.2(d)*

Ht 9.8; **diam lip** 13.5-14.0; **diam base** 5.0.   Pale orange clay (7.5YR 7/6), rather coarse and very micaceous.   White inclusions. Black to dark brown (5YR 3/3) paint. **Lip**, not offset, ht 1.3; flat **base**. **Ext**: two sets of seven semicircles, intersecting on one side only. Paint on lower part of body stops 2.5cm above the base. **Int**: painted. **Context**: as *166*.

Marmariani 28, pl.VII.

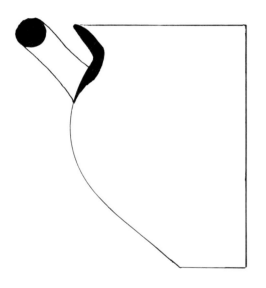

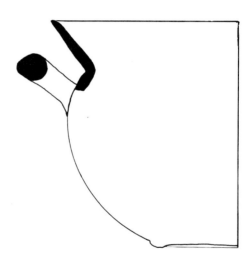

Fig. 24 Marmariani 118. Athens NM (*169*).   Fig. 25 Marmariani 122. Athens NM (*173*).

170.   Athens NM, Marmariani 119.   *Fig 36(b), Pl.4(c)*

Ht 11.5; **diam lip** 16.9-15.4; **diam base** 5.9; **th** 0.4-5. Brownish orange clay (5YR 6/6), hard-fired and micaceous.   A few white inclusions. Black to brown-red (2.5YR 5/8) paint. **Lip**, offset, ht 2.2; **foot** ht 0.8. **Ext**: two sets of nine semicircles, intersecting. **Int**: painted, except for reserved band on lip. **Context**: as *166*.

Marmariani 28, pl.VII; *GGP* 153, pl.32g; Coldstream (Chapter 1 n. 10) 38 Fig. 8a.

171.   Athens NM, Marmariani 120.   *Fig 35(c), Pl.3(d)*

    Ht 10.9; **diam lip** 15.6-16.5; **diam base** 6.3; **th** 0.5. Brownish orange clay (5YR 6/6), very coarse, with a few flecks of mica. Large white inclusions, Black to brownish red (2.5YR 5/6) paint. Dull reddish brown paint inside (2.5YR 4/4). **Lip**, offset, ht 2.0; **foot** ht 0.7. **Ext**: two sets of five semicircles, intersecting. **Int**: painted, except for reserved band on edge of lip. **Context**: as *166*.

    Marmariani 28, pl.VII.

172.   Athens NM, Marmariani 121.   *Fig 34(b), Pl.1(d)*

    Ht 10.9; **diam lip** 15.0-14.6; **diam base** 5.5; **th** 0.4. Brownish orange clay (5YR 6/6), hard-fired, with mica and small white inclusions. Mainly black paint, but patches of bright orange red (10R 5/8). **Lip**, not offset, but a slight ridge in places at the join between lip and body, ht 1.6; **foot** ht 0.6. **Ext**: two sets of seven semicircles, not intersecting. **Int**: painted, except for reserved band on edge of lip. **Context**: as *166*.

    Marmariani 28, pl.VII.

173.   Athens NM, Marmariani 122.   *Fig 25, Pl.2(c)*

    Ht 8.7-8.3; **diam lip** 14.1-14.6; **diam base** 6.2; **th** 0.3. Orange clay (5YR 7/6), hard-fired, with mica and dark coloured and white inclusions. Black to dark brownish red paint (2.5YR 4/8). **Lip**, offset and sagging badly in places, ht 1.5-2.0; minimal ring **foot**. **Ext**: two sets of five semicircles, intersecting on one side only. Hour-glass within the semicircles. **Int**: painted, except for reserved band on lip and small reserved circle in the centre. **Context**: as *166*. From tomb VI.

    Marmariani 28, pl.VII.

174.   Copenhagen NM 7025.[20]   *Fig 26*

    Ht 10.5; **diam lip** 16.0; **diam base** 5.0. Reddish clay. Brown, reddish paint. **Lip**, offset, ht 1.1; flat **base**. **Ext**: two sets of 11 semicircles, not intersecting. The paint on the lower part of the body is broken by a reserved band. **Int**: painted. **Context**: tholos tomb.

    CVA Copenhagen (2), pl.66.4.

MERSIN

175.   One probable fragment: J. Garstang, "Explorations in Cilicia, Excavations at Mersin 1938-9. The Historic Periods, Pts. III and IV", *Liverpool Annals of Archaeology and Anthropology* 26 (1940) 103, pl.LXXVI, 15; *PGP* 181.

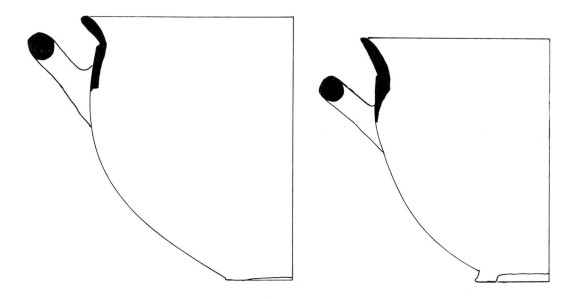

Fig. 26 Marmariani. Copenhagen NM 7025 (*174*).   Fig. 27 Nea Ionia (Iolcos). Volos K2235 (*178*).

METHYMNA

176.   A rim fragment was found in an undated context. (Buchholz (*82*) 90, Fig. 25[a].)

NAXOS

177.   Two shoulder fragments with the beginning of an offset lip are published by Walter-Karydi (Chapter 1 n. 23) 387, Fig. 1:10 (=396, Fig 17:10); Fig. 1:11, and 417 (Catalogue). Good quality clay similar to Attic, with white slip. **Context:** uncertain.

     See also Catalogue Appendix (p.193).

NEA IONIA (IOLCOS)

178.   **Volos** K2235.   *Fig 27, Pl.5(c)*

     Ht 9.7; **diam lip** 14.2-13.7; **diam base** 5.4; **th** 0.3. Orange clay (7.5YR 7/8), micaceous and rather soft. Mainly brownish red paint (2.5YR 5/6). **Lip,** offset, ht 1.4; **foot** ht 0.5. **Ext:** two sets of nine semicircles, intersecting on one side only. **Int:** painted, except for reserved band on lip. **Context**: cist tomb. late tenth–early ninth centuries.

 M.D. Theocharis, "Protogeometrikoi Taphoi N. Ionias Volou", *Thessalika E* (1966) 49, Fig. 13; *Lefkandi I* 288 n. 44.

179. **Volos K2237.**   *Fig 35(d), Pl.5(b)*

 Ht 9.9; **diam lip** 13.2–13.6; **diam base** 5.7; **th** 0.4. Orange clay (5YR 7/6), hard-fired. Black paint. **Lip**, offset, ht 1.7; **foot** ht 0.6. **Ext**: two sets of eight semicircles, intersecting. **Int**: painted, except for reserved band on lip. **Context**: as *178*.

 Theocharis, *Thessalika E* (1966) 51, Fig. 15.

NINEVEH

180. One Protogeometric sherd is reported: R. Campbell Thompson, "The Excavations on the Temple of Nabu at Nineveh", *Archaeologia 79* (1929) 138. This is described in *Sukas I* 144 n. 574 as a fragment of a pendent semicircle skyphos.

ORCHOMENOS (?)

181. There is a rather small skyphos on display in the Chaeronea Museum (February 1977) which is probably to be identified with that said by Desborough (*PGP* 190-2) to come from an unpublished tomb at Orchomenos. The decoration is of eight semicircles in both sets, and the two sets intersect. The lip is rather short, not offset, flaring outwards from the body. There is a low foot.

PALEKYTHRO

182. **Nicosia** 1972/IV-11/1

 Ht 9.5; **diam lip** 15.0; **diam base** (5.2). Yellowish clay. Dark brown paint. **Lip**, offset, ht (1.2); **foot** ht (1.4). **Ext**: two sets of 12 semicircles, intersecting on one side only. The lip is painted on its lower part and on the extreme top edge, but reserved between. **Int**: only top part of lip and lower section of body painted, reserved between. **Context**: unkown.

 H.W. Catling, "A Pendent Semicircle Skyphos from Cyprus and a Cypriot Imitation", *RDAC* (1973) 179, 181 no. 14, Fig. 1, pl.XVII; V. Karageorghis, "Chronique de fouilles à Chypre en 1972", *BCH* 97 (1973) 606 no. 9, Fig. 12; D. Chrestou, *ADeltChr* 29 (1973-4 [1980]), 1011 no. 9, pl.754 B; *GGAPC* 24 no. 22.

PAROS

183.   One unpublished sherd is reported by Desborough (*PGP* 186). Other fragments have recently been found in the geometric settlement at Koukounaries: D.U. Schilardi, "The Decline of the Geometric Settlement of Koukounaries at Paros", in R. Hägg (ed.), *The Greek Renaissance,* (Monograph XIV, Institute of Archaeology, University of Los Angeles, [1983]) 177.

PHAISTOS

184.   **Phaistos,** rim fr.

Diam lip ?   Pink clay with pinkish slip.   Red Paint. **Ext:** four arcs of one set. **Int:** painted. **Context:** on the lower floor of structure G, Protogeometric – Late Geometric.

L. Rocchetti, "La ceramica dell'abitato geometrico di Festòs", *ASAtene* 52-53 (1974-1975) 262-5; 296, Fig. 127:11.

Two other fragments, a shoulder and a wall, are illustrated among the surface finds (287, Fig. 167, top row, third and fourth from left).   Possibly another rim fragment in D. Levi, "Gli scavi a Festòs nel 1956 e 1957", *ASAtene* 35-36 (1957-58) 287, Fig. 125B.

PHOCAEA

185.   The occurrence of pendent semicircle skyphoi at Phocaea is commented on by Boardman (*67*) 117.

PHTHIOTIC THEBES

186.   Two pendent semicircle skyphos fragments are mentioned by Desborough (*PGP* 153, 189).

PONTECAGNANO

See Catalogue Appendix (p.193).

PTELEON

187.   One wall fragment of a pendent semicircle skyphos from a multiple burial tomb covering several centuries is mentioned in *PGRT* 28, no. 62).

RAS EL BASSIT

188.   One pendent semicircle skyphos: P. Courbin, "Rapport sur la 4ème campagne de fouilles (1974) à Ras el Bassit", *AAS* 25 (1975) 60. Others are referred to in "Rapport sur la sixième campagne de fouilles à Ras Bassit (Syrie)", *AAS* 27-28 (1977-1978) 30.

RHENEIA

The following six skyphoi are from one or more burials of local inhabitants and were not part of the material from the Delos Purification Trench. *PGP* 156-7, 186-9; *GGP* 156.

189.   **Mykonos** 25 (=A1463).

Ht 7.4; **diam lip** 12.3-12.8; **diam base** 5.0; **th** 0.3. Yellow orange clay (7.5YR 8/6) with pale orange slip (7.5YR 7/6). Mainly light brownish red paint (2.5YR 6/6). **Lip,** offset, ht 1.0; **foot** ht 0.5. **Ext:** two sets of ten semicircles, intersecting. **Int:** painted, except for reserved band on lip, and reserved circle in centre. **Context:** mixed burial groups.

PGP 156-7, pl.25B.

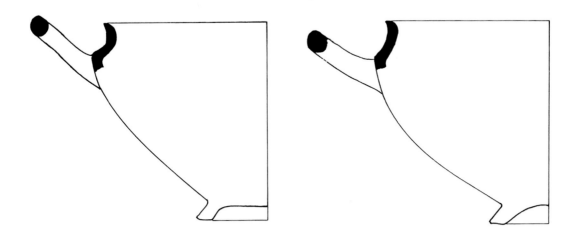

Fig. 28   **Rheneia** A1464. Mykonos 21 (*190*).   Fig. 29   **Rheneia** A1465. Mykonos 24 (*191*).

190.   **Mykonos** 21 (=A1464).   *Fig 28*

    Ht 7.9; **diam lip** 12.5–12.8; **diam base** 5.4; **th** 0.4. Light yellow orange clay (7.5YR 8/4) with brownish slip (7.5YR 7/4). Black paint. **Lip**, offset, ht 1.3; **foot** ht 0.8. **Ext**: two sets of nine semicircles, intersecting. **Int**: painted, except for reserved band on lip and reserved circle in centre. **Context**: as last.

    PGP 156–7, pl.25B.

191.   **Mykonos** 24 (=A1465).   *Fig 29*

    Ht 8.0; **diam lip** 12.5; **diam base** 4.7; **th** 0.4. Orange clay (7.5YR 7/8) with pale orange slip (7.5YR 7/6). Brownish red paint (2.5YR 6/8). **Lip**, offset, ht 1.5; **foot** ht 0.8. **Ext**: two sets of 13 semicircles, intersecting. **Int**: painted, except for reserved band. **Context**: as *189*.

    PGP 156–7, pl.25B; Descoeudres/Kearsley (Chapter 1 n. 3) 44 n. 121, Fig. 42.

192.   **Mykonos** 20 (=A1466).   *Fig 39(c)*

    Ht 7.9; **diam lip** 12.2–12.6; **diam base** 5.0; **th** 0.4. Yellow orange clay (7.5YR 8/6) with pale orange slip (7.5YR 7/6). Mainly light brownish red paint (2.5YR 6/8). **Lip**, offset, ht 1.4: **foot** ht 0.8. **Ext**: two sets of ten semicircles, intersecting. **Int**: painted, except for reserved band on lip and reserved circle in centre. **Context**: as *189*.

    PGP 156–7, pl.25B; *GGP* pl.32,h; [21] Coldstream (Chapter 1 n. 10) 89, Fig. 28d.

193.   **Mykonos** 22 (=A1467).

    Ht 7.4; **diam lip** 13.0; **diam base** 5.0; **th** 0.4. Pinkish brown clay (5YR 7/4) with pinkish orange slip (2.5YR 7/6). Black to light brownish red paint (2.5YR 6/6). **Lip**, offset, ht 1.1; **foot** ht 0.5. **Ext**: two sets of nine semicircles, intersecting. **Int**: painted, except for reserved band on lip. **Context**: as *189*.

    PGP 156–7, pl.25B.

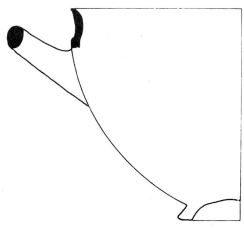

Fig. 30 Rheneia A1468. Mykonos 23 (*194*).

194.   Mykonos 23   (=A1468)   *Fig 30*

Ht 8.1-8.4; diam lip 13.1; diam base 5.0; th 0.3. Soft pale orange clay (7.5YR 7/6).   Very slight traces of a slip.   There are only very pale traces of paint, once black. Lip, offset, ht 1.2; foot ht 0.7. Ext: two sets, probably of 11 semicircles, intersecting. Int: painted. Context: as *189*.

PGP 156-7, pl.25B.

SALAMIS (CYPRUS)

195.   Nicosia, Salamis 106.

Ht (8.4); diam lip 13.0; diam base (5.4). Lip, offset (1.3); foot ht (0.4). Ext: two sets of eight semicircles, intersecting. Int: painted, except for reserved line on lip. Context: tomb associated with Attic skyphoi of *ca.*775-750 BC. End of Cypro-Geometric III – beginning Cypro-Archaic I.

P. Dikaios "A 'Royal' Tomb at Salamis, Cyprus", *AA* 78 (1963) 190, Fig. 35, no. 46, and Appendix II: Desborough (Chapter 1 n. 15) 204-6, Fig. 42; *GGP* 157; Catling, *RDAC* (1973) 180 no. 1; *GGAPC* 24 no. 5, pl.I,5; *Lefkandi I* 341 n. 411; Karageorghis (*100*) 529.

196.   Nicosia, Salamis 119.

Much restored, diam lip 12.7. Ext: two sets of eight semicircles, intersecting. Context: as last.

Dikaios, *AA* 78 (1963) 191 and Desborough, 204-6, Fig. 42; *GGP* 157; Catling *RDAC* (1973) 180 no. 2; *GGAPC* 24 no. 6, pl.I,6.

SARATSE

197.   Thessaloniki II 854, rim fr.

A marked white slip covers the clay. Pinkish brown paint. Short, offset lip. Ext: two sets of 13 semicircles, intersecting. Int: painted.

W.A. Heurtley and C. Ralegh Radford, "The Toumba of Saratsé, Macedonia, 1929", *BSA* 30 (1928-9, 1929-30) 141, Fig. 281.[22]

SARDINIA

See Catalogue Appendix (p.193).

SARDIS

198.   Two rim fragments from Sardis are published in G.M.A. Hanfmann, "The Ninth Campaign at Sardis (1966)", *BASOR* 186 (1967) 27, Fig. 12 nos. 24, 27.

SAREPTA

199. A rim fragment decorated with pendent semicircles has been published from Sarepta: J.B. Pritchard, *Sarepta: a preliminary report on the Iron Age* (Philadelphia 1975) 96, Fig. 26:14. The profile of the fragment is compared with one of the skyphoi from Hama. However, it is possible also that the fragment comes from a plate, such as that from Tarsus (*Tarsus III* Fig. 146, no. 1513). The published profile does not allow a firm decision. **Diam lip** 14.0. **Clay** 10YR 4/3. **Paint** 7.5YR N41. **Context**: Kiln V, II-B-5.

See also Catalogue Appendix (p.194).

SESKLO

200.   Volos K2247, (Sesklo 9-65).   *Fig 36(a), Pl.3(c)*

Ht 10.5-11.0; **diam lip** 15.4-16.4; **diam base** 6.2; **th** 0.4. Pale orange clay (7.5YR 7/6), hard-fired and very micaceous. Light red paint (10R 5/6). **Lip**, offset, ht 1.8; **foot** ht 0.5. **Ext**: two sets of 11 semicircles, intersecting. **Int**: painted, except for reserved band on edge of lip and small circle in centre. **Context**:unknown. Perhaps from the tholos referred to in Theocharis *178* 50 n.3.

SKYROS

201.   Eight skyphoi were found in tombs excavated by Stavropoullos. These have not been published to date, but notes and sketches of six of these made available to me by Mr V.R. Desborough in 1976 indicate that they are of a similar type to the deep skyphoi with high flaring and offset lip such as that from Lefkandi S.T56. *PGP* 165-6 and 189-90; *GGP* 152. See V.R. Desborough, "A Group of Vases from Skyros", in *Stele N. Kontoleontos* (Athens 1980) 55-58.

SMYRNA

202.   Pendent semicircle skyphos fragments with high or medium lip were found in the Anglo-Turkish excavations at Old Smyrna during 1948-51. See *Lefkandi I* 292 n. 81.

SOLI

203.   Nicosia

Ht (7.0); **diam lip** (11.2); **diam base** (4.6). **Lip**, offset, ht (ca. 1.3); **foot** ht (0.5). **Ext**:two sets of five semicircles, intersecting. **Int**: painted, except for reserved band on edge of lip. **Context**: looted tomb, dated by Cypriot/Syrian pottery to the end of the eighth century.

V. Karageorghis, "Chronique des fouilles à Chypre en 1960",
BCH 85 (1961) 277, Fig. 28a; *GGAPC* 24 no. 7, pl.I,7; Catling, *RDAC*
(1973) 180 no. 3.

204.   Nicosia

Preserved ht (5.5); **diam lip** (12.2). Lip, not offset. **Ext**: two sets
of seven semicircles, intersecting. **Int**: painted, except for reserved
band on edge of lip. **Context**: as last.

Karageorghis, *BCH* 85 (1961) 277, Fig. 28a; *GGAPC* 24 no. 8,
pl.I,8; Catling, *RDAC* (1973) 180 no. 4.

TABBAT AL HAMMAM

205.   A wall fragment thought to be from a pendent semicircle skyphos
is illustrated in R.J. Braidwood, "Report on Two Sondages on the Coast
of Syria, South of Tartous", *Syria* 21 (1940) 193, Fig. 4.9; *PGP* 181;
GGP 311; *Sukas I* 142, 152.

TARSUS

206.   **Adana, Tarsus** 1500, rim fr.

Ht 5.7; **diam lip** (reconstructed) 12.0; **th** 0.4.   Dark reddish
brown clay, well levigated with very small particles of mica.   Light
brown slip.   Dark brown-black paint, thinning out occasionally to red.
Lip, offset, ht (1.2). **Ext**: two sets, intersecting. **Int**: painted, except
for reserved band on lip. **Context**: Middle Iron period (*ca.* 850-700 BC),
early part.   For dates see *Tarsus III* 115.

Tarsus III 306 Fig. 146.

207.   **Adana, Tarsus** 1501, rim fr.

Ht 5.5; **diam lip** (reconstructed) 15.0.   Fabric as above, but
slip turned to grey. **Lip**, offset, ht (1.2). **Context**: as last, possibly the
early part.

Tarsus III 306 Fig. 146.

208.   **Adana, Tarsus** 1505, base fr.

Ht 3.0; **diam base** 4.5.   Fabric as above. **Foot** ht (0.7).
Context: early part of Middle Iron.

Tarsus III 306 Fig. 146.

209.   Adana, Tarsus 1508, rim fr.

Ht 3.6; w 5.5. **Lip**, offset, ht (1.1). **Ext**: eight arcs of one set. **Context**: unstratified, but 12 or more fragments of this type were found in the destruction fill.

Tarsus III 307, Fig. 146.

210.   Adana, Tarsus 1509, rim fr.

Ht 2.0; w 3.7. **Lip**, offset, ht (1.1). **Ext**: five arcs of one set. Only top edge of lip is painted. **Context**: as last.

Tarsus III 307, Fig. 146.

211.   Adana, Tarsus 1510, rim fr.

Ht 2.5; w 3.7. Red paint. **Lip**, offset, ht (1.2). **Ext**: eight arcs of one set. Lip is painted only on top edge. **Context**: as *209*.

Tarsus III 307, Fig. 146.

More than 80 fragments (from at least 40 vases) were found at Tarsus, among which were nos. 1506-7 for which no profiles are given on Fig. 146. (*Tarsus III* 305-7).

TEKE - see KNOSSOS

TELL ABU HAWAM

212.   **Jerusalem**, PAM 37.318, rim fr.   *Fig 40(c)*

Ht 6.4; w 6.2; diam lip 14.0.   Fine hard red-buff clay with buff slip.   Red paint. **Lip**, slightly offset, ht (1.4). **Ext**: part of one set of nine semicircles only. **Int**: entirely painted. **Context**: level III-date disputed.

Hamilton *23*, 24 no. 96, pl. XII; W.A. Heurtley, "Note on Fragments of Two Thessalian Proto-geometric Vases found at Tell Abu Hawam", *QDAP* 4 (1934-1935) 181 pl. LXXXVIII; *PGP* 181-5, pl. 26,4; *GGP* 303-310; *Sukas I* 142-152, Fig. 47a; P. Courbin, "Une Pyxis géométrique argienne (?) au Liban", *Berytus* 25 (1977) 157 n. 54.   Popham *et al*. (Chapter 1 n. 3) 151.
See also Catalogue Appendix (p. 194)

TELL HALAF

213.   Location unknown.

Ht 8.0; diam lip (11.5); diam base (5.0). Dark paint. **Lip**, offset, ht ?; **foot** ht ? **Ext:** two sets of 11 semicircles, intersecting. **Context:** unknown.

B. Hrouda, *Tell Halaf IV* (Berlin 1962) pl.69, 188; Buchholz (Chapter 1 n. 14) 224; *GGP* 311; *Sukas I* 144, Fig. 48e.

TELL JUDAIDAH

214.   One fragment with rim and handle.   Eight arcs of one set: *PGP* 181, pl.26,6; *Sukas I* 144.

TELL SUKAS

215.   **Aleppo TS 2018,** rim fr.

Ht 5.2; **w** 7.0; **diam lip** ?   Fine, pale buff clay with tiny white grits and a little mica.   Black to light brown paint. **Lip,** offset, ht (1.3). **Ext:** two sets of 11 semicircles, intersecting. **Int:** painted, except for reserved band on lip. **Context:** Hellenistic fill.

P.J. Riis, "L'activité de la mission archéologique danoise sur la côte phénicienne en 1959", *AAS* 10 (1960) 123, Fig. 13; *Sukas I* 50 n. 143, 142-144, Figs. 53b, 54,a; *Sukas II* 15, Fig. a,37, pl.IIA.

There is also a wall fragment from Tell Sukas (TS 1012). *Sukas I* 50 n. 143, 142-4, Figs. 53,c, 54,b; *Sukas II*, pl.IIA, 38. **Context:** as *215*.

TELL TAYINAT

(*PGP* 181-185; *Sukas I* 144).

216.   **Chicago, Oriental Institute** 646, rim fr.[23]

..t 2.1; **w** 3.7; **diam lip** (reconstructed) 13.0; **th** 0.4. Light dull brown clay (7.5YR 6/3) with very discoloured slip.   Faded paint, mainly black on outside and black-dark brown (5YR 3/3) on the inside. **Lip,** offset, ht 1.2. **Ext:** four arcs of one set; **Int:** painted. Unpublished.

217.   **Chicago, Oriental Institute** 625, rim fr.

Ht 3.7; **w** 3.2; **diam lip** (reconstructed) 11.0; **th** 0.4. Brownish clay (7.5YR 7/4) with brownish-pinkish beige slip (7.5YR 7/4-3).   A few small white inclusions.   Mainly black paint but reddish brown arcs (5YR 5/6). **Lip,** offset, ht 1.3. **Ext:** four arcs of one set and two of the other, intersecting. **Int:** painted, except for broad reserved band on edge of lip.   Unpublished.

218.   Chicago, Oriental Institute, no number, rim fr.

Ht 3.6; w 3.3; diam lip (reconstructed) 15.0; th 0.3.   Pinkish brown clay (5YR 7/4) with light brown slip (7.5YR 6/4).   One or two specks of mica.   Mainly black paint, but light reddish brown arcs (5YR 5/4). Lip, offset, ht 1.4. Ext: seven arcs of one set. Int: painted, except for reserved band on edge of lip. Unpublished.

219.   Chicago, Oriental Institute 634, rim fr.

Ht 2.9; w 3.1; diam lip 14.0; th 0.4.   Cream-yellow clay (5YR 8/2-3) with light brown slip (7.5YR 6/4).   White inclusions.   Brownish black paint (5YR 2/1). Lip, offset, ht 1.2. Ext: seven arcs of one set and five of the other, intersecting. Int: painted, except for reserved band on lip.   Unpublished.

220.   Chicago, Oriental Institute 615, rim and handle fr.

Ht 5.7; diam lip ca.10.0. Pinkish beige clay (7.5YR 7/3) without mica.   Light brown slip (7.5YR 6/4). Lip, offset, ht 0.8. Ext: two arcs of one set preserved. Int: painted, except for reserved band on lip. Unpublished.

There is a more complete example from Tell Tayinat (T.2947) in the Oriental Institute.[24] *PGP* 181, pl.26,5; *Sukas I* 144, Fig. 48,c; Hanfmann (Chapter 2 *34* 175 n. 36); *GGP* 311.   There are also several wall fragments.

TENOS? (TINE)

221.   A possible grave group, now in the Vatican, said to be from Tine and containing two pendent semicircle skyphoi is published by C. Albizzati, *Vasi antichi dipinti del Vaticano* (Rome 1925) fasc. i 1-2, nos. 1-5.   One pendent semicircle skyphos (no. 4) is illustrated on pl.1,4 and also in *PGP* pl.25A. Ext: two sets of 14 semicircles, intersecting.   The second skyphos, no. 5, is not illustrated. *PGP* 158-9, 186-9; *GGP* 152.

THASOS

222.   Thasos, rim fr.

Ht 6.0; w 7.5.   Fine hard pale clay with some white particles. Brown to black paint. Lip, not offset, ht (1.2). Ext: part of one set of 11 semicircles preserved. Int: painted, except for reserved band on lip. Context: associated with material of the first half of the seventh century: probably displaced, according to the excavator.

P. Bernard, "Céramiques de la première moitié du VIIe siecle a Thasos", *BCH* 88 (1964) 140, Figs. 10 and 52.

THESSALY

223.   **Volos K1144.**   *Fig. 31, Pl. 6(c)*

Ht 10.4-6; **diam lip** 14.9-16.5; **diam base** 6.1; **th** 0.4.   Light yellow-orange clay (7.5YR 8/4), micaceous and rather soft.   Very faded dark paint. **Lip,** offset, ht 0.9; **foot** ht 0.3. **Ext:** two sets of nine semi-circles, not intersecting. **Int:** painted. **Context:** unknown. [25]

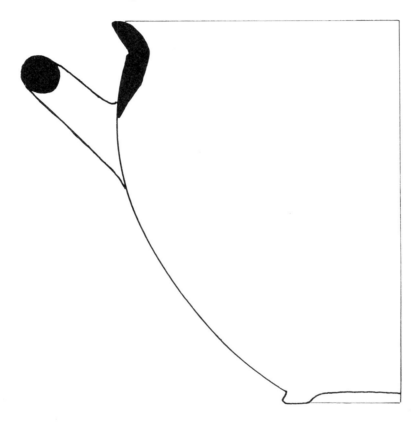

Fig. 31   Thessaly. Volos K1144 (*223*).

224.   **Volos K1117.**   *Fig. 37(b), Pl. 6(d)*

Ht 10.5; **diam lip** 15.5-15.9; **diam base** 5.7; **th** 0.4. Yellow-orange clay (7.5YR 8/6), micaceous and rather soft. Mainly dark brown paint (2.5YR 3/3) with streaky patches of dark reddish brown (2.5YR 3/4). **Lip,** offset, ht 1.2; **foot** ht 0.5. **Ext:** two sets of nine semicircles, intersecting on one side only. **Int:** painted, except for reserved band on lip. **Context:** unknown.

TORONE

See Catalogue Appendix (p.194).

TROY

225.　**Troy VIII** 124, rim fr.

Reddish-buff clay with buff surface.　Brown paint.　**Lip**, not preserved to full height.　**Ext**: six arcs of the left set and eight of the right.　Not intersecting.　**Context**: Settlement VIII.　No pottery of earlier date than 700 BC.

C.W. Blegen *et al., Troy IV* (Princeton 1958) 279, pl.303,8.

226.　**Troy** no number, rim fr.

Light red-brown clay.　Dark brown lustrous paint. Short **lip**. **Ext**: only one set, probably of eight semicircles, preserved. **Context**: with pottery of VIIb,1 but probably out of context. (Settlement VIIb ends *ca.*1100 BC).

Blegen, *Troy IV,* 233, pl.278,26.

TYRE

227.　Rim fr.

Dark brown clay (5YR 3/2).　Dark brown metallic paint (5YR 4/2). **Lip**, offset. **Ext**: seven arcs of one set. **Int**: painted, except for reserved band on edge of lip. **Context**: stratum IX: mid 9th century on.

P.M. Bikai, *The Pottery of Tyre* (Warminster 1978) 53, pl.XXII,4.

Twenty-four fragments in all were found.　A shoulder fragment is also illustrated from Stratum X,1 (after 850).　Bikai, 53, pl.XXIV,6; *Lefkandi I* 341 n. 412.

VATI (RHODES)

228.　Two complete skyphoi are illustrated in I.Ch. Papachristodoulou, "Geometrikos Taphos eis Vati, Rodou", *AAA* 8 (1975) 226, Fig. 3.

See also Catalogue Appendix (p. 194).

VEII

229.　**Rome, Villa Giulia** 60255.[26]　　　　　　　　　　*Fig. 40(d)*

Ht 6.1; diam lip 10.0; diam base 4.0.　Recomposed and partly restored.　Clay well levigated without mica; hard-fired.　Core pink (7.5YR 7/4), surface (completely worn) very pale brown (*ca.*9YR 7/4).

Black paint, dull or only slightly lustrous; diluted brown (6.5YR 5/4). **Lip**, offset, ht 1.0; **base**, flat. **Ext**: very worn. Faint traces of two sets of five semicircles in handle zone, not intersecting. Broad encircling bands on rim and lower part of wall. **Int**: painted, except for thin band reserved on lip. **Context**: Quattro Fontanili cemetery, square F13 (surface find).

A. de Agostino *et al.*, "Veio", *NSc* 17 (1963) 89–90, Fig. 4a; 166, Fig. 59d; D. Ridgway and O.T.P.K. Dickinson, "Pendent Semicircles at Veii: a Glimpse", *BSA* 68 (1973) 191–2, Fig. 1; Descoeudres/Kearsley (Chapter 1 n. 3) 41 no. 18, Fig. 43.

230.   **Rome, Villa Giulia, Veii no number.**[27]

Ht 6.3; **diam lip** 12.3; **diam base** 5.3. Light coloured clay. Red paint. **Lip**, not offset, ht (0.7); **foot** ht (0.4). **Ext**: two sets of five semicircles, intersecting. **Int**: painted, except for reserved band on lip. **Context**: Quattro Fontanili Tomb AABγ – IIA phase.

E. Fabbricotti, "Veio" *NSc* 26 (1972) 246, Fig. 36. E. La Rocca, "Due tombe dell'Esquilino", *Dialoghi di Archeologia* 8 (1974–1975) 97, Fig. D; Descoeudres/Kearsley (Chapter 1 n. 3) 41 no. 19.

VERGINA [28]

231.   **Thessaloniki, Vergina Δ 15.**

Ht 9.9; **diam lip** 13.9–14.3; **diam base** 5.4; **th** 0.4. Buff clay (10YR 7/2), hard-fired. Black paint. **Lip**, offset, ht 1.9; **foot** ht 0.5. **Ext**: two sets of ten semicircles, intersecting. **Int**: painted, except for reserved band on lip. **Context**: multiple burials extending from 1000 – 700 BC.

M. Andronikos, *Vergina I. To Nekrotapheion ton Tumbon*, (Athens 1969) 169, Fig. 23, pl.34.

232.   **Thessaloniki, Vergina P 1.**

Ht 11.9; **diam lip** 17.0–16.0; **diam base** 6.5; **th** 0.2. Fabric as above, but a few flecks of mica. Black paint. **Lip**, offset, ht 1.7; **foot** ht 0.4. **Ext**: two sets of nine semicircles, not intersecting. **Int**: painted. **Context**: as last.

Vergina I 169, Fig. 23, pl.49.

233.   **Thessaloniki, Vergina P 21.**

Ht 10.9; **diam lip** 14.4–16.7; **diam base** 6.6; **th** 0.4. Light yellow beige clay (10YR 8/2), very micaceous, Light brownish red paint (2.5YR 6/8). **Lip**, offset, ht 1.8–1.6; **foot** ht 0.6. **Ext**: two sets of nine semicircles, intersecting. The paint on the lower part is broken by two reserved bands. **Int**: painted. **Context**: as *231*.

Vergina I 169, Fig. 23, pl.50.

234.   Thessaloniki, Vergina T 1.

Full **ht** not preserved; **diam lip** 19.0.   Brownish red clay with a lighter surface.   Dark red paint. **Lip**, not offset, ht (1.5).   **Ext:** two sets of ten semicircles, not intersecting.   **Int:** upper half painted. **Context:** as *231*.

Vergina I 170, Fig. 24, pl.51.

235.   Thessaloniki, Vergina AΓ 24.

Ht 10.5; **diam lip** 14.0; **diam base** 5.8; **th** 0.4.   Beige clay (7.5YR 8/3), very micaceous. Dark brownish red paint (2.5YR 4/8) with black patches.   Very worn. **Lip**, a slight ridge where lip joins body, ht 1.5; **foot** ht 0.6. **Ext:** two sets of seven semicircles, touching only. **Int:** painted. **Context:** as *231*.

Vergina I 169, Fig. 23, pl.63.

236.   Thessaloniki, Vergina AZ 16.

Ht 8.2; **diam lip** 12.1-12.6; **diam base** 5.2;   **th** 0.4.   Pale yellow clay (7.5YR 8/4), micaceous.   Dark brownish red paint (2.5YR 4/8). **Lip**, slightly offset, ht 1.9; **foot** ht 0.3. **Ext:** two sets of seven semicircles on one side and eight on the other.   Both sides intersecting. **Int:** painted. **Context:** as *231*.

Vergina I 169, Fig. 23, pl.72.

At least three other skyphoi have been found at the site, see M. Andronikos, *Vergina I* 171.   (One of these may be that illustrated in M. Andronikos, "Vergina, The Prehistoric Necropolis and the Hellenistic Palace", [*Studies in Mediterranean Archaeology* 13, London 1964] 11, Fig. 9).

VILLASMUNDO[29]

237.   Syracuse National Museum 78407.

Ht 6.1; **diam lip** 12.2; **diam base** 5.6. (Recomposed from several fragments, both handles and part of one side missing).   Hard-fired clay with some white inclusions.   Core reddish brown (4-7.5YR 5-6/4-5). Fine slip, light brown (10YR 7.5/3-4).   Slightly glossy surface. Paint black, fading to reddish brown/brown (2.5-7.5YR 4-5/5-6). (The clay is of Eretrian type.) **Lip**, offset, ht 1.4; **base** flat. **Ext:** two sets of six semicircles, intersecting. **Int:** painted all over. **Context:** a violated tomb in the cemetery at Villasmundo dated to the eighth century.

G. Voza, "L'attività della Soprintendenza alle Antichità della Sicilia Orientale, Parte II", *Kokalos* 22-23 (1976-77) 570, pl.CVIII,1;

R. Romeo (ed.), *Storia della Sicilia I* (1979) pl.33; G. Voza, "La necropoli della valle del Marcellino presso Villasmundo", in "Insediamenti coloniali greci in Sicilia nell'VIII e VII secolo A.C.", (various authors), *Cronache di Archeologia* 17 (1978) 104-110, pl.27,1; Descoeudres/Kearsley (Chapter 1 n. 3) 41 n. 106.

VRANESI COPAIDOS[30]

238.   **Chaironeia 161.**

Ht 16.1; **diam lip** 24.0.   Soft brown clay.   Dull red paint. **Lip**, slightly offset, tall and flaring; **foot** low conical. **Ext**: two sets of 18 semicircles, intersecting. **Int**: painted except for reserved band on lip. **Context**: mixed tombs ranging from Late Protogeometric to Late Geometric.

PGP 191-2, 196-7, pl.17,5.

ZAGORA

239.   **Andros** C67 (formerly 145).

Ht 10.5; **diam lip** (15.0); **diam base** (6.1). Dark yellow surface, slightly micaceous clay.   Black-brown paint.   Island ware. **Lip**, not offset, ht (1.3); **foot** ht (0.7). **Ext**: two sets of ten semicircles, intersecting. **Int**: painted, except for reserved band on lip. **Context**: mixed burials, Protogeometric-Early Geometric material: 900-875.

PGP 161-3, 189-9, pl.16; *Lefkandi I* 292 n. 73; A. Cambitoglou, *Archaeological Museum of Andros.   Guide* (Athens 1981) 101, no. 341.

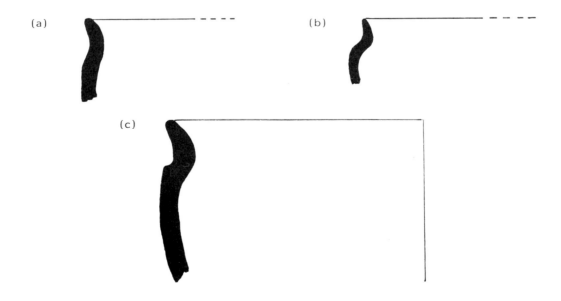

Fig. 32 **Zagora.**   (a) Zagora 1739 (*240*); (b) Zagora 2466 (*241*); (c) Zagora 2602 (*242*).

240.   Andros, Zagora 1739, rim fr.[31]   *Fig. 32(a)*

Ht 2.3; w 2.6; **diam lip** ?   Island ware. **Ext:** six arcs of one set. **Int:** painted except for reserved band on lip. **Lip,** not offset, ht (0.7). **Context:** WE/14, deposit 2-mixed deposit: 900-750.

Cambitoglou, *Andros Guide,* 47 no. 62.

241.   Andros, Zagora 2466, rim fr.   *Fig. 32(b)*

Ht 1.8; w 1.9; **diam lip** ?   **Lip,** not offset, ht (0.5).   **Ext:** five arcs of one set. **Context:** H19, bench fill, deposit 2-early Late Geometric, with some Middle Geometric.

242.   Andros, Zagora 2602, rim fr.   *Fig. 32(c)*

Ht 4.4; w 7.0; **diam lip** 13.6. **Lip,** offset, ht (1.2). **Ext:** only one set of nine semicircles. **Int:** painted, except for reserved band on lip. **Context:** FW6, deposit 8 (mainly Middle Geometric I with some Early Geometric and, possibly, a little early Middle Geometric II).

There is also at least one shoulder fragment from the Zagora excavations (inv. 2510).

UNKNOWN PROVENANCE: IN VARIOUS COLLECTIONS

243.   Geneva, Coll. Dorig.

Ht 7.0; **diam lip** (10-11.0); **diam base** (4.1). Brownish clay. Black paint. **Lip,** offset, ht (0.8); **foot,** ht (0.6). **Ext:** two sets of nine semicircles, intersecting.   **Int:** painted, except for reserved band on lip.

J. Dörig, *Art Antique. Collections Privées de Suisse Romande* (Geneva 1975) no. 118.

244.   Sydney, Nicholson Museum 73.03.[32]   *Fig. 38(b), Pl.8(a)*

Ht 8.8; **diam lip** 14.6-15.6; **diam base** 7.3; **th** 0.4-5.   Light pinkish brown clay (5YR 7/4) with brownish surface (7.5YR 7/4).   A few fine white inclusions.   Brownish black (7.5YR 2/2) to brownish (2.5YR 5/6) paint, with yellowish brown (7.5YR 6/6) for the arcs. **Lip,** offset, ht 0.9; **foot** ht 0.4. **Ext:** two sets of 11 semicircles, intersecting. **Int:** painted, except for reserved band on lip.

245.   Ischia. Private Collection (once Athens Market).[33]

Ht 7.1-7.2; **diam lip** 11.0. **Lip,** offset, ht 1.1; **foot** ht 0.8. **Ext:** two sets of nine semicircles, intersecting. **Int:** painted except for reserved band on lip.

72

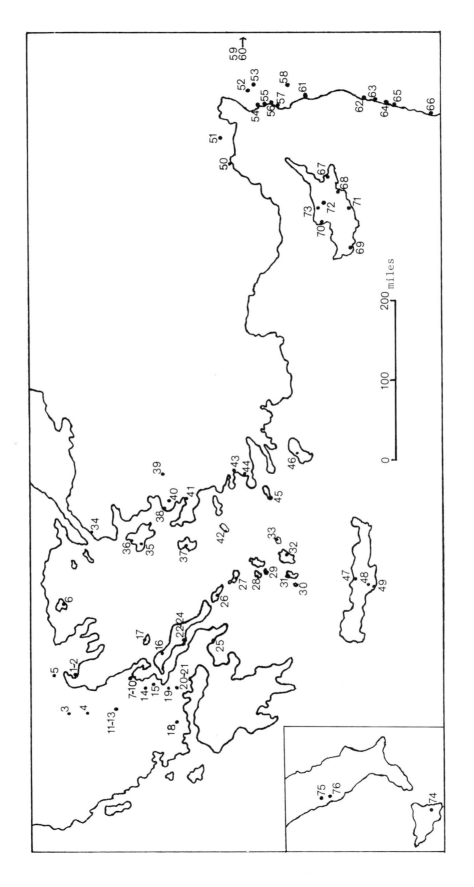

Figure 33: Distribution of Pendent Semicircle Skyphoi throughout the Mediterranean.

KEY TO DISTRIBUTION MAP OF PENDENT SEMICIRCLE SKYPHOI[35]

1.	Kalamaria	39.	Sardis
2.	Karabournaki	40.	Larisa, Aeolis
3.	Chauchitsa	41.	Smyrna
4.	Vergina	42.	Ikaria
5.	Saratse	43.	Didyma
6.	Thasos	44.	Iasos
7.	Iolcos	45.	Cos
8.	Kapakli	46.	Vati
9.	Nea Ionia	47.	Knossos
10.	Sesklo	48.	Gortyn
11.	Argyropouli Tirnavou	49.	Phaistos
12.	Larisa	50.	Mersin
13.	Marmariani	51.	Tarsus
14.	Phthiotic Thebes	52.	Tell Tayinat
15.	Pteleon	53.	Tell Judaidah
16.	Kerinthos	54.	Al Mina
17.	Skyros	55.	Ras el Bassit
18.	Delphi	56.	Ibn Hani
19.	Kalapodhi	57.	Tell Sukas
20.	Orchomenos	58.	Hama
21.	Vranesi Copaidos	59.	Tell Halaf
22.	Chalcis	60.	Nineveh
23.	Lefkandi	61.	Tabbat al Hammam
24.	Eretria	62.	Khaldeh
25.	Athens	63.	Sarepta
26.	Zagora	64.	Tyre
27.	Kardiani	65.	Tell Abu Hawam
28.	Rheneia	66.	Askalon
29.	Delos	67.	Salamis
30.	Antiparos	68.	Kition
31.	Paros	69.	Kouklia
32.	Naxos	70.	Soli
33.	Donousa	71.	Amathous
34.	Troy	72.	Palekythro
35.	Antissa	73.	Kazaphani
36.	Methymna	74.	Villasmundo
37.	Emporio	75.	Veii
38.	Phocaea	76.	Rome *

*
(A fragment in the S. Omobono area may represent a wall fragment of a pendent semicircle skyphos, although La Rocca restores it as a full circle skyphos. E. La Rocca (230) 91 no. 1, Fig. A; "Ceramica d'importazione a Roma", in *Civiltà del Lazio Primitivo* [Rome 1976] 369 no. 124,2, pl. XXI,B; "Note sulle importazione greche in territorio Laziale nell'VIII secolo A.C.", *Parola del Passato* 32 [1977] 386 f., Fig. 2/A, no. 1.)

246.   **University College London** UCL 720, rim fr.[34]

    Ht 3.0; **w** 3.0. Fine clay, rather pink-red, with one large inclusion visible. Surface paler, creamy-buff. Matt paint, mid- to dark-brown. **Lip,** offset and curved. **Ext:** six arcs of one set. **Int:** painted except for reserved band on lip. Unpublished.

CHAPTER 3

F A B R I C

The source of pendent semicircle skyphoi found in the Near East and Cyprus has always been one of the dominating problems connected with the class. As skyphoi with the same characteristic decoration are found at many different sites in Macedonia, Thessaly, Euboea and the Northern Cyclades, it is not possible to determine by stylistic analysis the origin of those in the East Mediterranean. The fabric of the skyphoi has thus assumed an increased importance, despite the fact that published information about the clay of skyphoi from either the Near East or the Aegean has usually been only of the most general kind.[1] Although soil colour charts have been used to describe clay colour in more recent excavation reports, providing an absolute standard for comparison with other clays,[2] it is not possible adequately to describe the composition of a clay, even though this appears the only reliable means of determining its origin.

Such a situation is by no means restricted to the pendent semi-circle skyphos: it applies equally to much other Greek pottery. Several attempts have been made since the 1960s to identify the chemical composition of clays by techniques such as spectrographic or X-Ray fluorescence analysis, and more recently, by neutron activation.[3] These techniques have had only limited success in determining the origin of pottery, owing to some extent to the difficulty of obtaining archaeologically-suitable samples for analysis as much as to limitations of the technique.[4] For example, the depth of the analysis carried out by Catling, Richards and Blin-Stoyle to determine the provenance of certain Mycenaean and Minoan pottery was hindered by the need to include pottery from many different areas and the difficulty of obtaining sufficient quantities of all the relevant material.[5] As a result, the information provided by the project was not as complete as might be hoped, since although broad geographical regions could usually be distinguished and separated according to the varying nature of their clays, a more informative breakdown by site in the Peloponnese, for example, was not possible.[6] In the northern mainland also, sherds from some sites in Thessaly and

Euboea were found to be of the same type, making impossible the separation of even these two areas.[7]

In 1964 another •spectrographic analysis was carried out by Ridgway. This time the aim was to characterize the chemical composition of vases known to come from Euboea, Pithecusae-Cumae and Veii, as a first step towards distinguishing between Greek geometric imports in Italy and local Italian imitations.[8]   As in the previous projects, its failure seemed to be due, at least in part, to unsolved archaeological problems as well as to the limitations of the technique.[9]

By way of contrast, the focus of the analysis of Popham, Hatcher and Pollard on pottery from Euboea and Al Mina was very narrow.   It sought to link the Al Mina pendent semicircle skyphoi to two Euboean sites, and in particular to that of Lefkandi, by demonstrating that the pottery from there was of closely similar chemical composition.[10]   The clarity of the results was obscured, however, by sampling difficulties such as the lack of suitable material from the second Euboean site, Chalcis; the small size of the sample analysed (a maximum of ten sherds from any site); and the need to include heterogeneous material of another class because of uncertainty of the reliability of the main data bank.   The determination of this fairly straightforward archaeological problem assumed a complicated aspect when the analysis revealed that some groups thought to be homogeneous archaeologically proved not to be so chemically.[11]   Hence although the problem was framed as a simple alternative, the sample introduced more variables and the results did not provide a clear answer one way or the other.   For some reason un-specified by the authors, no material from the third important Geometric site in Central Euboea, Eretria, was included: thus the possibility of a clear Euboean origin to the Al Mina sherds remains a possibility.   If material from Eretria, had also proved dissimilar to that from Al Mina, then only sampling on a much wider scale would help to determine the origin.   The unexpected results of the analysis – that the pottery from Lefkandi could not be linked firmly with that from Al Mina – led Popham *et al.* to consider the role that could be played by levigation techniques, variability in the composition of clay beds and the affect of ground water during burial in colouring the chemical results.   The answers to these questions remain unknown and must result in a certain caution when assessing the results of chemical analyses of ancient pottery.[12]

It is precisely the type of problems discussed above which would be encountered in a broader investigation into the composition of the clays of the pendent semicircle skyphos class as a whole.   As in the case of the Catling and Ridgway analyses, the logistic task of assembling sufficient samples of both skyphoi and comparative material would be daunting.   Because of the many centres of production of the skyphoi a large bank of sherds would be needed from Greece alone.   Samples from sites in the Near East where pendent semicircle skyphoi have been found would also be necessary, to ensure that all eventualities, including the possibility of local manufacture in the Near East, would be covered. And there is also the problem of assembling sufficient material from each area to be sampled. Moreover, because of the concentrated geographical distribution in Greece of most pendent semi-circle skyphoi, there is the need for an even greater degree of precision in the division of clays by area than was the case in the analysis of the Mycenaean pottery. For example a clear distinction between the clay of neighbouring areas, such as coastal Thessaly and Euboea, would be fundamental to the success of any analysis of the pendent semicircle skyphoi. As mentioned above, however, in the analysis of Catling *et al*. some sherds from these two areas appeared to have the same chemical composition, and no distinction could be made.

Could these difficulties be overcome, however, statistical evaluation of the chemical variations in clays is the most reliable means of deter-mining differences between them. As Stern and Descoeudres point out, if certain conditions are fulfilled, there is a reasonable chance that the general character of a clay will emerge despite oddities in individual sherds due to variability in clay sources and differences in the treat-ment of their clay by local potters. It must be underlined that the results of chemical analysis have their value in terms of probability only, not in absolute certainty.[13]

A successful analysis of the clay of the pendent semicircle skyphoi would be of great value, and the need is illustrated by the confusion that has already resulted from attempts to attribute skyphoi from the Near East on the basis of the appearance of their clay. [14]

Meanwhile, although visual classification of pottery fabric can provide information only of a very general nature, the following is a survey of some of the material studied. The pottery is discussed from two points of view: firstly, according to broad geographical areas (A), and secondly (B) according to the characteristic elements of the clays.

A. Geographical areas
(The size of the sample is indicated at the beginning of each section).

1. EUBOEA: (Lefkandi two fragments and one complete skyphos; Eretria eight fragments;[15] Chalcis five fragments; Kerinthos two fragments).

At Lefkandi and Chalcis slightly more than half of the material examined contains a few specks of mica while the Kerinthos fragments are divided equally. None of the Eretrian examples has any mica at all. The colour of the clay from all four sites falls roughly within the range 5YR 6/3-8/4 to 7.5YR 7/4-8/6 (dark pinkish-brown to yellow-orange). All Lefkandi material is slipped; in contrast, none of the Eretrian fragments nor those from Kerinthos has slip. Those from Chalcis, with the exception of one wall fragment, are also without slip.

2.   TENOS (Kardiani one skyphos).

The clay is very micaceous and its colour falls at the brighter end of the range found in Euboea - 7.5YR 8/4 (light yellow-orange). No slip.

3.   DELOS (16 skyphoi, many largely restored).

Of all the skyphoi from Delos only one, *56*, has a little mica. The clay varies in colour from 2.5YR 6/3 (dark pink) through 5YR 6/3 (dark pinkish brown) to 7/4 and 7.5YR 7/6-8/4 (light yellow-orange). The range is thus fairly wide and the clay occasionally has a redder hue than is found elsewhere among the sites surveyed. Fourteen of the 16 skyphoi are slipped; however, the two without slip are both almost entirely restored from small fragments and appearances could be deceptive.

4.   RHENEIA (six skyphoi).

None has any mica, and the clay colour is very homogeneous, ranging only from 5YR 7/4 (pinkish brown) to 7.5YR 7/8-8/6 (yellow-orange). All are covered with a slip.

5.   THESSALY (21 skyphoi: Kapakli seven; Marmariani seven; Nea Ionia two; prov. unknown two; Larisa one; Sesklo one; Argyropouli Tirnavou one).

Of the skyphoi examined, 15 are of micaceous clay. These include all those from Marmariani, four of the seven from Kapakli, the two of unknown provenance, that from Sesklo and one of the two from Nea Ionia. The exceptions are Kapakli 56, 57 and 63; Larisa; Nea Ionia K2237; and Argyropouli Tirnavou. All the skyphoi which contained no mica are slipped apart from Nea Ionia K2237 *179*. On the other hand, none of those of micaceous clay is slipped. In the case of the unslipped, micaceous skyphoi, the clay tends to be rather soft and powdery, while the slipped skyphoi have a harder, better-fired fabric. The clay colour extends from 5YR 6/6 (brownish orange)-7/4 (pinkish brown), 7.5YR 7/4 (brownish)-8/6 to 10YR 8/3 (yellow-beige). Thus it sometimes has a more yellowish hue than occurs further south.

6.   MACEDONIA (eight skyphoi: Vergina five; Kalamaria two; Chauchitsa one).

All the Vergina skyphoi except one, and also that from

Chauchitsa, have micaceous clay. The exception from Vergina
231, together with the two from Kalamaria, are without mica. The
colour ranges from 5YR 7/6 (orange)-7.5YR 6/3-8/4 to 10YR 7/2
(buff), thus resembling Thessaly in the occasional occurrence of
a more yellowish hue than in other areas. None of the Macedonian
skyphoi is slipped.

7.   DELPHI (six fragments and one complete skyphos).

Mica is not found in any of the material from Delphi. The
clay colour almost exactly parallels that from Euboea, ranging from
5YR 7/3 (light pinkish brown)-7/6 to 7.5YR 6/3-8/6 (yellow-orange).
All except one fragment are slipped.

8.   THE NEAR EAST AND CYPRUS

(a)   **Al Mina**: 25 fragments

The occurrence of mica in the pottery was found to be
slight and sporadic: 16 fragments have no mica at all, while
nine others have a few specks. The clay varies from 2.5YR
6/3 (dark pink)-7/3; 5YR 7/4 to 7.5YR 7/6-8/6 (yellow-
orange) with most fragments (15 in all) falling in the 5YR
7/3-4 category. Of the fragments, all except two have
a slip.

(b)   **Tell Tayinat**: Ten fragments.

Eight fragments contain no mica at all, while two have
a few specks. The colour of the clay varies from 5YR 7/3
(light pinkish brown)-8/4 to 7.5YR 6/3-7/4 (brownish).
Seven of the fragments are covered with a slip.

(c)   **Cyprus**: Two skyphoi

Neither the skyphos in the Fogg Museum *34* nor that
in the Fine Arts Museum of Boston *33* consists of micaceous
clay. That of the former is 2.5YR 7/6 (pinkish orange)
and the latter 7.5YR 8/4 (light yellow-orange). Both
are slipped.

9.   THE WEST MEDITERRANEAN (two skyphoi)

Mica is not present in the clay of either the skyphos from
Villasmundo or that from Veii *229*. The colour of the Villasmundo
example is very similar to that of the Veii skyphos, and both
fall within the range 7.5YR 5/4 to 7/4. Only the Villasmundo
skyphos is known to be slipped, although, because of the poor
state of preservation of the surface of the Veii example it is
possible it also was originally slipped. The clay of the Villasmundo
skyphos contains some white inclusions. The skyphos from Veii
has none.

B. Characteristic elements

Clay colour and texture

There is a great basic similarity in the range of colour found in the clay of the pendent semicircle skyphoi. From every area under consideration, most of the material falls in what may be called the middle range of colour - around 5YR 7/4 (pinkish brown) and 7.5YR 8/6 (yellow-orange).

There are, however, one or two variations. The clay of one fragment from Delos *51* has a reddish hue (2.5YR 6/3-7/6), as does one from Eretria *68*. This does not occur in any of the other areas around the Aegean. Five examples are also found in the Near East, one on Cyprus *34* and three at Al Mina *14* (a and b) and *16*. In addition, six skyphoi from two sites in Thessaly and Macedonia (Kapakli *89, 90, 92* and Vergina *231-233*) have a noticeably more yellowish clay (10YR 8/3) than elsewhere.

The pendent semicircle skyphoi are usually of a good, hard-fired fabric with walls *ca.* 0.4cm thick. Among those from Thessaly, however, are seven, mainly from Kapakli and Marmariani *89-92, 167* and *223-224*, where the clay has a soft and powdery texture. In Macedonia the only skyphos of poor quality clay is Chauchitsa *31*, in which the fabric is also soft and crumbly. Three other areas have some pots or fragments of softish clay: Delphi *62,* Kardiani *95* and Rheneia *194*.

Mica

The areas where mica is found in large quantities in the clay are Macedonia, Thessaly and Tenos. A few pots from both Macedonia and Thessaly are without mica, however, for example 84-5, 87-88 and these come mainly from coastal sites. Further to the south there is no sign at all of mica in any of the fragments from Delphi.

The skyphos from Tenos is the only one from the islands, whose clay contains mica to any great extent. In Euboea, mica occurs in occasional specks sometimes difficult to distinguish with the naked eye and it is found in only about one third of the fragments. Mica is rarer still on Delos and Rheneia. Of the 22 skyphoi from these two islands, only one *56* from Delos, has any mica

The clay of the two skyphoi from Cyprus which I have seen is completely free of mica, as are many of the fragments found on the mainland at Al Mina and Tell Tayinat. It does occur in a minority of fragments, but then in only very small quantities. There is no mica in either of the skyphoi from the West.

Inclusions

The clays of the northern mainland areas are generally free of observable grits. In Macedonia, the only skyphos where inclusions are apparent in the clay is one of the two from Kalamaria *84*. Although all seven Marmariani skyphoi have both dark-coloured and white inclusions, this is unusual for Thessaly as a whole and no other site has similar clay. Elsewhere in Thessaly there are no grits. The same inclusion-free clay is found on Tenos and also on both Delos and Rheneia. Among the 22 skyphoi from the latter islands, only one (*48* from Delos) had some small white grits.

By contrast, the clay of the central mainland site of Delphi usually contains white inclusions. In the clay of Lefkandi, Chalcis and Kerinthos on Euboea there are frequently, though not always, small white or dark-coloured grits. The Eretrian fragments, on the other hand, are completely free of any inclusions.

In the Near East there is a difference between the fabric of the skyphoi from Cyprus and those from the two mainland sites. No inclusions occur in those from Cyprus: at Al Mina and Tell Tayinat, however, small white and occasionally dark-coloured inclusions are found in about half the material. In the West Mediterranean, inclusions are present in the Villasmundo skyphos, but not that from Veii.

Slip

Slip is not found on any of the Macedonian skyphoi. It is on five skyphoi from Thessaly (Kapakli *87-88* and *93*, Larisa *106* and Argyropouli Tirnavou *22*), but they are still a distinct minority of the sample. In all the other areas under consideration, however, the material is more frequently slipped than not. The Kardiani skyphos is slipped. At Delphi all fragments but one *62* are slipped and so are 14 of the 16 skyphoi from Delos and all six from Rheneia. The exceptions from Delos are *50* and *51*. In Euboea there is some difference between the various sites. All the Lefkandi material is slipped but that from Eretria is all unslipped. The Chalcis and Kerinthos fragments are mainly unslipped also.

In the Near East the clay is most commonly covered with a slip. Both skyphoi from Cyprus are slipped, as are 23 out of the 25 fragments from Al Mina and seven of the ten from Tell Tayinat. The unslipped fragments from these two sites are one rim fragment *8* and four uncatalogued wall fragments. Only Villasmundo, of the two skyphoi from the West, is slipped.

The following table summaries in graphic form the characteristics discussed above:

TABLE 1: CHARACTERISTICS OF THE CLAYS

	Sample size	Clay colour	Clay texture	Mica	Inclusions	Slip
Macedonia:						
Vergina	5	A c	A	A c	B	B
Kalamaria	2	A	A	C	AB	B
Chauchitsa	1	A	B	A	B	B
Thessaly:						
Sesklo	1	A	A	A	B	B
Kapakli	7	C a	B a	A c	B	B a
Nea Ionia	2	A	AB	AC	B	B
Marmariani	7	A	A b	A	A	B
Larisa	1	A	A	C	B	A
Argyropouli Tirnavou	1	A	A	C	B	A
Provenance Unknown	2	A	B	A	B	B
Delphi	7	A	A b	C	A b	A b
Euboea:						
Chalcis	5	A	A	B c	A b	B a
Kerinthos	2	A	A	BC	B	B
Lefkandi	3	A	A	B c	A b	A
Eretria	8	A b	A	C	B	B
Tenos:						
Kardiani	1	A	B	A	B	A
Delos	16	A b	A	C b	B a	A b
Rheneia	6	A	A b	C	B	A
Cyprus	2	A b	A	C	B	A
Al Mina	25	A b	A	C b	A b	A b
Tell Tayinat	10	A	A	C b	B a	A b
The West	2	A	A	C	AB	AB

KEY

	A	B	C
Colour	Middle range	Reddish	Yellowish
Texture	Hard-fired	Soft and Powdery	–
Mica	Yes	A little	None
Inclusions	Yes	No	–
Slip	Yes	No	–

The difference between upper- and lower-case letters in the above table is one of quantity. Upper case letters indicate the strongest characteristic of the site, lower case the weaker. Where the distribution is equal, two upper-case letters are used.

The inability of the above survey to provide detailed information on which conclusions about the origin of the pendent semicircle skyphos may be based is obvious.

From Table 1 it can be seen that only two sets of two sites have clay which appears to be the same. The first pair, Chauchitsa and the two skyphoi from Thessaly whose provenance is unknown, makes little sense since one does not know the origin of the Thessalian skyphoi and in any case one would expect that sites within either Macedonia or Thessaly might have provided better parallels. In the case of the second pair, Larisa and Argyropouli Tirnavou, the connection is reasonable, for both are inland sites in Thessaly, and in quality and general appearance these two skyphoi are fairly similar.

For the bulk of the material, however, the very general terms of this visual comparison creates a vagueness in the delineation of the character of clays from geographically distinct regions and prevents the establishment of any kind of exclusive profile for a clay. Furthermore, in every area where the sample consists of more than one pot, there is a certain amount of variety and overlap in the five elements considered, and this also prevents the character of a local clay being clearly defined.[16] For example, while it seems true that the clay of Thessaly is generally micaceous and that pots are frequently unslipped, there are exceptions, even among pots from a single site such as Kapakli. No solution is found here, either, for the problem of the origin of pendent semicircle fragments in the Near East. None of the three sites in the East Mediterranean is linked unequivocally with any Aegean area, although there are similarities to several.

Thus the lack of reliable information to be gained from the fabric of the pendent semicircle skyphoi leads to a conclusion suggested many years ago by Desborough, and recently re-emphasised:[17] that a study of the shape of the skyphos offers a greater hope of increasing our understanding of its centres of manufacture.

CHAPTER 4

T Y P O L O G Y[1]

TYPE 1(a) (Figure 34)

Kardiani *96* – Pl.1(b)

Chauchitsa *31* – Fig. 34(c); Pl.2(a-b)

Delphi *58* – Fig. 34(a); Pl.1(c)

Vergina AΓ24 *235*

Marmariani 121 *172* – Fig. 34(b); Pl.1(d)

The skyphoi of this group all have a deep rounded body. None is less than 10cm in height, and the Delphi skyphos is the tallest at 12cm. In each case the lip is tall (between 1.5 and 2.0cm) and straight. It is joined to the body smoothly without being offset. Sometimes, however, there is a slight ridge where the lip meets the body. Although the type of lip is uniform, the angle at which it is set varies from almost upright (on the Delphi skyphos) to more accentuated and flaring (on the Chauchitsa skyphos). Of these five skyphoi, only Kardiani has a well-articulated low conical foot. It is about 1cm high. The Delphi skyphos, on the other hand, has a low ring foot less than half that height. The shape of the feet o the other three falls between. They are closer to the Delphi skyphos however, in both height and angle.

On four of the five the semicircle decoration consists of seven arcs in each set, and the Kardiani skyphos is the only one painted with eight. On the Delphi, Marmariani and Vergina skyphoi the two sets of semicircles are not intersecting, while on the Chauchitsa skyphos they only just overlap. On the Kardiani skyphos, however, the semicircles intersect. There are also distinctive decorative elements in addition to the normal pendent semicircles. The Delphi skyphos has an hour-glass motif in the centre of each set of semicircles. The Chauchitsa skyphos has reserved bands beneath the semicircles, and the Kardiani skyphos appears to have them also.[2] In addition, the Chauchitsa skyphos is decorated with semicircles on one side only. The handle zone on the reverse has been left blank.

(a)

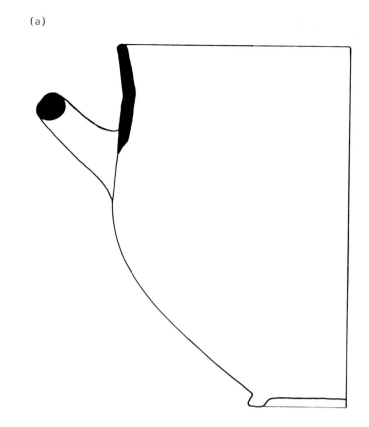

(b)

(c)

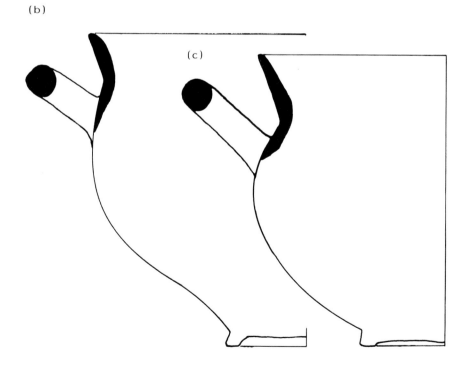

Fig. 34 Type 1. (a) Delphi 5909 (*58*); (b) Marmariani 121. Athens NM (*172*);
(c) Chauchitsa. Thessaloniki 4647 (*31*).

The proportions of these five skyphoi can be described by a ratio of the diameter of rim to the height (expressed as 100) to the diameter of the base.[3] They are:

Kardiani	127:100:50
Chauchitsa	130:100:57
Delphi	133:100:54
Vergina	133:100:55
Marmariani	137:100:50

A rim fragment of a large skyphos from the Palia Perivolia cemetery at Lefkandi *119* also has a smooth transition between lip and body and the same reserved bands below the semicircles as the other two skyphoi. Three other rim fragments from Lefkandi, two from the settlement *124*[4] and *126,* and one from the lower fill of the North Channel in the Palia Perivolia cemetery *122*, have similar profiles. It is possible that skyphoi from Knossos *102* and Vergina *234* belong here also.

TYPE 1(b)

Marmariani 118 *169* – Fig. 24; Pl.2(c)

Marmariani 122 *173* – Fig. 25; Pl.2(d)

These skyphoi fall into a sub-group of Type 1 because elements of both shape and decoration suggest strongly that they belong in close relationship with the preceding group, even though neither has a proper foot. Marmariani 118 has a completely flat base and Marmariani 122 a minimal ring foot.   Their height ranges from 8.7 to 9.8cm and both have the deep body profile, together with a tall lip that flares outwards but is not offset from the body.   The shape of Marmariani 122 has been badly distorted.   The body has sagged and the lip dropped downwards and outwards on one side, making the vessel very lopsided.   The decoration consists of sets of five semicircles which intersect on one side of the pot but not on the other, with an hour-glass filler painted in the centre of each set.

Marmariani 118 is also a rather poor example, for the paint has been applied in a very careless and sloppy manner. However, it is still possible to see that the paint on the lip has deliberately been extended downwards in a broad band across the top of the body, with the result that the usually broad reserved handle zone becomes a narrow band; another peculiarity in the decoration of this skyphos is that the paint on the lower part of the pot stops about 2.5cm above the base on all sides. The semicircles, with seven in each set, intersect on one side of the vase only.   Because of the irregularities in the shapes of this sub-group there is little coherence in their ratios.[5]

TYPE 2(a) (Figure 35)

> Lefkandi P.T2:1 *116*
>
> Lefkandi Skoubris T33:1 *108*
>
> Nea Ionia K2237 *179* – Fig. 35(d); Pl.5(b)
>
> Lefkandi-Xeropolis *129*
>
> Vergina P1 *232*
>
> Kardiani, Tenos B79 *95* – Fig. 20; Pl.3(a)
>
> Kapakli 58 *89* – Fig. 35(a); Pl.5(a)
>
> Vergina Δ 15 *231*
>
> Vergina P 21 *233*
>
> Marmariani 120 *177* – Fig. 35(c); Pl.3(d)
>
> Lefkandi Skoubris T59A:4 *114*
>
> Lefkandi Skoubris T56:3 *111*
>
> Vranesi Copaidos *238*
>
> Amathous *17/1*
>
> Vergina AZ 16 *236*
>
> Argyropouli Tirnavou *22* – Fig. 35(b); Pl.3(b)
>
> Larisa *106* – Fig. 22; Pl.4(d)

An offset lip is the most distinctive characteristic of this large sub-class, and it marks an important change from Type 1. All the skyphoi are large, ranging in height from 9.3 to 11.9cm, with the exception of Vergina AZ 16 (8.2cm) and Vranesi Copaidos (16.1). All the bodies have deep, rounded profiles. Although offset, the lip of most of the 17 skyphoi is similar to that of Type 1 in being straight and tall. It varies between 1.2 - 2.2cm in height, with the emphasis on the upper part of the range. On most skyphoi the lip flares at an angle similar to that on the Chauchitsa skyphos of Type 1, and only on Lefkandi P.T2:1 and Marmariani 120 does the more upright lip of the Delphi skyphos reappear. The foot of the skyphoi ranges between 0.3 and 1.1cm in height. The skyphos from Vranesi Copaidos has a low conical foot. The foot of Kapakli 58, Kardiani, Arg. Tirnavou, Marmariani 120, Amathous and the Lefkandi skyphoi, on the other hand, is a low ring. Between those two extremes fall the remaining six skyphoi: Nea Ionia K2237; Larisa; Vergina P 1, Δ 15, P 21 and AZ 16.

There is a greater proportion of intersection of the semicircles than in Type 1. Only four (Lefkandi P.T2:1; Lefkandi-Xeropolis; Vergina P1 and Kapakli 58) have semicircles that do not intersect at all. The use of reserved bands below the semicircle decoration is also found to a lesser extent (Vergina P21), and only on Lefkandi P.T2:1 and Skoubris

(a)

(b)

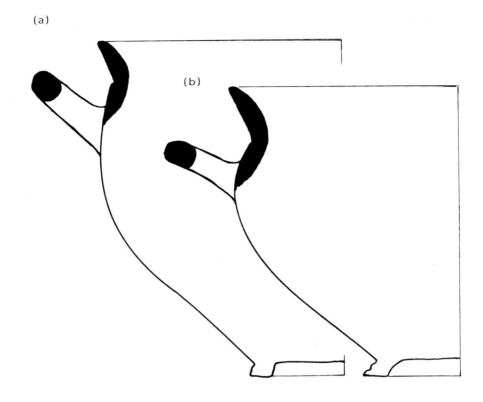

(c)

(d)

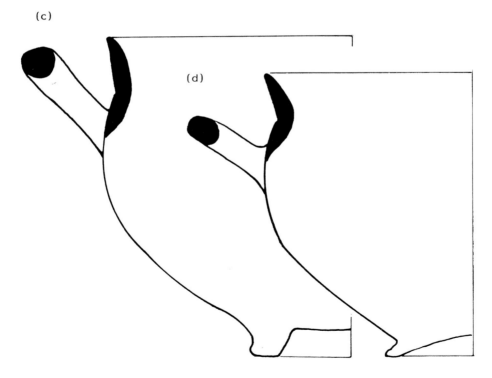

Fig. 35 Type 2. (a) Kapakli 58. Volos K1356 (*89*); (b) Argyropouli Tirnavou.
Volos K3022 (*22*); (c) Marmariani 120. Athens NM (*171*);
(d) Nea Ionia. Volos K2237 (*179*).

T56:3 is the Type 1 feature of reserving the lower part of the foot or base retained.

Further, while sets of seven semicircles are overwhelmingly popular on the skyphoi of Type 1, there is greater variety here. There is one example each of five *171*, six *129*, seven *95*, eight *179*, 12 *22*, 16 *111* and 18 semicircles to a set *238*; sets of ten arcs appear three times *17/1, 106, 231*; as do nine *89, 232, 233*, and 14 *108, 114, 116*. On Vergina AZ 16 *236* there are sets of seven semicircles on one side and eight on the other. It is interesting to observe that rarely is any particular number of semicircles restricted to a single site, at least where the site provides more than one example. Lefkandi is the only exception, with sets of 14 arcs. Similarly, no site seems specially characterised by the use of a particular number of semicircles, although it is at Lefkandi that the greatest number in each set appear most frequently.

The ratios of this class of skyphoi are very close despite the large number of pots. Their relationship to the skyphoi of Type 1 is seen in a gradual increase in the ratio of the diameters of rim and base to the height of the pot:

Lefkandi P.T2:1	112:100:40
Lefkandi Skoubris T33:1	132:100:49
Nea Ionia K2237	135:100:57
Lefkandi-Xeropolis	137:100:57[6]
Vergina P1	139:100:55
Kardiani, Tenos B79	140:100:58
Kapakli 58	141:100:54
Vergina Δ15	142:100:54
Vergina P21	142:100:60
Marmariani 120	147:100:58
Lefkandi Skoubris T59A:4	148:100:55
Lefkandi Skoubris T56:3	149:100:62
Vranesi Copaidos	150:100:53
Vergina AZ 16	150:100:63
Amathous	151:100:63
Argyropouli Tirnavou	156:100:64
Larisa	160:100:55

At least six of the eight skyphoi from Skyros *201* probably belong here; as do Lefkandi *123/2* and Kition *100*. There are also 13 fragments with tall, flaring offset lips that appear to fit with this class: 11 from Lefkandi *115, 121, 123/1, 123/3, 125, 127, 128, 131-133, 135;* one from Delos *56* and another from Anti-Paros *20.*

TYPE 2(b) (Figure 36(a))

Sesklo *200* - Fig. 36(a); Pl.3(c)

Delos 19 *57* - Fig. 9

Lefkandi Skoubris T.59:2 *112* - Fig. 23(a)

The skyphoi of this sub-class are similar to Type 2(a) except in that they have a less rounded body with a tighter and more direct line from shoulder to foot. Those from Sesklo and Delos are both large (10.5 and 11.0cm respectively) and have tall flaring offset lips. Although Lefkandi also has a similar tall lip, it is small (6.7cm). On all three skyphoi the height of the foot falls between 0.5 and 0.8cm. Lefkandi T59:2 has something approaching a low conical foot. Delos 19 has one that is very low and flattened out horizontally towards the bottom to form a splaying ring. The shape of the foot on the Sesklo skyphos falls between the two, but is closer to Lefkandi than to Delos 19.

The semicircles intersect on all three skyphoi, but different numbers of semicircles have been used on each. Sesklo is painted with 11 in each set, Delos with eight and Lefkandi with ten.

The ratios of this small sub-class fall mainly within the range of Type 2(a):

Sesklo   149:100:58

Delos   158:100:56

Lefkandi   164:100:63

The rim fragment from Emporio *67* probably belongs with these skyphoi.

TYPE 2(c) (Figure 36 (b-c))

Lefkandi Skoubris T33:2 *109*

Lefkandi P.T3:14 *117*

Marmariani 119 *170* - Fig. 36 (b); Pl. 4 (c)

Lefkandi Skoubris T59A:3 *113*

Kapakli 56 *87* - Fig. 36 (c); Pl. 4 (a)

Kapakli 57 *88* - Fig. 16; Pl. 4 (b)

These six skyphoi are also large, ranging in height from 9.4 to 11.5cm, except for Lefkandi *113* which is 7.1. Their rounded body profile makes

(a)

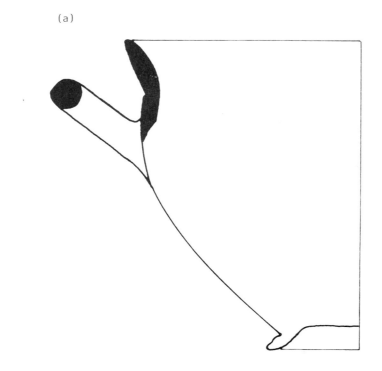

(b)

(c)

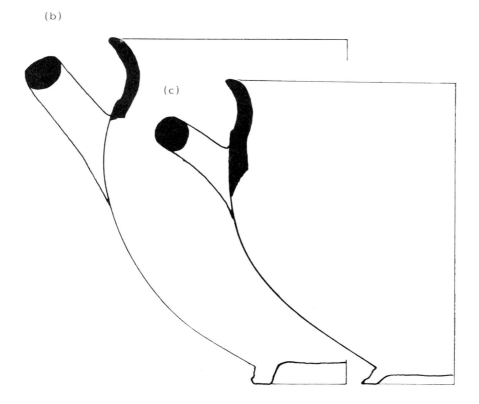

Fig. 36 Type 2. (a) Sesklo. Volos K2247 (*200*); (b) Marmariani 119.
Athens NM (*170*); (c) Kapakli 56. Volos K1354 (*87*).

92

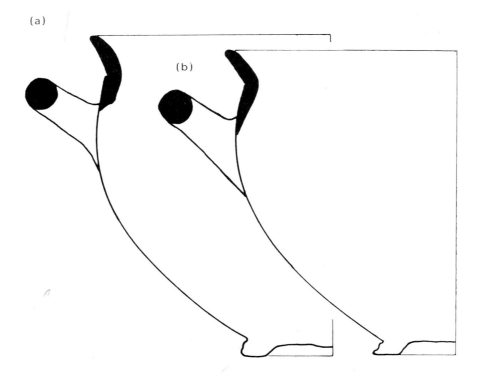

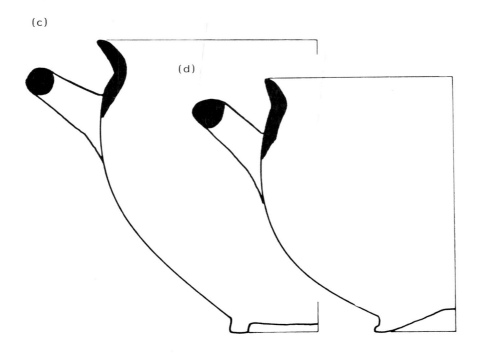

Fig. 37. Type 3. (a) Kapakli 60. Volos K1358 (*91*); (b) Thessaly.
Volos K1117 (*224*); (c) Marmariani 116. Athens NM (*167*);
(d) Marmariani 115. Athens NM (*166*).

them more similar to Type 2(a) than to Type 2(b), but they are set apart because their lip is slightly different. They differ from all the preceding Type 2 skyphoi by having a tall lip on which the outward-flaring profile is not rigidly maintained and instead has a concave curve. The foot of these vessels ranges from 0.4 to 0.8cm in height. The Lefkandi skyphoi have a ring foot that flares outwards, as do the two from Kapakli. The foot of the Marmariani vessel is set at a near-vertical angle to the body.

The skyphoi from Marmariani, Kapakli and Lefkandi T59A:3 all have nine intersecting semicircles in each set, while on Lefkandi T33:2 there are ten intersecting semicircles. Lefkandi T3:14 has sets of seven semicircles and there is no intersection but an hour-glass motif within each set.

The ratios of this class fall within the range of the other Type 2 skyphoi:

Lefkandi T33:2	132:100:47
Lefkandi T3:14	134:100:58
Marmariani 119	140:100:51
Lefkandi T59A:3	141:100:63
Kapakli 56	152:100:61
Kapakli 57	163:100:63

Four rim fragments, three from Lefkandi *130, 134, 165,* and one from Delphi *60*, are very similar and probably belong here. [7]

TYPE 3 (a) (Figure 37 (a-b))

Nea Ionia K2235 *178* - Fig. 27; Pl.5(c)

Kapakli 60 *91* - Fig. 37(a); Pl.5(d)

Thessaly, Volos K1144 *223* - Fig. 31; Pl.6(c)

Thessaly, Volos K1117 *224* - Fig. 37(b); Pl.6(d)

Kapakli 59 *90* - Fig. 17; Pl.6(a)

Kapakli 61 *92* - Fig. 18; Pl.6(b)

Marmariani *174* - Fig. 26

Kalamaria 5710 *84* - Fig. 15

Type 3 skyphoi are characterised by a deep, rounded body combined with a short lip that does not exceed 1.4cm in height. The overall height is within the range 9.7 to 11.0cm. All have short lips similar to that of the following sub-class, but are especially linked with each other by the fact that the lip is offset. The foot is between 0.3 and 0.7cm in height, except for Marmariani *174* which has a flat base. A thick-set ring foot, (as found on Kapakli 59-61) is the predominant type.

In decoration the variety is not great. Kapakli 60 and 61 are decorated with sets of nine semicircles, as also are Nea Ionia K2235, Volos K1144 and K1117. Kapakli 59 has eight; Kalamaria 5710 ten and Marmariani eleven. Two skyphoi have intersecting semicircles on both sides (Kapakli 61 and Kalamaria 5710); three on one side of the pot only (Kapakli 59, Nea Ionia K2235 and Volos K1117); and three have semicircles that do not intersect (Kapakli 60, Marmariani and Volos K1144). The Marmariani skyphos has a reserved band on the lower body.

The ratios of these skyphoi are very similar to those of the five in Type 3(b) and the two classes together also lie within the range already found in Type 2:

Nea Ionia K2235	143:100:56
Kapakli 60	144:100:53
Volos K1144	148:100:58
Volos K1117	149:100:54
Kapakli 59	149:100:56
Kapakli 61	151:100:46
Marmariani *174*	152:100:48
Kalamaria 5710	152:100:54

Three rim fragments probably also belong to this class. Two are from Euboea: Chalcis *28* and Lefkandi *136*, and the other from Delphi *61*.

TYPE 3(b) (Figure 37 (c-d))

Lefkandi P.39B:5 *120*	
Marmariani 115 *166*	- Fig. 37(d); Pl.7(b)
Marmariani 116 *167*	- Fig. 37(c); Pl.7(a)
Andros 145 *239*	
Lefkandi P.T21:10 *118*	

The skyphoi of Type 3(b) range in height from 8.9 to 10.5cm, with the exception of those from Lefkandi, which are 7.2 and 5.7cm. The five skyphoi are subdivided from the eight in the preceding sub-class because their short lip is simply everted and not offset: in all other respects they are very similar. The foot of the Andros skyphos is a low conical shape while both those from Lefkandi, Marmariani 115 and 116 have ring bases. The height of the foot varies between 0.4 and 0.7cm.

Each is decorated with a different number of semicircles. Sets of five were used on Lefkandi P:T21:10; sets of eight on Marmariani 116;

95

nine on Lefkandi P.T39B:5; ten on Andros 145, and on Marmariani 115,
sets of 11 semicircles. They intersect on both sides of Marmariani 115,
the Andros skyphos and Lefkandi *120,* but on one side of the pot only
on Marmariani 116 and Lefkandi *118.*

The ratios are as follows:

Lefkandi P.T39B:5	143:100:65
Marmariani 115	144:100:58
Marmariani 116	146:100:57
Andros 145	147:100:60
Lefkandi P.T21:10	154:100:74

The skyphos from Orchomenos *181* and a rim fragment from Thasos
222 appear to belong with this class.

TYPE 4(a) (Figure 38(a-c))

Lefkandi Skoubris T45:3 *110*

Delos 8 *46* - Fig. 38(c)

Kapakli 63 *93* - Fig. 19; Pl.7(d)

Knossos, Teke 123 *103* - Fig. 21(a)

Knossos, Teke 124 *104* - Fig. 21(b)

Sydney 73.03 *244* - Fig. 38(b); Pl.8(a)

Delos 16 *54* - Fig. 38(a); Pl.8(c)

These skyphoi are generally smaller than Types 1 to 3, ranging in height
from 9.8-6.9cm, and have a rather squat appearance. The lip is offset,
short and straight. It ranges from 1.4 to 0.9cm. Teke 123 has a very
substantial high ring while the foot of the Sydney skyphos, Teke 124
and Delos 16 is simply a low ring. Between these two extremes lies Delos
8, with a somewhat higher and more splaying foot than the Sydney
skyphos. The height of the foot in this class lies mainly between 0.4
and 0.9cm, although Kapakli 63 has a flat base.

On all the skyphoi the semicircles are intersecting. Kapakli 63 is
decorated with sets of seven; the Sydney skyphos with sets of 11; Lefkandi Skoubris T45:3, Delos 8 and Delos 16 with ten to a set; and on
the two skyphoi from Teke 14 semicircles have been used.

The increasing shallowness in the shape of the Type 4 skyphoi is
reflected in the greater ratio of diameter of rim and foot to the height
of the pot:

96

(a)

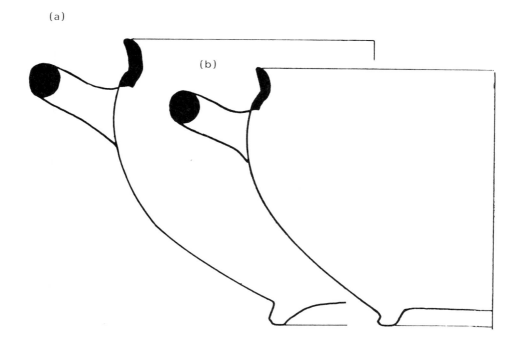

(c)

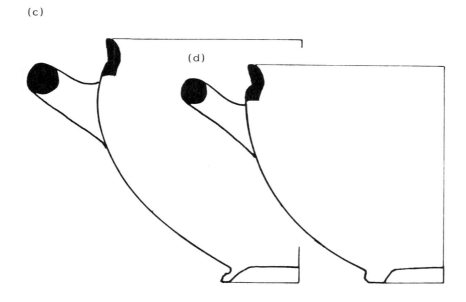

Fig. 38 Type 4. (a) Delos 16. Mykonos 755 (*54*); (b) Provenance unknown.
Sydney 73.03 (*244*); (c) Delos 8. Mykonos 756 (*46*);
(d) Delos 10. Mykonos 959 (*48*).

Lefkandi Skoubris T45:3	151:100:69
Delos 8	154:100:63
Kapakli 63	160:100:80
Teke 123	163:100:60
Teke 124	170:100:68
Sydney 73.03	171:100:83
Delos 16	171:100:66

From the settlement at Lefkandi, 20 of the 28 fragments published from the latest material of the pit at Xeropolis appear to be of Type 4 variety, *137, 138, 143-150, 152, 154-162*. In addition, two skyphoi of unknown provenance from Cyprus, *38, 41*; one from Tenos *221*; and rim fragments from Zagora *242*, Delphi *59*, Tell Tayinat *216, 218* and Al Mina *4* all seem to belong with this class.

TYPE 4(b) (Figure 38(d))

> Chalcis A1385 *30* – Fig. 3(e)
> Delos 4 *42* – Fig. 5
> Delos 10 *48* – Fig. 38(d)

The skyphoi of this sub-class are closely related to the preceding ones in shape, but have shallower profiles (the average height is 7.5cm) and a shorter lip (0.8-1.2cm). The height of the foot falls between 0.4-0.6cm. The foot of Delos 10 is set at an almost vertical angle to the body, and Delos 4 has a flaring foot that approaches a conical shape.

Sets of eight semicircles were painted on Delos 10. On Delos 4 and the Chalcis skyphos there are sets of seven. The semicircles intersect on Delos 10 and Chalcis A1385, but not on Delos 4.

The ratios are:

Chalcis	164:100:52
Delos 4	169:100:73
Delos 10	178:100:69

A rim fragment from Delos *53* appears to belong here and, from the published photographs, it is not unlikely that both the skyphos from Tell Halaf *213* and that which is now in Switzerland *243* should also be included.

(a)

(b)

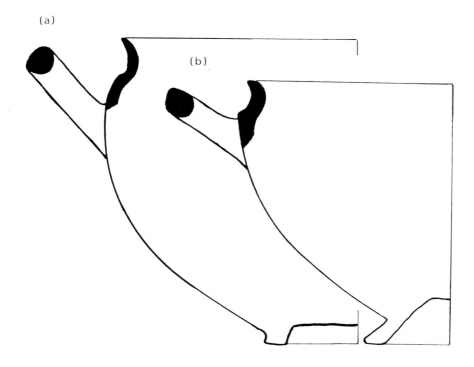

(c)

(d)

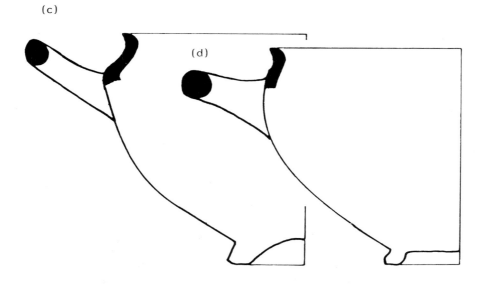

Fig. 39 Type 5. (a) Kalamaria. Thessaloniki 4714 (*85*); (b) Cyprus. Boston 72.76 (*33*); (c) Rheneia A1466. Mykonos 20 (*192*); (d) Delos 7. Mykonos 753 (*45*).

TYPE 5(a) Figure 39(a-c))

> Delos 5 *43*
>
> Cyprus *34* - Fig. 4
>
> Cyprus *35*
>
> Cyprus *33* - Fig. 39(b)
>
> Hama *77* - Fig. 12
>
> Kalamaria 4714 *85* - Fig. 39(a); Pl.8(b)
>
> Salamis *195*
>
> Rheneia A1465 *191* - Fig. 29
>
> Rheneia A1466 *192* - Fig. 39(c)
>
> Hama *76*
>
> Hama *78* - Fig. 13
>
> Rheneia A1464 *190* - Fig. 28
>
> Rheneia A1468 *194* - Fig. 30
>
> Soli *203*
>
> Delos 6 *44* - Fig. 6; Pl.8(d)
>
> Cyprus *36*
>
> Rheneia A1467 *193*
>
> Rheneia A1463 *189*
>
> Cyprus *37*

The overall appearance of all Type 5 skyphoi is not dissimilar to those of Type 4 as, again, a rather shallow body and short lip appear in combination. The chief difference, however, is in the lip. In Type 5 the lip does not flare outwards with a straight profile; it is set back from the shoulder and is concave in the centre. These 19 skyphoi have an average height of 8.0cm and usually the wall of the body slopes sharply to the foot rather than having a rounded profile - see, for example, Cyprus *33*. The skyphoi have an average lip height of 1.1cm and the average height of the foot is 0.7cm. Some vessels have a low conical foot that is well-formed - Cyprus *33* but Cyprus *34, 36*, for example, have a lower foot which is merely a splaying ring foot.

The semicircles intersect on all these skyphoi and there is a great variety in the number used. Sets of five (Soli), six (Hama *76*), 11 (Rheneia A1468) and 13 (Rheneia A1465) all appear once. Seven semicircles to a set appear three times (Cyprus *33*, Cyprus *36*, Hama *77*) as do eight semicircles (Delos 5, Hama *78*, Salamis). Sets of nine (Cyprus *34*, Delos 6, Rheneia A1464 and A1467) and ten (Cyprus *35* and *37*, Rheneia A1463 and A1466) are used four times each. Kalamaria 4714 is

100

decorated with one set of six and one set of seven semicircles on one side and two sets of seven on the other.

The ratios of this large sub-class are remarkably consistent and it is notable that they, and those of the other Type 5 sub-class, coincide almost completely with the ratios of Type 4(a) and (b). In addition, like Type 4, they represent a gradual transition from the range of Type 1-3 towards an even greater ratio of diameter of rim and base to the height.

Delos 5	140:100:73
Hama *78*	146:100:64
Hama *77*	149:100:49
Cyprus *34*	149:100:66
Cyprus *35*	150:100:67
Cyprus *33*	152:100:62
Kalamaria 4714	155:100:56
Salamis	155:100:64
Rheneia A1465	156:100:58
Rheneia A1466	156:100:63
Hama *76*	157:100:40
Rheneia A1464	159:100:68
Rheneia A1468	160:100:60
Soli	160:100:66
Delos 6	160:100:70
Cyprus *36*	164:100:60
Rheneia A1467	168:100:64
Rheneia A1463	168:100:67
Cyprus *37*	168:100:76

Five more skyphoi from Cyprus appear to belong here: Kition 4062 *101*, Amathous *18*, Kazaphani *97*, Cyprus *39*, *40*. Rim fragments from Lefkandi *139*, *153*, Tell Sukas *215*, Tarsus *206*, *207*, Hama *79* and Methymna *176* also seem to belong here, as do five others from Delos *47*, *50*, *51*, *52*, *55*.

TYPE 5(b) (Figure 39(d))

Delos 7 *45* - Fig. 39(d)

Delos 11 *49*

The two skyphoi of this sub-class are characterised by a greater shallow-ness (each is only 7.5cm high), together with an extremely short lip of 0.8-9cm. They represent a modification in the shape of the popular sky-phos of Type 5(a) in the same way that the sub-group Type 4(b) is related to 4(a). Both 4(b) and 5(b) seem to be a degeneration of a more highly developed shape. The foot of both is simply a small ring (0.6cm high) with a slightly splaying profile similar to that of Cyprus *34* in Type 5(a).

The semicircles intersect on both vases, and each is decorated with sets of ten semicircles.

The ratios are:

Delos 7   168:100:66
Delos 11   180:100:73

TYPE 6 (Figures 40-41)

Veii 60255 *229* - Fig. 40(d)

Kouklia *105*

Khaldeh *99* - Fig. 41(a)

Villasmundo *237*

All four skyphoi are very small and shallow, ranging from only 6.0 to 7.0cm in height. Each has a curved lip which is offset and either over-hangs the shoulder slightly or else stands almost directly above it. In this respect there is a difference from the lips of the Type 5 skyphoi which are set back noticeably from the shoulder. On all these three skyphoi, either a flat base or a tiny disc base has been substituted for the substantial foot usually found in Types 1-5.

Both the skyphoi from Kouklia and Khaldeh have been painted with sets of seven semicircles. On the Villasmundo skyphos there are six semicircles to a set. The semicircles intersect on all these three vases, but on the Veii skyphos there are sets of five semicircles and no sign of intersection.

The ratios are:

Veii   164:100:66

Kouklia   176:100:71

Khaldeh   190:100:86

Villasmundo 200:100:92

There are also 31 rim fragments very similar in shape to these four skyphoi:[8] 12 are from Al Mina *1-3, 8, 9, 11, 12, 13,* and *14* - two

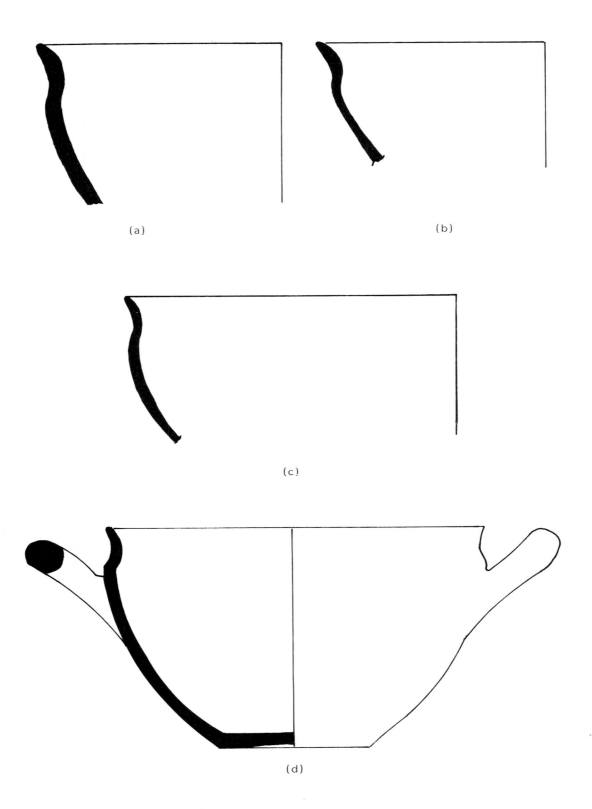

Fig. 40 Type 6. (a) Al Mina. London 1955.4-22.2 (*1*); (b) Eretria
FK E/8 B639 (*70*); (c) Tell Abu Hawam (*212*);
(d) Veii. Villa Giulia 60255 (*229*).

103

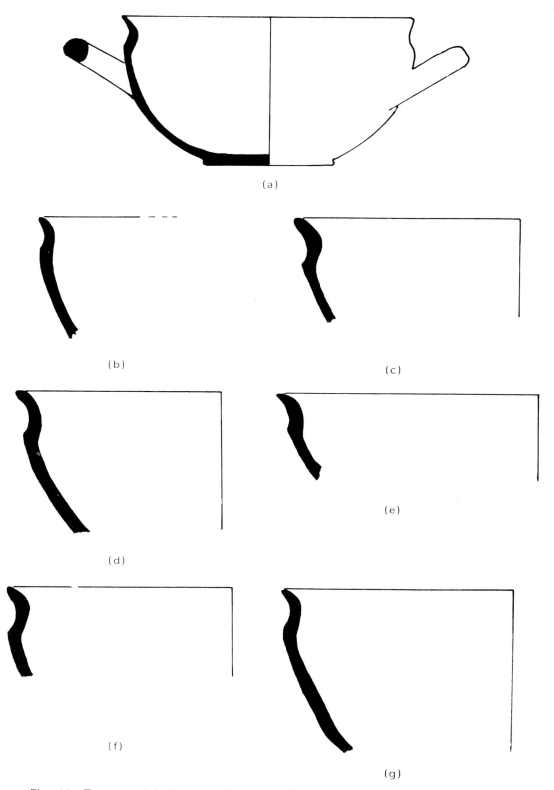

Fig. 41   Type 6.   (a) Khaldeh. Nat.Mus., Damascus (99); (b) Eretria
FK 1643.19 (73); (c) Al Mina. London 1955.4-22.4 (3);
(d) Al Mina. London 1955.4-22.11 (8); (e) Al Mina.
Oxford 1954.271/1 (9); (f) Al Mina. Oxford 1954.271/5 (12);
(g) Al Mina. Oxford 1954.271/6 (15).

fragments each, *15;* nine from Eretria *68-73;* three from Lefkandi *151, 163, 164;* two from Tell Tayinat *217, 219;* two from Tarsus *209, 211;* one each from Tyre *227* and Tell Abu Hawam *212* as well as one provenance unknown *246.* Seven of the fragments have evidence that the semicircles are intersecting. On Eretria *72* there are two sets of five semicircles which do not intersect. On most, only part of one set of semicircles is preserved. Most of these rim fragments have the same marked shoulder and curved lip as on the skyphoi Veii, Kouklia, Khaldeh and Villasmundo. Judging by the angle of the lip, some may have come from pots even shallower than these three. (Fig. 40(d) and Fig. 41 (b-g).)

Four fragments, Al Mina *1,* Eretria *70, 72* and Tell Abu Hawam *212,* stand apart because they have a less emphatic curve in the lip and a much smoother transition between lip and shoulder. (Fig. 11(d) and Fig. 40(a-c).) If complete skyphoi had been preserved, these would have undoubtedly constituted a sub-class of Type 6. As it is, however, the differences must merely be noted at this stage: the reason will be discussed in Chapter 7.

CHAPTER 5

RELATIVE CHRONOLOGY

The typology was formed purely on the basis of the shape of the sky-phoi. Classified in this way, the vessels form six well-defined types or classes, but do not necessarily form groups related stylistically by decoration.[1]

The features used above were the ratios of the diameter of the rim to the height, and the diameter of the base to the height; the shape and height of the lip, and the foot. Reconstructed on this basis, the development of the shape is from large skyphoi of 10-12cm in height to smaller ones of about 7.5cm or less. Associated with this decrease in height is an increase in the ratios of the diameter of the rim to height and of diameter of base to height. This is demonstrated in the ranges for each Type:

Type 1	127:100:50	–	137:100:50
Type 2	132:100:47*	–	164:100:63
Type 3	143:100:56	–	154:100:74
Type 4	151:100:69	–	178:100:69
Type 5	140:100:73	–	180:100:73
Type 6	164:100:66	–	200:100:92

(*Lefkandi P.T2:1 *116,* with a ratio of 112:100:40, strictly speaking marks the beginning of the range of Type 2. But although its other characteristics place it in this Type, the skyphos has an unusually low ratio between the diameter of the rim and the height. The next six skyphoi in the Type fall between 132:100 and 139:100).

The lip appears in several different forms during the sequence, but two consistent trends can be observed. The first is the disappearance of the smooth transition between the everted lip and body, and its replacement by an offset lip with marked shoulder. This change, which fundamentally occurs after Type 1, is almost always followed, for the offset lip is the only variety found in Types 2, 4 and 5. There are, however, five exceptions in Type 3 and four in Type 6. The second major development is the gradual movement from a high lip of about 2.0cm to a short one usually less than half that height. Type 6 alone does not fit this general pattern: the reason will be considered in Chapter 7.

A comparison between the number of alterations in the overall shape of the skyphos (as illustrated by the ratios) and the shape of the lip makes it apparent that different sorts of lips occur on vessels of very similar shape. For example, there are six varieties of lip (represented by the six Types), but only four broad changes in the shape of the skyphos. The ratios of Types 2 and 3, and 4 and 5, overlap to a large extent and the proportions of the vessels in each of these two groups are basically the same. This fact, taken together with the distribution of the Types, appears to be significant and will be discussed further below and in Chapter 8.

By contrast, all indications are that variations in the shape of the foot do not fall into any pattern of development. Such differences as there are appear to occur either continuously throughout the sequence, or at random. For example, if one ignores transitional forms and takes two of the three chief varieties in shape – the conical and ring foot – it can be seen that these occur side-by-side in almost all of the first five Types:

	Low conical	*Ring*
Type 1	Kardiani *96*	Delphi *58*
Type 2	Vranesi Copaidos *238*	Kapakli 58 *89*
Type 3	Andros 145 *239*	Volos K1144 *233*
Type 4	–	Sydney *244*
Type 5	Cyprus *33*	Cyprus *34*

Flat bases, the third variety of foot, are found only sporadically within the first five Types: twice in Type 1 and once each in Types 3 and 4.

A further indication that the foot can give little assistance in tracing the development of the pendent semicircle skyphos is the lack of variation in height from Type to Type. Indeed, the range in Types 1 – 5 is almost identical:

Type 1:	0.4 – 1.0 cm
Type 2:	0.3 – 1.1 cm
Type 3:	0.3 – 0.7 cm
Type 4:	0.4 – 0.9 cm
Type 5:	0.5 – 0.9 cm

Since the height of the foot varies so little, there are no grounds for proposing a development from a true conical foot to a poor imitation, or *vice versa*. Furthermore the hypothesis that the use of either a conical or a ring foot may fall into any regional pattern seems negated by the fact that of the six skyphoi from Rheneia, four have a conical foot and two have a lower foot that is flattened out and more similar to a ring.[2] These skyphoi are remarkable for their homogeneity in shape and in the quality and style of their decoration. Regardless of the question of where they were actually made, they give the appearance of having come from the same workshop. Yet, even so, they have two different sorts of foot.

In summary, at this stage no explanation can be offered for the differences in the shape of the foot in Types 1-5. Type 6 alone is uniform in this respect: all these skyphoi have virtually flat bases.

The shape of the skyphos alone was used in forming the typology because it was obvious from the outset that individual decorative elements were neither numerous nor complex enough to allow any meaningful stylistic analysis. Furthermore, a cursory survey revealed that even among vessels which appear to be of chronological proximity and are also from the same site (such as the material from the Pit fill at Xeropolis *130 - 136* or the two skyphoi from Skoubris T33 at Lefkandi *108, 109*) there is not necessarily any definitive similarity in the decoration.[3] Conversely, it occasionally happens that vessels with no other apparent sign of relationship look very much the same in decoration, two such examples being the skyphoi from Kapakli *93* and Kouklia *105*.

Despite this, however, after the skyphoi had been classified according to shape, the occurrence of some elements of the decoration did indeed fall into a pattern, and these now appear to have diagnostic value for tracing the development of the skyphos.[4] First are several decorative features over and above the basic semicircle design found in Types 1 and 2, which occur only very rarely after that. These are the filling motif in the semicircles on, for example, the skyphoi from Lefkandi *117* and *129*, Delphi *58* and Marmariani *173* and the reserved bands or areas on the lower part of the body or on the foot of the skyphos. These latter are seen, for example, on Marmariani *174*, Vergina *233*, Kition *100*, and Lefkandi *111, 116, 119*. Secondly, there is the position in which the two sets of semicircles are painted. Non-intersecting semicircles occur in greatest proportion in Type 1, while in Types 2 and 3 there is a transition to skyphoi decorated with separate sets of semicircles on one side of the pot and intersecting sets on the other. In Types 4, 5 and 6 intersection on both sides is most common.

It is fortunate that typological conclusions such as those above can now be checked against stratified evidence. At Xeropolis, pendent semicircle skyphos fragments have been found in a pit consisting of three deposits. These are, from bottom to top: the Moulds deposit, the Pit fill and the Levelling material.[5]

Among the pendent semicircle skyphos rim fragments in the Moulds deposit all but one have tall lips. Mostly the lip is offset, but occasionally it is merely everted. A ring foot is the only kind found. As to the decoration, both reserved bands below the semicircles and a half hour-glass filler motif appear. In addition, in this the lowest deposit, the two sets of semicircles are frequently set separately on the pot and do not intersect.[6] In the second deposit, the Fill material, there is a marked increased in the number of the pendent semicircle skyphos fragments in proportion to the other wares. Most fragments still have tall lips, although a shorter version is also found. Now all the lips are offset. The shape and height of the foot has remained the same as in the Moulds deposit. In decoration there is little evidence now of subsidiary features such as reserved bands or hour-glass motifs.[7] The pendent semicircle skyphos continues to be very popular in the Levelling material of the pit, but with a certain further modification to its shape. The majority of lips are now short, and the body of the vase is broader and shallower. Nevertheless, the profile of most lips has not altered basically, still flaring and very slightly overhanging the shoulder. In addition to the many examples, there are, however, eight fragments with a different lip: two are curved and set well back from the shoulder; another three also have a curved lip which is not set back from the shoulder.[8]

This three-stage stratification of fragments at Xeropolis appears to confirm the typological sequence, at least in its broadest lines. Some pottery of the Moulds deposit is closely related to the skyphoi of Type 1, such as those from Kardiani *96* and Delphi *58*,[9] while the Pit fill confirms the waning of some of the extra decorative elements, together with the almost exclusive use of the tall offset lip of Type 2. In view of the increased variety of lip types found in Type 2, it is also particularly interesting to note the increased popularity of the pendent semicircle skyphos as represented by its marked increase in the latter deposit.[10] The occurrence of a few short lips in the Pit fill suggests a close chronological relationship between Types 2 and 3.[11]

The Levelling material of the pit also contains a mixture of Types, with fragments belonging to Types 4, 5 and 6.[12] The typology is confirmed to the extent that all three are shown to belong later than Types 1-3, and yet there must also be a certain degree of contemporaneity.

Here, too, as in the Pit fill, the Types are in unequal quantities. The large majority, 20 out of 28, are of Type 4 and these, together with the complete skyphos from Skoubris cemetery *110*, illustrate the popularity of this Type at Lefkandi. It is noteworthy, however, that Type 5, which is found in great numbers at other sites, is represented here only by two fragments, even though its lifetime apparently overlaps that of Type 4. The same is true of Type 6, represented at Lefkandi by only three fragments despite its frequent appearance at East Mediterranean sites. Distribution indicates, therefore, that factors which are not strictly chronological influenced the shape of the skyphos: these will be discussed further in Chapter 8.

The origin of the Pendent Semicircle Skyphos

In his study of Protogeometric pottery in 1952, Desborough advanced the hypothesis that most Protogeometric styles of Greece, including that of Thessaly, were to some degree dependent on Athenian influence. His interpretation of the way the regional styles began followed his opinion that it was unlikely for technical innovations such as the compass and "multiple brush" to appear without antecedents in areas which were not influenced by each other. [13] In a detailed discussion of the origin of the Thessalo-Cycladic pendent semicircle skyphos, he further suggested that Athenian influence was crucial, and that the skyphos evolved somewhere in the Northern Cycladic region after the adaptation of the Attic Protogeometric skyphos shape. He illustrated his argument by some vases in Protogeometric style from Andros which included, among others a high-footed Atticising skyphos (no. 45), a pendent semicircle skyphos with low foot (no.145), and a second high-footed skyphos (no. 146) quite unlike the first. He felt that no. 146 illustrated an intermediate stage of development between the Atticising type and the low-footed variety with pendent semicircle decoration (no. 145), while the close chronological relationship of nos. 146 and 145 was supported by the fact that they were reported to have been decorated with the same "multiple brush". [14]

Six years later an extensive survey of the Thessalian Protogeometric style was published by Verdelis, who disagreed with Desborough and emphasised strongly both the native content of the style and what he felt were locally-inherited Mycenaean elements. [15] His conclusion was that the Thessalian style (of which the pendent semicircle skyphos is an important part) had evolved completely independently of Athens, being a mixture only of these two elements. His view was supported by Theocharis, who felt that his excavations at Iolkos indicated a similar deduction on stratigraphic grounds. [16]

The difference of opinion remained unresolved, for although Desborough acknowledged the truth of Verdelis' delineation of native features, and even the continued existence of some Mycenaean shapes – such as the deep bowl – until after the beginning of the Protogeometric style in Thessaly, he could not accept that the style had commenced without any contact at all with Athens. [17] The basic weakness in the argument, he felt, was that Verdelis did not attempt to account for the appearance of the compass and "multiple brush" in Thessaly and that, in lieu of any better explanation, their transference from Athens was the most likely explanation.

Even apart from this question, however, there remains a problem in Desborough's hypothesis that the pendent semicircle skyphos is a Cycladic adaptation of the Attic Protogeometric skyphos, for there is a basic difference between the Atticising skyphos no. 45 and skyphos no. 146 which makes questionable a direct relationship. The latter has a tall offset lip as well as decoration of only two sets of concentric

circles – both of them quite definitely "unAttic" features. [18] A closer
parallel to skyphos no. 146 than any Attic Protogeometric skyphos is
provided by a vase found in Amathous in Cyprus which was believed
by Desborough to be imported from either the Northern Cycladic region
or Euboea:[19] it also has the high offset lip, pedestal foot and two sets
of concentric circles. Here, too, as in the case of the Andros skyphos,
resemblance to the pendent semicircle skyphos shape had been pointed
out,[20] and the apparent connection is strengthened because the two sets
of concentric circles on the reverse of the Amathous skyphos are intersecting.

From these two skyphoi in particular and also from other similar
ones found in Thessaly, it appears likely that an independent tradition
of bowl shape existed in that region during the Protogeometric period,
even when the Attic skyphos shape was occasionally being imitated. [21]
That this local bowl shape was produced with both low and high pedestal
foot simultaneously may be indicated by the similarity in decoration
between Andros nos. 146 and 145. But a third skyphos, from the site
of Koundouriotissa Pieria in Macedonia, leads even more definitely to such
a conclusion. [22] This is very similar in shape to Andros no. 145 and
also had the fully-developed pendent semicircle decoration. As well as
these canonical features, it has a high pedestal foot (Fig. 42, Plate 7(c)).

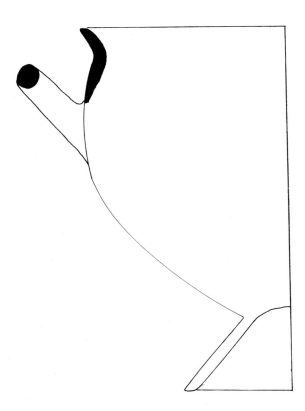

Fig. 42 Koundouriotissa Pieria. Thessaloniki 4709.

However, the fact that an alternative variety of skyphos to the Atticising type was popular in the Thessalo-Cycladic region, and that it is always on this rather than on the Atticising skyphoi that pendent semicircle decoration is found, is of greater importance for the question of the origin of the pendent semicircle skyphos than is the co-existence of two versions of this kind of bowl. As early as the 1920s it was suggested that the pendent semicircle skyphos shape was a direct derivative of the Mycenaean deep bowl,[23] and this was reasserted many years later by Verdelis;[24] but it is only since the excavation of Lefkandi that the connection can be demonstrated in detail, for the site provides a large number of Late Mycenaean deep bowls, from which direct comparison with the pendent semicircle skyphos may be made.[25]

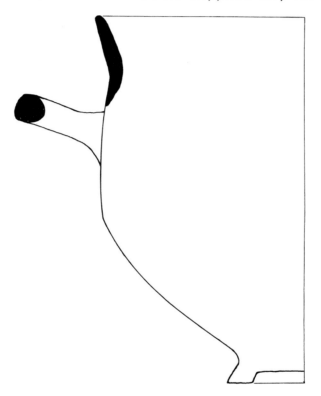

Fig. 43 Delphi 7697. Mycenaean deep bowl.

Many deep bowls from the IIIC and Sub-Mycenaean periods have already been published from Lefkandi.[26] A profile drawing of a similar Late Mycenaean deep bowl, this time from Delphi, is shown in Fig. 43 Pl.1(a).[27] Its ratio is 115:100:47, while the ratios of several other deep bowls from both Lefkandi and Delphi are as follows:

116:100:43

120:100:48

122:100:46

122:100:53

123:100:47

129:100:36

131:100:53[28]

Usually accompanying the deep rounded body is a high flaring lip that is not offset, and a low conical foot.

The Delphi skyphos from Type 1 *58* demonstrates a close similarity to the shape of a Mycenaean deep bowl. Its ratio is 133:100:54 and it has the same tall slightly everted lip. This variety of Mycenaean deep bowl with a lip more upright than flaring has also been found at Lefkandi. [29] The large bell-shaped pendent semicircle skyphos of Type 1 from Kardiani *96* is extremely similar to the Late Mycenaean bowls with more flaring lip. Its ratio is 127:100:50; it has the same kind of tall flaring lip joined to the body in a simple curve; and also the conical foot. [30] Sub-Mycenaean deep bowls at Lefkandi and the pendent semicircle skyphoi of Type 1 also have several specific decorative elements in common, for occasionally there is some variation in the solid dark wash so typical of the Mycenaean bowls. Other features, found either separately or together, are reserved bands just below the handles, a reserved area extending over the lowest part of the body and the foot, a totally reserved foot, or a reserved band between the handles either left blank or filled with a horizontal wavy line. [31]

Evidence for an intermediate stage of the transitional process from the Sub-Mycenaean to Protogeometric style at Lefkandi is now provided by a deep bowl found in the recently-excavated tomb adjacent to the Toumba cemetery. The bowl bears three sets of pendent semicircles in the handle zone with a reserved band below. The context is Middle Protogeometric to early Late Protogeometric, thus slightly antedating any of the canonical pendent semicircle skyphoi known from the site,[32] which belong to Late Protogeometric at the earliest.[33]

Nevertheless, all the Mycenaean decorative elements still appear at one time or another on pendent semicircle skyphoi of Type 1.[34] For example, the reserved bands on the body beneath the concentric semicircles are found on at least two skyphoi - from the Marmariani tholos tomb *174*, and the cemetry at Vergina *233*. On skyphoi such as Skoubris T56:3 *111* and P.T2:1 *116* from Lefkandi the lowest part of the foot has been left unpainted, while on one of the flat-based skyphoi from Marmariani *169* the whole of the lower part of the body is reserved. This same Marmariani skyphos also has the paint from the lip extended downwards in a broad band across the top of the body so that only a narrow decorative panel is left in the handle zone,[35] and on the skyphos from Chauchitsa *31* there is pendent semicircle decoration in only one handle zone: the panel on the other side is completely empty.

It was also noted above that it is common among the pendent semicircle skyphoi of Type 1 for the sets of semicircles to hang independently, and not to intersect. In this can be seen a continuation of the basically zonal scheme of decoration so common in IIIC and found also in the Early Protogeometric period on the skyphos from Lefkandi Skoubris T.20.[36] Thus the overall decorative scheme that became standard on psc skyphoi - a painted lip, lower body, foot and handles, together with painted stripes where the handles join the body and a large reserved zone between the handles – is in use from the IIIC, 3 phase at Lefkandi continuously until Late Protogeometric, when the pendent semicircle skyphos appears.[37]

The Thessalo-Cycladic pendent semicircle skyphos, therefore, appears to be a mixture of old and new components. It contains both Late Mycenaean and Protogeometric features, as do the two pedestal skyphoi from Andros (no. 146) and Amathous.[38] Such a mixture of styles is not unique to this region: several vases from Argos, for example, are Sub-Mycenaean deep bowls on a high pedestal foot of Attic Protogeometric type, their only decoration the typically IIIC reserved lower body and foot, however, the occurrence of one of these bowls in a tomb together with a purely Protogeometric oinochoe with compass-drawn decoration emphasizes their transitional nature.[39] Another example comes from the Kerameikos in Athens.[40]

In terms of relative chronology, this combination of Mycenaean shape with Protogeometric decoration or other features such as a pedestal foot, clearly represents a period earlier than that of the true Athenian Protogeometric skyphos shape. It would thus be inconsistent to consider the same basic archaism of shape with Protogeometric decoration as a development from the Attic Protogeometric skyphos when it occurs in the Thessalo-Cycladic region, even if it could be shown without doubt that Athenian influence was involved. In fact, the question of any stimulus from Athens in the creation of the Thessalo-Cycladic Protogeometric style must be considered unlikely since the excavation of Lefkandi. Although the presence of a pedestal foot on vases with Protogeometric decoration in the Thessalo-Cycladic region has sometimes been thought to indicate Athenian influence,[41] there is a basic difference in shape between the Thessalo-Cycladic and Attic versions.[42] Now, in addition, Lefkandi has revealed that a high foot was in use at that site even in the period before the arrival there of the compass-drawn Protogeometric style.[43] Equally important is the fact that Lefkandi has also revealed a large settlement in the centre of the Thessalo-Cycladic area which is similar to Athens in the extent of its wealth and the frequency of its overseas contacts at the time of the beginning of its compass-drawn Protogeometric style.[44] In particular, the site is known to have had direct contact with Cyprus,[45] and as this island is suggested as a possible source for the new features of the Protogeometric style in Greece,[46] it is no longer necessary to assume that the distinctive Thessalo-Cycladic style could only have originated and developed through contact with Athens.[47]

Finally, it is impossible to leave a discussion of the origin of the psc skyphos without considering the low-footed skyphos with two sets of concentric circles, for in 1952 Desborough suggested that this might represent a further transitional step between the Atticising skyphoi with pedestal foot and the low-footed skyphoi with pendent semicircles. Any attempt to base conclusions on this class of skyphoi is still beset with problems. As Desborough pointed out at the time, examples are much less frequent than the pendent semicircle skyphos and so the evidence available on their shape, distribution and chronology is limited. [48]

The best reliable evidence about the concentric circle skyphos, and especially about its relationship with the psc skyphos, appears to be Lefkandi-Xeropolis, although here too, the concentric circle skyphoi are found only in small numbers. They are considerably fewer than the pendent semicircle skyphos fragments in the Moulds and Pit fill deposits at Xeropolis, and in the Levelling material scarcer still. There are none in the tombs. Nevertheless it is clear from the pit that the two kinds of skyphoi did exist side by side during most of the Subprotogeometric period, even though the concentric circle skyphos is decidedly the less popular.[49] Such changes as there are in its rim indicate that the development of shape in the class is not radically different from the pendent semicircle skyphos. [50]

Certainly all indications are that the two varieties are contemporary and there is nothing from cemeteries or settlement to suggest that the low-footed concentric circle skyphos begins earlier than the pendent semicircle skyphos. They appear to exist concurrently as two different aspects of the local Protogeometric style. This evidence for contemporaneity and similarity in development between the two classes of skyphoi at Lefkandi, together with their almost identical distribution throughout the Mediterranean, suggests that the concentric circle skyphos should be considered simply as a poor cousin of the pendent semicircle skyphos, and not as an ancestor.

CHAPTER 6

N U M E R I C A L   A N A L Y S I S

Introduction

Numerical analysis of archaeological material has become common only in
fairly recent times for, although there were isolated examples of numerical ordering as early as the nineteenth century, it has been during
the last 40 years or so that the subject has become a topic of frequent
discussion among archaeologists and a full appreciation has arisen of the
role which such techniques can play in complementing traditional methods
of analysis and classification.[1]

The impetus for development in the twentieth century was provided
by two Americans, W.S. Robinson and G. Brainerd, who collaborated in
devising a numerical method for the chronological ordering of archaeological assemblages according to the frequencies of types in each assem-
blage. [2]   Since publication of their work in 1951 it has become standard
practice to follow their procedure of constructing a similarity matrix before starting the analysis of data, but because the method as a whole
was developed purely for archaeological situations where assemblages
were involved, their approach was soon found to be of rather limited
use.   Initially, attempts were made simply to modify the method and to
combine it with a kind of similarity analysis suitable for individual units
rather than assemblages, but this led to methodological problems[3] and
it was not until the mid-1960s that experiments with the more flexible
forms of multivariate proximity analysis produced ways of dealing suc-
cessfully with a wide variety of archaeological data.[4]   Of particular
advantage also was the general adoption of a presence/absence matrix
for analysis of individual units.   As this is based purely on features
of the units themselves, even material which would be completely un-
suitable for the type-frequency approach can be included. [5]

Research into multivariate techniques for ordering archaeological
data has produced a large range of methods, many of which rely on
highly sophisticated computerised programmes. In addition to these more
complex approaches, however, attention has also been directed to deve-
loping various rapid seriation methods which, though still based on a

matrix of coefficients, involve considerably less manipulation to produce a coherent result.[6]   One such technique is the Double-Link Method devised by Renfrew and Sterud;[7] this is a multi-dimensional technique which orders the material while yet permitting any clusters to become apparent. Thus it combines much of the advantage of the computerised techniques with the simplicity of a graphical representation.   The method was originally tested by Renfrew on pottery from Cycladic cemeteries of the Early Bronze Age, and has been used more recently by Frankel in his work on Cypriot White-Painted Ware.[8] It was felt that this technique would also be suitable for an analysis of the pendent semicircle skyphos, where the aims were

(a) to discover whether the clustering into Types by purely visual classification would be confirmed by a more overtly defined numerical analysis;

and

(b) whether such indications of sequential arrangement of the material as were perceived on stylistic ground would be revealed by links between the individual clusters.[9]

Because of the necessity for completely reliable data, only skyphoi for which the information had been gathered at first hand were included.[10] The number of skyphoi analysed was also governed by a second criterion, namely, that the vessels should have all of the elements or features necessary for the analysis. Thus incomplete skyphoi or those where the decoration was too faded to be described with certainty were excluded, leaving a total of 55 skyphoi to be subjected to a proximity analysis. The examples included representatives from each of the first five Types, in the following quantities: [11]

Type 1: 4 skyphoi

Type 2: 23 skyphoi

Type 3: 11 skyphoi

Type 4: 6 skyphoi

Type 5: 11 skyphoi

Description of the units

Each skyphos is described by 11 attributes of either quantitative or qualitative nature. These are, in the order they appear on the computer print-out:

1. Ratio of diameter of lip to height of the vessel;[12]

2. Percentage of height of lip to total height of the vessel;

3. Percentage of height of foot to total height of the vessel;

4. Type of lip;

5. Height of lip;

6. Number of pendent semicircles in each set;

7. Height of the vessel;

8. Presence or absence of an offset lip;

9. Presence of absence of intersection in the semicircle decoration;

10. Presence or absence of an hour-glass motif within the semicircles;

11. Presence or absence of a reserved area below the semicircle decoration.

For convenience, the attributes were coded by numerical symbols, since this notation could be applied both to the directly measureable and to the descriptive features.[13] The symbolisation is tabulated below:

TABLE 2: ATTRIBUTES USED IN PROXIMITY ANALYSIS

ATTRIBUTE	1	2	3	4	5	6	7	8	9	12	13	14
1.	calculated directly from the relevant measurements											
2.	8-11%	12-16%	17-19%	20-23%	-	-	-	-	-	-	-	-
3.	3-4%	5-7%	8-10%	11%+	-	-	-	-	-	-	-	-
4.	flaring or near vertical straight lip	flaring or near vertical curved lip	curved lip set back from the shoulder	-	-	-	-	-	-	-	-	-
5. (cm)	0.9 or less	1.0-1.3	1.4-1.7	1.8+	-	-	-	-	-	-	-	-
6.	5	6	7	8	9	10	11	12	13	7 & 8 combined	14	16
7. (cm)	8.3 or or less	8.4-10.2	10.3-12.0	12.1-16.0	-	-	-	-	-	-	-	-
8.	Yes	No	-	-	-	-	-	-	-	-	-	-
9.	Yes	No	one side only	-	-	-	-	-	-	-	-	-
10.	Yes	No	-	-	-	-	-	-	-	-	-	-
11.	Yes	No	-	-	-	-	-	-	-	-	-	-

Attribute 1, the ratio of the diameter of rim to the height of the vessel, was calculated to several decimal places. Only one decimal is shown in the matrix, however, since this was felt to be the significant degree of accuracy. The calculation of the ratios of Attribute 1 for each pair of pots is felt to be an important measure of the difference and similarity between pairs, and in view of this and the significant differences which may result in the ratio from even an 0.3 cm measuring error,[14] each individual ratio (that is, $\frac{\text{Attribute 1 of unit 1}}{\text{Attribute 1 of unit 2}}$) is used, rather than classes of ratios.

Attributes 2, 3, 5 and 7 are all quantitative features which, though directly measurable, required classifying into ranges before coding. Two factors were considered when deciding where divisions should be made within the total range of any measurement: first the inherent clustering of the units as revealed by histograms of each attribute, and second a combination of irregularities in the vases themselves and the assumption of the possibility of a 0.3cm error in measurement.[15]

Neither the shape of the foot nor its absolute height was included in the analysis. As demonstrated in chapters 4 and 5, the shape of the foot is not well-defined on the pendent semicircle skyphos, and in addition, where feet have been classified, the categories distinguished occur either together or at random throughout the typology. In the height of the foot, all units tend to cluster around 0.4cm and thus it is of no significance in determining similarities or differences between vessels. Similarly, the decorative feature of a reserved band on the inside of the lip was omitted because of its ubiquity and lack of use as an item for differentiating between units.[16]

Before the calculation of a similarity coefficient for each pair, consideration was given to the question of the relative weighting of the eleven attributes. The coding method excluded any natural weighting due to the number of columns used for any single attribute, so it became a matter of personal judgement.[17] Experience suggested that certain attributes were more significant in differentiating between units,[18] but as this could not explicitly be justified in terms of this type of analysis, it was decided that each attribute should be allotted equal weight – with the exception of attribute 1: for this a weighting of 2 was given, on the grounds that this single attribute in fact involves two separate features of each unit. As Diagrams 2 and 3 in Appendix 3 show, there is a very high correlation between the change in the diameter of the rim to the height and in the diameter of the foot to the height, although it is true that the rate of increase in the diameter of rim is approximately three times that of the rate of increase in the diameter of the foot. Therefore, attribute 1 implicitly also represents the ratio of the diameter of the foot to the height of the vessel and its double weight can be justified on those grounds. As a result of this decision, the maximum possible agreement between any two units became 12.

The similarity coefficient

A FORTRAN programme written for the Cyber 70/72 at the University of New South Wales by Dr W. Kearsley, of the School of Surveying at that university, was used to produce an unordered presence and absence similarity matrix of coefficients. The coefficient itself is the Simple Matching Coefficient, devised by Sokal and Sneath, which is calculated as the number of attribute agreements out of the total number possible. [19] For example, in the case of units 1 and 2 in the matrix, there is a coefficient of 7.0 out of the possible 12.0. This was produced because five attributes are held in common and attribute 1 is contributing a score of 2 to the coefficient. The complete matrix of similarity coefficients is found in Appendix 1 (Table 3).

Results

All 55 units are connected to at least one other by a coefficient of 8.0 or more out of the possible 12.0. This is a 75 percent level of agreement, which is a high level of correlation, given the variation evident in the material as a whole. The highest coefficient between any two units is 12.0, occurring only once, between a pair of vessels belonging to Type 5, nos. 47 and 52. The lowest group of correlations is in the 2.5-2.9 range and involves nine pairs. In all but one case these contain one vessel from Type 1 and another from Type 5. [20]

Forty-four of the 55 vessels analysed are linked by their highest coefficient only to another pot from the same Type. Of the remaining 11, three (no. 12 - Vergina P21; no. 30 - Nea Ionia K2235; and no. 36 - Kalamaria 5710) have equally high links with vessels of their own Type and another from a different one. The other eight vessels (no. 1 - Delphi 5909; nos. 25-7 - Lefkandi T59, 2-4; no. 38 - Marmariani 115; no. 39 - Sydney 73.03; no. 44 - Delos 10; and no. 45 - Boston 72.76) have their highest coefficient with a pot that does not belong to their own Type. However, the discrepancy in all cases except one is less than the difference resulting from a complete attribute, since it is less than 1.0.

For example, no. 1 (Delphi 5909), classified in Chapter 4 as Type 1, has its highest coefficient with Lefkandi P.T3, 14 at the level of 8.0. But its second highest coeffcient with Marmariani 121 of its own Type, is just 0.1 less at 7.9. Similarly, no. 45 of Type 5 has a coefficient, of 10.0 with no. 42 (Delos 8) of Type 4. Its second highest coefficient, however, only 0.1 less at 9.9, linking it with nos. 47 and 52, both of Type 5.

Unit no. 38 (Type 3) has its highest correlation (9.7) with no. 39 from Type 4, which is 0.7 higher than its next highest correlation, with no. 37 (Marmariani 116) of its own Type. [21] Similarly no. 39 (Type 4) has its highest correlation (9.7) with no. 38 of Type 3, 0.9 higher than its secondary links with no. 44 (Delos 10) of Type 4 and no. 21 (Larisa) of Type 2.

Nos. 25-27 (Lefkandi S.T59, 2-4) may be considered as a group as all come from the same archaeological context. The three were classified as Type 2 in Chapter 4 but the primary link is with Type 4 in the case of nos. 25 and 27, and Type 5 in the case of no. 26. Nevertheless each is linked to a Type 2 vessel at a level less than 1.0 lower than their highest coefficient.

Only no. 44 (Delos 10) has neither its highest nor second highest coefficient with a vessel of its own Type. Both links are with pots in Type 5 - no. 53 (9.9) and no. 54 (9.0). The vessel's third highest coefficient is 8.9, with no. 39 (Sydney 73.03) of its own Type. Thus there is a total overall difference of 1.0 between no. 44 and a vessel of its own Type.

As stated above, it was intended originally to plot the results of this analysis according to the Double Link Method of Renfrew and Sterud, but because the extent of clustering within the material is so great and so complex the diagram produced is too confused to be of any assistance in clarifying relationships between the classes.[22] Thus Diagram 1, designed as an alternative, was drawn up by considering both primary and secondary links between pots. The *primary link* is defined as that which has the highest coefficient between pots; and the *secondary link* that which has the second highest coefficient.

All the units (identified by both matrix number and name) placed inside a box are related by their primary link to at least one other in the same box. (The exceptions are the eight vases - marked with asterisks - discussed above). Lines between boxes represent links to vessels outside the class, the arrows giving the direction of the link and the figures its levels or range. In addition, each boxed cluster defined by the analysis is labelled according to the visual typological classification of Chapter 4. Discussion of the results is arranged according to these Types:

TYPE 1

Three of the four vessels have their primary link with another member of the class. No. 2 (Vergina AΓ 24) and no. 3 (Marmariani 121) have high coefficients of 10.9. Chauchitsa (no. 4) has a primary link with no. 2 at the level of 8.0. In these cases the secondary links are mainly with pots of Type 2 - no. 10 (Kardiani B79), no. 11 (Vergina Δ 15), no. 12 (Vergina P 21), no. 13 (Vergina P 1) and no. 17 (Delos 19). Only no. 10 is linked to two different vessels in Type 1: these are nos. 2 and 4. Type 1 has one other secondary connection, apart from those with Type 2: this is between no. 4 (Chauchitsa) and no. 38 (Marmariani 115) and between no. 2 (Vergina AΓ 24) and no. 30 (Nea Ionia K2235), both of Type 3.

The fourth Type 1 vessel, no. 1 (Delphi 5909), has its primary link with no. 6 (Lefkandi 3, 14) of Type 2 and its secondary connection with no. 3 (Marmariani 121) of Type 1. Nos. 1 and 6 are the only two with the hour-glass filler within the semicircles, and this similarity is enough to tip the balance of similarity for no. 1 towards P.T3,14 in Type 2. Even so, the difference in its two highest coefficients, with Type 2 and Type 1, is only 0.1, so it differs little from the pattern of connections established by the other three units of Type 1.

TYPE 2

Most of the 23 Type 2 vases have strong primary and secondary links within the class, giving the impression of a very close-knit set of vessels. There are nine exceptions. Nos. 13 (Vergina P 1) and 19 (Kapakli 58) have a high coefficient of 11.9 with each other but are otherwise linked with their own Type only at 8.0 (no. 12 Vergina P 21).

Both nos. 13 and 19 have strong secondary links with Type 3, particularly with no. 32 (Kapakli 60), where there are coefficients of 9.9 and 10.0 respectively. A third pot from this Type, no. 12 (Vergina P 21), also has a link with no. 32 of Type 3. As the link is of equal value to the two links of no. 12 with Type 2, the close relationship of no. 32 with Type 2 is again emphasised.

Nos. 6, 9 and 24 have primary and secondary links within their own Type, but there are also secondary links to Type 1, Type 3 and Types 3 and 4 respectively. A more complex set of links outside Type 2 is provided by the three skyphoi from Lefkandi S.T59 (nos. 25-7). At the primary level they are linked to Types 4 (twice) and 5 (twice); at the secondary level to Type 2 (twice), Type 4 (once) and Type 5 (once). All links are at a level of between 9.8 and 9.0.

TYPE 3

These 11 pots also have a high degree of internal similarity, shown by the ten primary links of at least 9.0 within their own Type. No. 30 (Nea Ionia K2235) has two equally-high primary links within Type 3. It also has a secondary link to Type 1 (no. 2), five to Type 2 (nos. 9, 13, 16, 18, 27) and two more to Type 3 (nos. 31, 34). The primary and secondary links are at a level of 9.0 and 8.9, characterising Nea Ionia K2235 as a vessel with a high degree of similarity with 12 others. Both no. 32 (Kapakli 60) and no. 35 (Volos K1144) also have secondary links with Type 2. These are at 10.0 with no. 19 in the case of Kapakli 60, and at 9.9 with nos. 13 and 19 in the case of Volos K1144.

Like Type 2, Type 3 also has links with Type 4. No. 36 (Kalamaria 5710) has equal primary links to Type 4 by way of no. 40 (Lefkandi S.T45,3) and no. 42 (Delos 8) at 9.0, and in addition a secondary link to no. 17 (Delos 19) of Type 2. No. 38 (Marmariani 115) has a primary link to Type 4 at 9.7 and this was discussed above. One skyphos has a secondary link with Type 5: no. 29 (Lefkandi P.T39,5) with no. 55 (Fogg 1953.116).

122

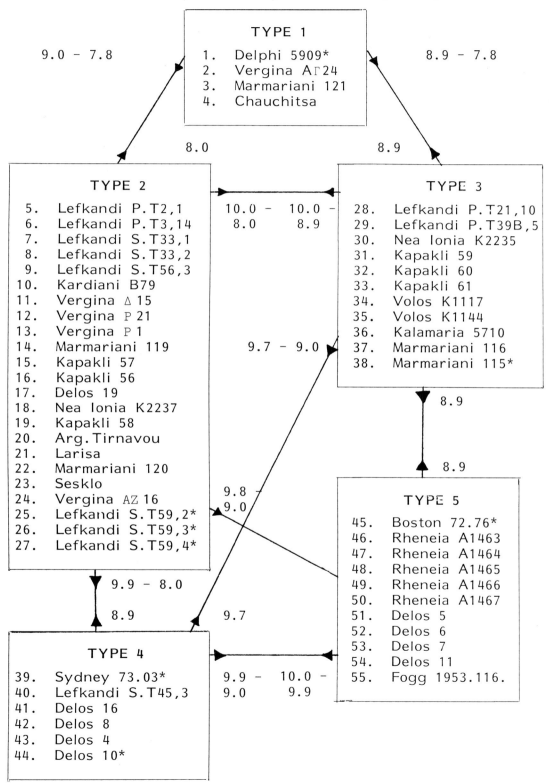

DIAGRAM 1
Clusters produced by the Proximity Analysis

TYPE 4

Four of the six vessels are linked at the primary level with another of their own Type. The exceptions, nos. 39 (Sydney 73.03) and 44 (Delos 10) are discussed above.

The link between Types 2 and 4 created from Type 2 by nos. 25-27 is here confirmed by a secondary link between the Sydney skyphos (no. 39) and no. 21 (Larisa). the same is true of the link between Types 3 and 4, illustrated here by the primary link between no. 39 (Sydney) and no. 38 (Marmariani 115). There are also two intercluster links between Types 4 and 5, both from no. 44 (Delos 10): one is at the primary level (9.9), the other is 9.0.

TYPE 5

Ten of the 11 skyphoi of this Type are interlinked by high coefficients of 9.8 or more at the primary level, and two vessels – nos. 47 (Rheneia A1464) and 52 (Delos 6) – are classified as identical, with a coefficient of 12.0. Furthermore, only three vessels have links outside the cluster. No. 45 (Boston 72.76) has a primary link with Type 4 at 10.0, although its two secondary links of 9.9 are to pots within its own Type – nos. 47 (Rheneia A1464) and 52 (Delos 6). There is also one other link with Type 4, provided by no. 53 (Delos 7). This vessel has both primary and secondary links within its own Type; but also has a further secondary link with no. 44 (Delos 10) of Type 4.

Finally, there is one link with Type 3, by no. 55 (Fogg 1953.116). This vessel has four primary and secondary links with its own Type at the levels of 9.8 and 8.9 respectively. In addition it has an equal secondary link with no. 29 (Lefkandi P.T39B,5).

CONCLUSIONS

With eight exceptions, the 55 skyphoi are clustered into five classes corresponding to Types 1-5 of the visual classification in Chapter 4. Since these clusters are formed by high similarity coefficients between the majority of vessels at both primary and secondary levels, it follows that they represent clearly definable classes, each with a unique combination of features. Variations in the average level of similarity between vessels of a given Type may be related to the number in each class. In Type 2, which has the largest sample, for instance, 17 out of 23 units have a similarity coefficient of 9.0 or higher with another in the same Type, while in Type 1, the smallest class, the level of similarity is a little lower, with three of the four vessels having a coefficient of 8.0 or more.

The skyphoi which have their only primary link with a vessel outside their own Type are so placed for various reasons. It should be noted, however, that all have strong links with pots of their own Type which are no greater than 1.0 below their highest coefficient. But it is in cases such as these that visual classification is more sensitive to similarities and differences to the extent that weight is given to those attributes instinctively felt to be more important. In these eight sky-phoi, weighting in favour of the ratios and the shape of the lip is necessary to counteract other, frequently fortuitous, similarities such as the occurrence of 11 semicircles in the case of both nos. 38 and 39.

The skyphoi which have primary and/or secondary links both with their own Type and with others provide the inter-cluster links essential to the establishment of a sequence. No. 30 (Nea Ionia K2235) and the group of three Lefkandi skyphoi from S.T59 (nos. 25-7) are the most extreme examples. Each has 12 primary and secondary links and is conected with two Types other than its own: no. 30 to Types 1 and 2 and nos. 25-27 to Types 4 and 5. This is an accurate reflection of their transitional character, which also led to problems in their typological classification.

The interpretation of the collective changes in the shape of the skyphos as indications of movement through time is illustrated by the way the Types are ordered according to the vertical links between them (Diagram 1). In addition, the horizontal links indicate that although a sequence is established there is no single line of development.

If Diagram 1 is extended, with those links which either travel in one direction only or are produced by a single pair of vessels rather than several now omitted, two possible configurations result:

(a)   (b)

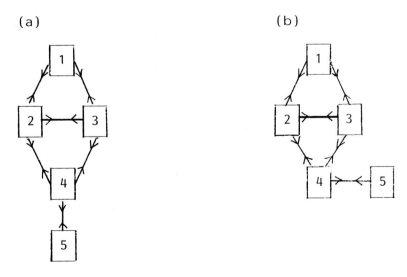

According to diagram (b), the development of the skyphos would fall into three stages, with two Types running parallel to each other in each of the last two stages:

(1)   Type 1

(2)   Type 2;   Type 3

(3)   Type 4;   Type 5

Of the two diagrams, this one seems more likely to reflect the true situation in the light of the archaeological evidence available at present, for stratified pendent semicircle skyphoi at Lefkandi also show a three-stage development in shape with the association of Types 2 and 3 on the one hand, and Types 4 and 5 on the other.

It is interesting that, according to the diagram, Type 3 retains a direct link with Type 1, and that this did not disappear when the weakest links were broken. Although this link is certainly not as strong - in either frequency or value - as those between Types 3 and 2, or 1 and 2, it calls for explanation. Similarly, there is the interesting situation that Type 5 is connected to Type 4 only once the weakest links have been broken. There are good archaeological reasons to suspect that both these cases are not accidents of the sample but a true reflection of the development of the skyphos. The interpretation is most readily indicated archaeologically by the distribution of the Types: a discussion follows in Chapter 8.

CHAPTER 7

A B S O L U T E   C H R O N O L O G Y

It was suggested by Desborough over 30 years ago that the life-span of the pendent semicircle skyphos was about 150 years, from *ca.* 900 to 750 BC, or a little later.[1]   At that time, however, the date of the appearance of the psc skyphos and the various stages of its development were based mainly on stylistic considerations and could not clearly be established from external chronological evidence because of the uninformative contexts in which the skyphoi had been found. [2] The discovery at Lefkandi of a pit which contained stratified pendent semicircle skyphos fragments associated with imported Attic wares thus had tremendous importance. It permitted, for the first time, a correlation of the psc skyphos with the securely-dated Attic Geometric pottery of the ninth and first half of the eighth centuries. [3]

The Moulds deposit at the bottom of the pit contained no Attic imports; but a few fragments of pottery in Attic Early Geometric style in the Pit fill immediately above indicate that the deposit must belong either to the late tenth or early ninth centuries. The Pit fill itself contained, as well as this Early Geometric ware, another fragment belonging to the Middle Geometric I period in Attica, so its date may well extend into the second half of the ninth century. Above the fill, the Levelling material of the pit contained about 30 fragments of Attic and Atticising Middle Geometric pottery, some of which belonged to Middle Geometric I, although most were typical of the Middle Geometric II period. [4]

In summary, the pit at Xeropolis indicates the following correlation between the Attic Geometric sequence and the development of the pendent semicircle skyphos at Lefkandi (always acknowledging, of course, that allowance must be made for some overlapping):[5]

Mouids deposit – pre-850 mainly LPG (late PG-EG) – TYPE 1[6]

Pit fill   – ninth century: SPGI/II-early SPGIII (EG-MGI)[7] – TYPES 2 and 3. The lower limit of MGI for the Pit fill appears to be confirmed by the discovery of an Attic MGI pyxis in Skoubris T59, which contains three Type 2 skyphoi, and another very similar Attic pyxis in Palia Perivolia T21, where there was a Type 3 skyphos). [8]

Levelling material – 825/800-750+: SPG III (MGI/MGII and into the second half of the eighth century, L.G.) – TYPES 4, 5 and 6. (Although the Late Geometric pottery in the Levelling material does suggest that the deposit expands beyond 750,[9] its limited quantity makes it difficult to be sure exactly how far.)

Apart from Lefkandi, there is clear contextual evidence for the date of Type 6 skyphoi at Eretria, where eight fragments of Type 6 have been found in two different Late Geometric deposits.[10]

The only other evidence in the Aegean for the absolute chronology of the pendent semicircle skyphos comes from the settlement of Zagora on Andros, where the fragment belonging to Type 4 was found in a context running down to Middle Geometric II.[11] This information is certainly less precise than that for Type 4 at Lefkandi, but is not out of harmony with the Middle Geometric II date indicated there.

At the lower end of the series, since three psc skyphoi have been found in the West, it might have been hoped that some help would be forthcoming from the traditional source of dating for the Late Geometric period, the Thucydidean foundation dates of Greek colonies.[12] But each skyphos comes from a non-Greek context. Of the two from Veii in Etruria, one *229* was a surface find. The other, *230*, was found in a tomb dated in the relative sequence of the site to the IIA phase conventionally attibuted to the first half of the eighth century on the basis of imported Greek skyphoi found at Veii.[13] The reliability of this date, however, has been thrown open by recent evidence for a more precise absolute chronology of the Cycladic (chevron) skyphoi themselves. This indicates that chevron skyphoi from Corinth, Euboea and East Greece, at least, continue well down into the Late Geometric period.[14] Furthermore, none of the Euboean chevron skyphoi, which form the majority of imports found in Veii, dates before 750 BC.[15] This has led to a proposed revision of dates for Veii IIA to 780-730.[16] The third skyphos from the West Mediterranean, that from Villasmundo in Eastern Sicily *237*, comes from a native grave robbed before excavation. It provides no information on the absolute chronology of the skyphos.

In the East Mediterranean the situation is similar: this region also provides much less information than might have been expected, given that contemporary records are not infrequent. However, there is some chronological information for pendent semicircle skyphoi of Types 5 and 6, relatively well-preserved examples of which have been found on Cyprus or at mainland sites. For example, the Amathous skyphos (*17/1*) was found in a tomb containing an Attic or Atticising MG I skyphos. This is in line with the lower limit for Type 2 indicated already at Lefkandi.[17] The Type 5 vessels from the tomb at Salamis (*195-6*) were found in association with other skyphoi of Attic Middle Geometric II type and plates with pendent semicircle decoration of the kind that occur in the Levelling material of the pit at Xeropolis no earlier than the Middle

Geometric period. [18]   Thus a date in the first half of the eighth century is indicated in Cyprus for Type 5 and on the mainland a firm *terminus ante quem* of 720 is provided for Type 5 by the destruction level on the citadel at Hama where two skyphoi were found.[19]   This evidence from the Near East coincides exactly with the presence of two Type 5 fragments in the Levelling material at Lefkandi, a deposit which extends from 825/800 to some time after 750 BC.[20]   Type 6 skyphoi are dated after 750 in the Near East by means of the skyphos from Kouklia. This was found in a tomb with two other Greek skyphoi which are undoubtedly of Late Geometric date. [21]

In summary, such reliable contextual information as there is on the absolute chronology of the pendent semicircle skyphos may be tabulated as follows:

Table 4: Absolute chronology of psc skyphoi

	AEGEAN		NEAR EAST		WEST MEDITERRANEAN
	Lefkandi	Eretria	Cyprus	Hama	
TYPE 1	pre 850	–	–	–	–
TYPE 2	900–825/800	–	850–800	–	–
TYPE 3	" "	–	–	–	–
TYPE 4	825/800–750+	·	–	–	–
TYPE 5	" "	–	800–750	*t.a.q* 720	–
TYPE 6	" "	750–700	750–700	–	–

Stylistic considerations also indicate a Late Geometric date for Type 6, for the shape is one which first appears in the Late Geometric period and has the old pendent semicircle decoration applied to it. [22]   For example, one of the fragments from Al Mina *1*, two from Eretria *70, 72*, and that from Tell Abu Hawam *212* are all close imitations in shape of the skyphos with slip-filled decoration, a type already found at Al Mina as well as at Eretria, Lefkandi and Chalcis.[23]   The shape is a good example of the well-established fact that the Euboean Late Geometric style is the result of a mixture of influence from Athens and Corinth. [24]   In the case of the psc fragments mentioned above, the Corinthian influence is especially prominent because the shape is an imitation of one of the variety of Corinthian chevron skyphoi.[25]   The relationship can be seen by comparison with the Corinthian chevron skyphos rim fragment from Pithecusae. [26]   This belongs late in the Corinthian series and is probably dated to Late Geometric I. [27]   A further example of the type occurs in an MG II–LG I context on Andros. [28]

The Euboean series of chevron skyphoi is eclectic in character and those published recently (mainly from Eretria)[29] reflect the same two influences as does the Late Geometric style in general. It is, however, in the later part of the series that the borrowing from Corinth becomes apparent and indicates that Euboean skyphoi of this shape are to be dated to the LG I period.[30] The use of the same shape for motifs other than chevrons or pendent semicircles is shown by an Eretrian metope skyphos from Veii which also dates to the third quarter of the eighth century, and there are other examples from Eretria itself.[31] The four well-preserved skyphoi of Type 6 (Khaldeh, Kouklia, Veii *229* and Villasmundo), and the rest of the rim fragments simply represent a development of this same shape which takes place after ca.720 at Eretria. They have a lip with a deeper curve and more sharply-defined shoulder.[32]

The occurrence of psc decoration on Euboean pottery of the Late Geometric period is not altogether unusual. In fact the use of pendent semicircles on shapes other than the canonical skyphos had already begun in a small way in the Middle Geometric period with its application to plates like those found in Lefkandi and Salamis.[33] The following is a list of fragments very different from each other in shape but sharing the fact that each is a Euboean Late Geometric skyphos shape decorated with pendent semicircles: Chalcis *26, 29*; Lefkandi *142*; Zagora *240, 241*; Soli *204*; Veii *230*; Delphi *63*; Al Mina *6, 10, 16*.

The two rim fragments fron Chalcis and that from Lefkandi are high-mouthed skyphoi, a shape for which Euboea was indebted to Athens in the last third of the eighth century.[34] Chalcis *29* is particularly interesting because, as well as being a Late Geometric shape, the pendent semicircle decoration is here combined with the typical Late Geometric skyphos motif, a cross-hatched lozenge.[35] The two fragments from Zagora also have parallels among Euboean Late Geometric shapes,[36] as do the skyphoi from Soli, Delphi, Veii[37] and the three Al Mina fragments.[38]

Fig. 44 Al Mina. Oxford 1954.271/7. Lekanis.

There is one other piece of evidence for the continued existence of pendent semicircle decoration into the Late Geometric II period, although it is not a skyphos but a fragment from Al Mina with a tiny wedge-shaped lip only 0.5cm high.[39] As well as the usual exterior psc decoration, there are groups of strokes across the reserved band on the inside of the lip: the shape and interior decoration are similar to a variety of lekanis produced at Eretria. Two examples of a slightly later type have already been observed at Tarsus.[40] This fragment, with the skyphoi discussed above and those of Type 6, forms unmistakable evidence that the pendent semicircle decoration outlives its original shape and appears on various new shapes of the Late Geometric period,

130

particularly the skyphos.[41]   The date assigned to the Euboean model of
the Type 6 skyphos so popular in the Near East indicates that it belongs
as late as Late Geometric II, or the last third of the eighth century.[42]

A similar date is indicated by the presence of pendent semicircle
skyphoi in the destruction level of 696 BC at Tarsus.[43]   While it is true
that the skyphos fragments included in Type 6 come only from the destruction fill which Boardman has shown to contain material of mixed date,[44]
other psc skyphos fragments were found in the destruction level itself,
in two areas which he has clearly identified as being in use to the very
end of the eighth century.[45]   No profiles of these fragments are published.[46]
While the information provided on the chronology of the pendent semicircle skyphos by the destruction level at Tarsus is admittedly limited,
it is certainly more definite than that of other Near Eastern sites – such
as Khaldeh, Tyre and Tell Abu Hawam – where Type 6 skyphoi have also
been found.   At all these sites the dates for the relevant strata have a
very wide range, caused mainly by the lack of a detailed relative chronology for local ceramics which prevents these sites being more firmly dated
by comparison with others where a destruction level has been identified
and dated.[47]

The situation is complicated further by divergent opinions among
Palestinian archaeologists on the correlation of strata from major sites
such as Megiddo, Samaria and Hazor.   This is so deep-seated that two
conflicting chronological schemes[48] at present cause considerable uncertainty also for the chronology of the smaller mainland sites and for Cyprus.[49]

One minor site of particular relevance here is Tell Abu Hawam.   It
has received a great amount of attention in discussions of the absolute
chronology of the pendent semicircle skyphos,[50] but has so far been of
little real assistance for chronology because four different dates are
proposed for the end of level III, in which the psc skyphos fragment
was found.   These dates cover more than two centuries, from the late
tenth to the seventh century.[51]

In all past attempts to date Tell Abu Hawam, its pottery – which
consists mainly of Cypriot Bichrome and of Red-Slip wares – has been
compared with that of Megiddo and to a lesser extent with Samaria.
There is little agreement among Palestinian archaeologists, however, and
the basic reason appears to be the long existence of the Hawam III pottery
types at Megiddo.   For example, the Cypriot Black-on-Red bowls peculiar
to level III at Hawam, and by far its most commonly-occurring form,[52]
are found at Megiddo in several strata.   The bowls first appear in level
V and continue through IV and into III,[53] so that on the basis of the
most common ceramic type in Hawam III, a correlation with any of three
different strata at Megiddo is equally correct.   According to the so-called
Hazorite chronology, the higher of the two current systems for the
Palestinian Iron Age, these bowls therefore have a firm *terminus ante
quem* at the site of 732.[54]

A class of finely burnished Red-Slip bowls was frequently associated with the Black-on-Red bowls in Hawam III[55] and this ware, now known generally as Samaria ware, also has a life extending over several centuries.[56] The straight-sided bowls with sagging bases found in Hawam III occur, like the Cypriot bowls, throughout levels V-III at Megiddo. They have also been found in level VI and deposit E207 at Samaria, both of which were destroyed in 722 by an Assyrian attack on the city, and occur even later at Ashdod in a context attributed to the time of the Assyrian attack of 712. [57] Therefore, a *terminus ante quem* of 722 is provided for the Hawam Red-Slip bowls on the basis of the evidence from Samaria, and it may perhaps be lowered to 712 if the Ashdod evidence is accepted. At Tell Keisan they do not appear before 750 and are especially popular in the second half of the eighth century. [58]

The result is that neither class of local pottery from Hawam III gives any ground for supposing that the more commonly accepted late tenth century or late ninth century dates are likely to be more correct that one as low as the late eighth century, and although certain reconstructions of the history of Tell Abu Hawam have been proposed on the basis of the varying correlations with the Megiddo strata, there is no direct evidence from the site itself for its connection with these events. [59] In fact, scholars' contradictory conclusions [60] suggest that a fourth proposal, of a less colourful nature, is likely to be equally valid. According to this view, the end of Hawam III is to be interpreted simply as a long-drawn-out period of stagnation which eventually tailed off in the seventh century. [61] This opinion is supported by the fact that ceramically a single level at Hawam extends over the period covered by several separate strata at Megiddo, themselves allotted over 200 years by *both* chronological systems. [62] In addition, a low date for the end of Hawam III does less violence to the interpretation of the stratigraphy of the site, obviating the need to postulate a long abandonment between levels III and II, for which there is no positive evidence but which is made necessary by a high chronology for the end of level III.

The high dates for the end of Hawam III and the period of abandon-ment between III and II were supported on purely ceramic grounds, but these also appear less reliable now than at the time of their publication. For example, it was suggested originally by Hamilton that the absence from Hawam III of the coarse Red-Slip wares typical of Israelite sites in the ninth and eighth centuries was of chronological significance and confirmed the need to place its end in the late tenth century.[63] Against this argument, however, Vincent immediately pointed out that cultural factors were more likely to be the cause, and since Hawam had never through-out its history shown close ceramic affinity with inland Palestine it was not surprising that level III continued this tradition.[64] As more sites along the coasts of Palestine and Syria are excavated, it does appear that this latter interpretation of a largely separate cultural and ceramic province is correct. [65]

The absence of wheel-burnishing on the pottery of Hawam III was felt to be another argument for a high chronology for the end of Hawam III.[66] The use of such an argument for chronological purposes has not been restricted to this site,[67] but its reliability must now be considered open to question in the light of evidence from several recently-excavated sites which indicates that there is no single or mutually exclusive line of technological development in the burnishing of pottery. [68]

It is still impossible therefore, to be dogmatic about the date of the end of Hawam III on the basis of the local pottery, and the most that can be said is that the *termini ante quos* established by reference to destruction levels in Palestine indicates that a date as low as the last quarter of the eighth century is quite as feasible as one in the late tenth or late ninth century. Iron Age ceramics in the Near East, including those considered diagnostic for the end of Hawam III, have such a long life and leave scholars a wide choice of dates.[69]

The third and final criterion for the chronology of Hawam level III has traditionally been the date of the two Greek imports found there.[70] At the time of the publication of the excavation report, it was felt that these fragments could positively be identified as Thessalian ware, although even then they offered little real assistance in dating the level, since they, too, could be dated only to within about 200 years. [71] Moreover, as more examples of the pendent semicircle skyphos have come to light, the identification of the fragments has become less certain, with regard not only to their chronology but also to their origin, and their use as a dating criterion for Hawam III has often been queried.[72]

Now, however, it has become possible, by a detailed study of the pendent semicircle skyphos class as a whole, to achieve a precise classification of the Hawam fragment,[73] and it is clear that the skyphoi from Marmariani originally suggested as parallels are quite dissimilar in shape,[74] and that several other skyphoi later put forward are no closer.[75] Because of its close connection in shape with Euboean Late Geometric skyphoi, the Hawam fragment can now reliably be placed close to the end of the long lifetime of the psc skyphos class, and assigned a date no earlier than the second half of the eighth century. As a result, Greek archaeology now has a positive contribution to make to the problem of the chronology of Tell Abu Hawam, for the date of the pendent semicircle skyphos fragment suggests that the end of level III is not likely to be before 750 BC, and that therefore the lower rather than the upper limit of the range provided by the Near Eastern pottery should be preferred.

CHAPTER 8

CONCLUSIONS

There can no longer be any doubt that the lifetime of the pendent semicircle skyphos was approximately 200 years, extending over the ninth
and eighth centuries BC.

On contextual and stylistic grounds, the appearance of the earliest
pendent semicircle skyphoi of Type 1 can be placed at the end of the
Late Protogeometric period, ca. 900 BC. [1] Soon after, the Pit fill deposit
at Xeropolis provides firm evidence for the contemporaneity of psc skyphoi of Type 2 with the Attic Early Geometric period and probably the
beginning of Middle Geometric. This chronological link between Lefkandi
and Athens is especially important in view of the strong indications now
that the creation of the Thessalo-Cycladic Protogeometric style, and the
pendent semicircle skyphos in particular, was independent of stimulus
from Athens. There is no other way at present to establish an absolute
chronology for the early development of the vessel. At the lower end
of the lifetime of the skyphos, in the second half of the eighth century,
the information once provided only by Kouklia and Tarsus in the East
Mediterranean is now corroborated in the Aegean by the consistent
Late Geometric contexts of the fragments from Eretria, and by the fact
that the latest skyphoi are seen to be imitations of Late Geometric Euboean
shapes. On the other hand, the question of where the psc skyphos
was actually created is not so easily detailed, for its widespread popularity over most of the Thessalo-Cycladic area from very early in its
development means that it is still impossible to be sure where it first
appeared. On present evidence, however, a strong case may be made
for the site of Lefkandi.

Throughout the large amount of pendent semicircle skyphos material
from Lefkandi, there is a high standard in both potting and decoration.
The clay is of a fine texture, and before decoration was applied it was
usually covered with a light brown slip. The skyphoi have been skilfully
formed in most cases, with a well-defined offset lip which, together with
the body of the pot, has a taut and crisp profile. This clarity of shape
is complemented by a precision in the decoration which gives even the
simple pendent semicircle scheme a certain attraction. The number of

134

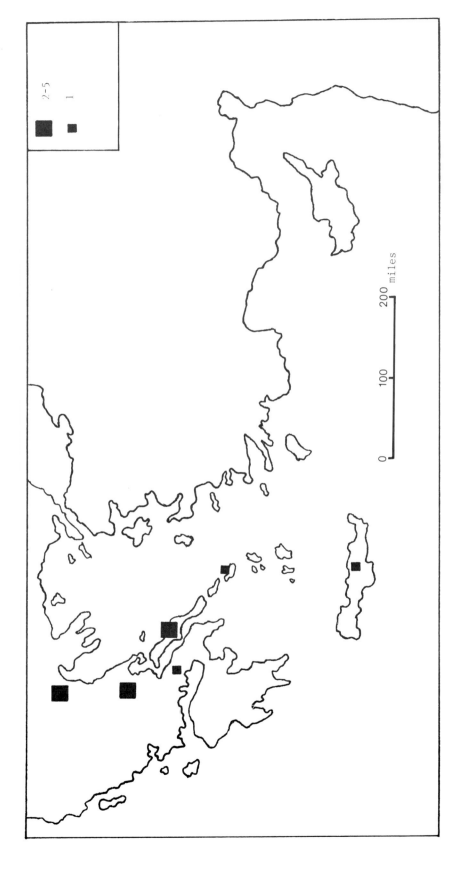

Figure 45: Distribution of Type 1.

135

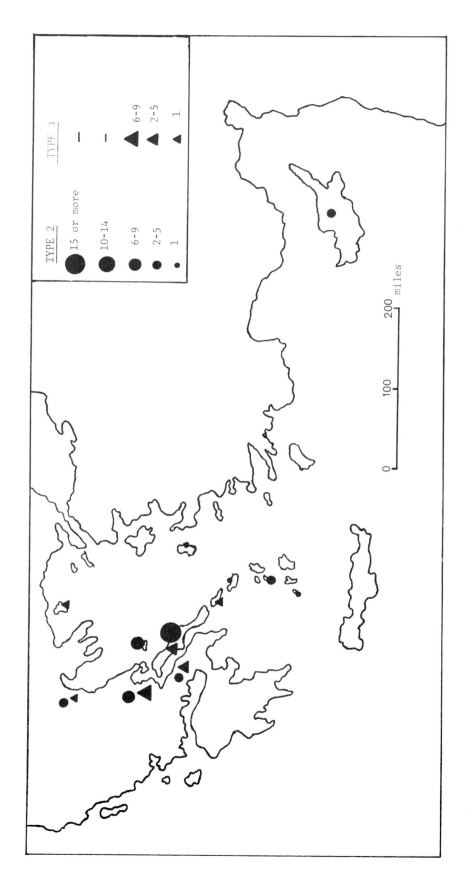

Figure 46: Distribution of Types 2 and 3.

semicircles in each set is usually large (between ten and 14 is most common), and these are painted with dexterity to produce a fine web of regularly-intersecting arcs. Indeed, the total impression given by the pendent semicircle skyphoi from Lefkandi is of vases produced by potters with a lively mental image of the finished product as they worked. There is no sense of the vessels being imitations or a model with which the potter was familiar only at second-hand.[2]

By comparison, the skyphoi from sites in Thessaly and Macedonia, such as Kapakli, Marmariani, Vergina or Kalamaria, are far inferior. In Northern Greece the clay is generally left in a rather coarse condition, and the application of a slip is rare. Irregularities in shape occur frequently in the total height of pot or lip, in the positioning of the handles, or the formation of the foot. The decoration on most is also badly executed, and although the number of arcs in each set usually does not exceed ten the semicircles are often incomplete and run into each other. This rather sloppy appearance is reinforced by imprecision and streakiness in the painting of the other parts of the vase.[3]

Thus there is strong contrast between the skyphoi of Lefkandi and those of the mainland north of Euboea. Since these are the two areas where skyphoi of the very earliest kind are mainly found, it seems probable at this stage that it was on Euboea, and in particular at Lefkandi rather than elsewhere, that the initiative of modifying an old bowl shape and applying to it a new decoration occurred.[4] It is certainly some indication of Lefkandi's close involvement in the production of the pendent semicircle skyphos that it alone of all sites has revealed fragments from each of the six Types.

Furthermore there are two skyphoi *116* and *117* from the site which have the distinct appearance of being something of a prototype for developments in the shape. The first comes from P.T2. It is the only pot from that tomb, so no attempt may be made to date it by association; but the skyphos itself has a basically early look: its overall proportions are still entirely those of the Mycenaean deep bowl, rather than of the pendent semicircle skyphos. Its roots in the preceding period are also indicated by the reserved area on the lower part of the foot and another early feature is the lack of intersection by the two sets of semicircles. The second vase, from P.T3, has been dated by associated finds to the LPG period, and stands as the earliest pendent semicircle skyphos from any cemetery at Lefkandi.[5] Like the skyphos from T2, the profile of the body is still close in proportion to the Mycenaean deep bowl and its semicircles, which do not intersect, contain an hour-glass filler. The characteristics of these two vases in shape and decoration would normally have placed them in Type 1; but each has a well-defined offset lip, the first development marking a move away from the old Mycenaean bowl.[6]

During the Late Helladic III period there was a flourishing settlement at Lefkandi and its pottery reflects a certain innovative spirit in both potting and decoration. Signs of experimentation and vitality are also found in the LPG period.[7] So although some doubt exists as

to the continuity of occupation from the Late Helladic to the Protogeometric period,[8] the fact that the PG settlement was also substantial,
with contacts that included both northern and southern areas of the
Greek mainland as well as the East Mediterranean, makes it quite feasible
that Lefkandiot potters should have created a vessel with the wide
geographical appeal of the pendent semicircle skyphos.[9] Indeed, the
protogeometric style at Lefkandi had such internal strength that it
remained popular as late as the end of the first half of the eighth century, when other areas were usually imitating Athenian Middle Geometric
pottery.[10]

Such matters must remain conjectural at this stage, however, and
it is the distribution of Types in relation to changes in the shape of
the skyphos which allows firmer conclusions to be drawn. The distribution of the deep-bodied skyphoi of Types 1, 2 and 3 (Figs. 45,46)
is very similar. They are distributed chiefly in Delos and the regions
stretching to the north, such as Andros, Tenos, Euboea, Skyros, Delphi,
Boeotia and both coastal and inland Thessaly and Macedonia. Of the
three Types only Type 2 is found outside this geographical area, with
isolated pieces at Paros and Chios and in the East Mediterranean on
Cyprus.[11]

The mainland areas of Northern Greece become noticeably less important in the distribution of the more shallow skyphoi of Types 4 and 5
(Fig. 47). Only one example comes from Macedonia (Kalamaria – Type
5) and Thessaly (Kapakli – Type 4), and since these skyphoi both occur
at coastal rather than inland sites, it is clear that influence from the
south no longer penetrates the region so deeply. Type 4 skyphoi come
mainly from Lefkandi, Chalcis, Zagora, Tenos, Delos and Delphi indicating
that these areas are still part of the cultural sphere which is unified
to some extent by use of the pendent semicircle skyphos. In addition,
skyphoi of Type 4 appear in Crete and Cyprus, and even further afield
on the Levantine coast (Al Mina) and hinterland (Tell Tayinat and Tell
Halaf).[12]

The distribution of Type 5 is also divided between the Central Aegean
and the Near East, but it is noteworthy that, within Greece, the skyphoi
are found mostly at sites other than those with Type 4 skyphoi: Delos
and Rheneia, and to a much lesser extent at Kalamaria, Methymna and
Lefkandi in the Aegean. In the Near East, they are most frequent on
Cyprus, but have also been found at Hama and Tell Sukas on the mainland.

In summary, the distribution of the first five Types of the pendent
semicircle skyphos appears to fall into two phases which parallel changes
in the overall shape of the vessel.

In the first phase there is the basically Thessalo-Cycladic distribution
of the large, deep skyphoi of Types 1, 2 and 3. In the second, Macedonia
and Thessaly produce virtually no examples, and the smaller, squatter

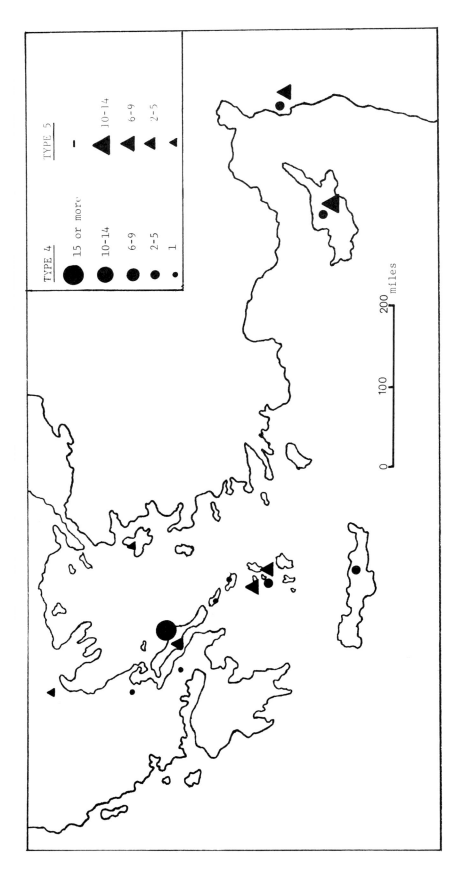

Figure 47: Distribution of Types 4 and 5.

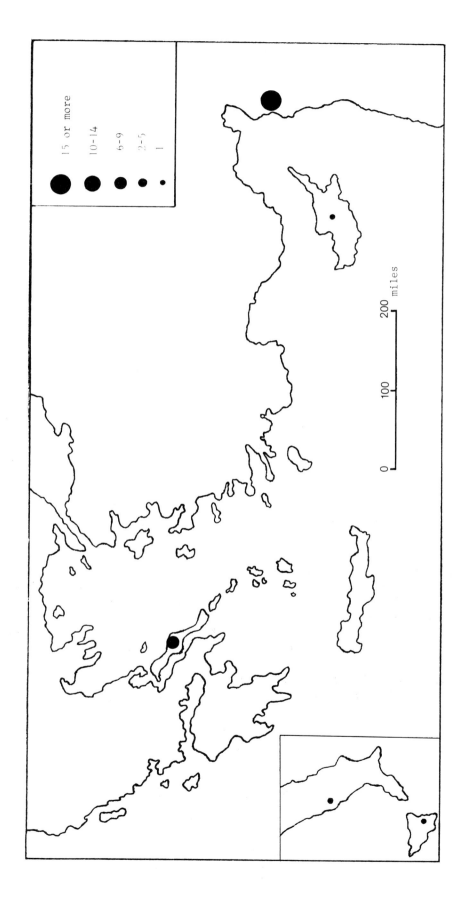

Figure 48: Distribution of Type 6.

skyphoi of Types 4 and 5 are found mainly in the Central Cyclades (Delos – Rheneia) and in Euboea, Andros and Tenos just to the north. There are also several skyphoi of both Types in the East Mediterranean. In terms of absolute chronology, the first phase extends over most of the ninth century, and the second covers *ca.*825/800–750/720 BC.[13]

Thus the most important aspects of the shape of the pendent semi-circle skyphos – the overall proportions of the body (expressed by the ratio used in Chapters 4 and 5) and the shape of the lip – reflect not only change through time but also distinct and geographically coherent distribution patterns. Since it is clear also that changes in the lip shape and body profile do not always occur in step, it appears that even further information may be extracted from the distribution of the Types. For example, there is great similarity between the ratios for Types 2 and 3, but each has a distinctly different lip. Similarly, Types 4 and 5 overlap considerably in the range of their ratios, but they too have differently-shaped lips. The explanation appears to be that, while the ratio expresses only change through time, alterations in the shape of the lip may represent either change through time or the occurrence of regional preference. The clearest illustration that this is the case is provided by the discrete distribution of the Types.

First, Types 2 and 3: the tall-lipped skyphos of Type 2 is found fairly equally spread between Euboea, Thessaly, Macedonia and the Northern Cyclades. The Type 3 skyphos with the short lip, in contrast, is found mainly in Thessaly. This Thessalian bias toward Type 3 may plausibly be interpreted either simply as preference by Thessalian potters or, in view of the general quality of skyphoi from that region, as a result of the relatively coarse and unmalleable clay which meant that the tall, flaring lip could not be produced with ease. Whichever is the case, Type 1 skyphoi in Thessaly would seem to be followed not by Type 2 but by skyphoi such as Marmariani 116 *167* of Type 3, the only changes being a slight broadening in the overall shape of the vessel and the shortening of the lip.[14] In decoration, occasional intersection of the semicircles occurs. They, in turn, are followed by the introduction of the offset lip, as seen, for instance, on skyphoi from Kapakli *90-92*. In Euboea and the Northern Cyclades, on the other hand, the tall lip of Type 1 retains its popularity in the Type 2 version and lasts until Type 4 takes over at about the end of the ninth century.

Thus the direct links between Types 1 and 3, seen in the extension of Diagram 1 of the numerical analysis (see p. 124)

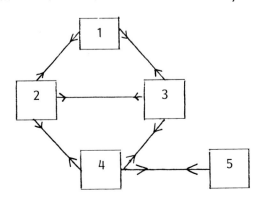

would seem to be due mainly to chronological factors. The multiple links in both directions between Types 2 and 3 are explained both by their contemporaneity and their geographical proximity. In particular, skyphoi such as Kapakli 58 *89,* Kapakli 60 *91,* and Nea Ionia K2235 *178,* all of which exhibited special ambivalence in their connections, should probably be interpreted as examples of the close contacts between coastal Thessaly and Euboea at this time. In spite of the general preference of the Thessalian potters for the shorter-lipped skyphos, it is understandable that Euboea's contacts with the mainland would lead to some imitations of the tall-lipped Type 2 vessel. It is interesting to note that of all the Thessalian skyphoi it is the tall-lipped ones that are most frequently given the added refinement of a slip. Thus superior quality in the pottery usually goes hand-in-hand with added care in decoration. [15]

The relationship between Types 4 and 5 appears to be of the same nature as that of Types 2 and 3. Skyphoi of Types 4 and 5 all have a rather shallow and squat bowl, and yet the classes have different lips. Chronological evidence has suggested that they are contemporary, but distribution indicates that, to a large extent, each circulated in a separate sphere within the Aegean area. For example, apart from Delos and Crete, Type 4 occurs only at sites north of the Central Cyclades. Furthermore, if frequency of occurrence is any guide, Type 4 appears to be centred on Euboea and its immediate neighbours, such as Andros and Tenos. By contrast, the incurved lip typical of Type 5 is found chiefly on Delos and on nearby Rheneia. There are rare examples at sites further north, some of which appear to be imports, for instance, Methymna *176,* and others local imitations, for example, Lefkandi *139* and *153.* But the very scarcity of Type 5 at Lefkandi at a time when Type 4 skyphoi were being produced so prolifically underlines the impression that Type 5 is not at home there. [16]

It seems that the proximity analysis has reflected accurately the archaeological situation. The contemporaneity and geographical affinity of centres producing Types 4 and 5 are represented by multiple links between the two Types. Even more significantly, the lack of any links between Type 5 and Types 2 or 3 is an indication that Type 5 belongs in areas which did not have close links with Thessaly and Macedonia. While the fact that all Type 5 links are with Type 4 (and there is nothing with the earlier Type 2) suggests not only that Types 4 and 5 are contemporary but also that Type 5 begins no earlier than subprotogeometric III, *ca.*825 BC. If this be so, it is yet another reason in favour of seeing Euboea rather than the Cycladic islands as the creator of the pendent semicircle skyphos.

Despite the difference in their distribution at home in Greece, it should again be emphasised that Types 4 and 5 are both found in Cyprus and on mainland sites of the Near East. In the past it has sometimes been assumed that all the skyphoi from the East Mediterranean are of the same shape and the same origin,[17] but if the variety in the shape of the lip does – as seems probable – represent production by regional centres, then it follows that more than one Greek state was trading with the Near East during the first half of the eighth century.

There is a third and final phase in the diffusion of the pendent semicircle skyphos. Represented only by the skyphoi of Type 6, it constitutes a marked break from the distribution patterns of the previous two phases. In both of these the Greek mainland and island sites were the chief focus of activity for the five Types, even though there were differences in the details of their distribution. In Types 4 and 5 the Near East also appeared as an important area of interest, but nevertheless involvement in the Aegean area remained of greatest importance. By the time of Type 6 the situation has altered (Fig. 48). Of the 35 skyphoi or fragments in the class, 20 come from the East Mediterranean and 12 are from Greece itself. In addition, two skyphoi are from Veii and one from Villasmundo, both sites in the West Mediterranean.[18] One fragment is of unknown provenance.

It is not entirely unexpected that those Greek sites represented in Type 6 are both Euboean, in view of that island's apparently vigorous participation both in the manufacture of the pendent semicircle skyphos and in Near Eastern trade during the ninth and eighth centuries.[19] Nonetheless, it does seem strange that the proportion of the total material which comes from Euboea is so low if centres such as Lefkandi and Eretria are to be viewed as the chief producers of the Type 6 skyphoi.[20]

Other evidence of a more general nature from the three main Euboean sites – Lefkandi, Chalcis and Eretria – also indicates that the degree of Euboea's involvement in the production of the pendent semicircle skyphos had dropped drastically by the Late Geometric period, the date that Type 6 was in existence. At Lefkandi, for example, the psc skyphos was rare during the Late Geometric period. Type 6 fragments are very scarce in the Levelling material of the pit, and as other kinds of Late Geometric pottery are also scarce it must be concluded that this deposit is mainly of Middle Geometric II date and does not extend much beyond 750. Even so, at this early stage of the Late Geometric period, production of the pendent semicircle skyphos had waned considerably and the stricter lines of the tradition had broken down, with the decoration now being applied to various skyphos shapes, such as the three Type 6 fragments and another that belongs to the high-mouthed skyphos class *142*. Later still in the Late Geometric period at Lefkandi, the skyphos appears non-existent: no fragments were found in the house constructed over the pit.[21]

The evidence from Chalcis is very patchy, owing to the difficulty of excavation in the ancient city, but there are two Late Geometric psc skyphos fragments, *26* and *29*. The picture they give is similar to that at Lefkandi. Both are of a different sort of Late Geometric shape (neither of which is Type 6), and *29* indicates further that at least by 725 at Chalcis the canonic decoration of the pendent semicircle skyphos had also been broken up.

At Eretria, the extensive excavations by the Swiss School are now producing some pendent semicircle skyphoi, but only the Type 6 variety of the LG period, and only in small quantities. This has special significance if Eretria is indeed the site to which the Lefkandiots removed themselves during the first half of the eighth century. Lefkandi is thought by many to be the "Old Eretria" referred to by Strabo because in addition to its geographical proximity, it seems to have been founded at the time when the population of Lefkandi was declining, and there is also marked continuity in most aspects of the ceramic industry of the two sites.[22] Therefore it is at Eretria that one would expect to find continuity of the tradition of pendent semicircle skyphoi of the Type 6 variety – the last known at Lefkandi – in sufficient quantity to sustain the overwhelming number of examples found in the Near East. So far, however, this has not occurred.[23]

Indications that production of the pendent semicircle skyphos (and especially of Type 6) was very limited in Euboea itself during the second half of the eighth century are supported by the recent excavations at Zagora. A great amount of the decorated ware at Zagora was imported from Euboea during the second half of the eighth century[24] but among the large quantity of Late Geometric I and II pottery, only three fragments of psc skyphoi have been found. One seems to be of Middle Geometric II date *242* the others, *240* and *241,* like those from Lefkandi and Chalcis, reflecting the disappearance of the traditional pendent semicircle skyphos shape in favour of Late Geometric ones. Neither, however, is of Type 6, the shape on which psc decoration is so commonly found in the Near East.

The most obvious inference from the above, together with the predominantly Near Eastern distribution of Type 6, is that during the Late Geometric period the main place or places of production had ceased to be in the Aegean and were now in the East Mediterranean.[25] This could be either because Euboeans were then living in that area, or that there were other imitators of Euboean pottery there. Even apart from its distribution, the pottery itself suggests such an interpretation, for although so many of the pendent semicircle skyphos fragments from Al Mina are of the Type 6 variety – which does occur also at Lefkandi – there is no similarity between the Lefkandi pendent semicircle skyphoi in general and the Al Mina fragments.

Similarly the Eretrian fragments, apart from *69,* give no sign of the obvious decline in the quality of the decoration seen at Al Mina. While both the treatment of the clay and its shaping are competent at Al Mina, the decoration is generally streaky and uneven, and the arcs frequently painted in a very irregular and untidy manner. In other words, although the shapes are Euboean, the pendent semicircle skyphoi from Al Mina (with few exceptions) could not be mistaken for Euboean products.[26] Locally-produced Euboean pottery has already been recognised in the Near East, particularly at Al Mina. In his preliminary report of the excavations, Woolley remarked that much of the "sub-geometric" pottery in levels X-VIII was of local origin. Later, a class of bichrome skyphoi imitating Euboean Late Geometric shapes was singled out as a product of the site, but it has always been presumed that most of the other Greek pottery, including the pendent semicircle skyphoi, were imported.[27]

Since, however, the occurrence of psc skyphoi in the area as a whole reached its peak just at the time when the skyphoi had fallen off significantly in the Aegean, and since fragments of psc skyphoi have been found near kilns at both Tarsus and Sarepta, local production of the vessel at several centres during the Late Geometric period seems likely. [28] Indeed, as a recently-published fragment of the bichrome skyphos class from Al Mina is an imitation of the same Euboean model as the many Type 6 pendent semicircle skyphoi from site, it seems possible that the same shape was being decorated there in two different ways. [29]

While it is true that the usual reason for overseas production of Greek pottery appears to be the presence locally of Greek residents, the large concentration of vases of Greek type (including pendent semicircle skyphoi) at Tarsus, in a structure in use during the last half of the eighth century, has led to the hypothesis that there was a market for Greek drinking vessels and associated vases at that time. It is certainly noteworthy also that at Salamis, where another large group of Greek vases was found, all were of this type and in much greater quantity than would be necessary for purely personal use by the tomb owner. [30] A local market would lead to production in the sort of quantity observed at Tarsus and would explain the presence of so many vases of a certain type in a single structure. It would also explain the frequency of pendent semicircle skyphoi in the Near East – but not in the Aegean – during the Late Geometric period.

The attribution of Type 6 skyphoi at Al Mina to Euboeans, or at least to Euboean-inspired potters, confirms current opinion of the importance of Euboean participation in the early years of the site's history. In this connection it is important to stress that no skyphoi of Type 5, the Delos-Rheneia class, were found among the material from Al Mina. Although they occur at other mainland sites such as Hama and Tell Sukas their main concentration in the Near East is Cyprus. The only pendent semicircle skyphos fragment from Al Mina that is not either Type 6 or some other Euboean Late Geometric shape belongs to Type 4 – the Euboean-centred class of the Middle Geometric II period. This Type has been shown to occur most commonly at Lefkandi. [31] Nevertheless, it is not yet possible to say with certainty which Euboean city-state was chiefly involved at Al Mina in the eighth century. At present it appears that Lefkandi, Chalcis and Eretria must be the main candidates, but future excavation may reveal some other site also in Euboea which flourished during this period. [32] Even in assessing the relative merits of Lefkandi, Chalcis and Eretria, the imbalance in the amount of evidence available from each must be a cause for hesitation in drawing conclusions. But bearing in mind these reservations, it may be said at this stage that either Lefkandi or Eretria – or both – could well have been the origin of any Euboean settlers at Al Mina. (A large question-mark must qualify the extent of Chalcis' involvement until more pottery is available from the site.) For example, the one canonical variety of pendent semicircle skyphos that appears at Al Mina (Type 4) is found abundantly at Lefkandi, and not at all at Eretria. Nevertheless it is only a single fragment, and of the two sites it is Eretria which provides better evidence for production of Type 6, the predominant class of psc skyphos found at Al Mina.

Another class of Late Geometric skyphos, the lozenge skyphos, provides a second ceramic link between Al Mina and Lefkandi specifically: this kind of skyphos, common at Al Mina, is also well known at Lefkandi. It is not usual at Eretria.[33]   On the other hand, imitations of Corinthian kotylai which are clearly Eretrian have also been found at Al Mina.[34] Thus it is not possible at this stage to judge between the competing claims of Lefkandi and Eretria to have played the leading role at Al Mina. At most, the analogy of the history of the two sites in Euboea itself might lead us to postulate that Lefkandi's interest preceded that of Eretria, but that Eretria's role was growing in the last decades of the eighth century at a time when Lefkandi's activity was declining.

As for the chronology of the early levels at Al Mina, the single pendent semicircle skyphos fragment of Middle Geometric II date, together with the half-dozen other sherds which appear to belong to the same period, indicate that Greeks probably visited the site some time before the middle of the eighth century.[35]   Since, however, the majority of the Greek pottery from levels IX and VIII has already been dated to the Late Geometric period, and it is now clear that most psc skyphos fragments are also of that date, occupation is unlikely to have begun before *ca.*750 BC.[36]   In addition, Woolley's observation that levels IX and VIII appeared to represent only a short period of time, such as 50 years or so,[37] now appears firmly supported by the pottery.   Several Late Geometric pendent semicircle skyphos fragments occurred in level VIII[38] with a considerable amount of other Late Geometric pottery of very similar nature to that found in level IX.[39]

Therefore the grounds for dating levels IX-VIII at Al Mina between 750-700 are substantial.   There has certainly been no indication provided by the pendent semicircle fragments that a foundation date of 825 is acceptable.   On the contrary, it is of particular significance in this respect that none of the popular Type 2 skyphoi - which belong in the ninth century - and only a single fragment of the Middle Geometric II Type 4 have been found among the pendent semicircle fragments at Al Mina.

NOTES TO CHAPTER 1

1. S. Smith, "The Greek Trade at Al Mina: A Footnote to Oriental History", *AJ* 22 (1942) 87-112 is still the fullest discussion of the place of Al Mina in trade between Greece and the Near East, but see also T.F.R.G. Braun, "The Greeks in the Near East", *CAH* III, Pt. 3 (Cambridge 1982) 11-14. For excavation reports of other sites, see P.J. Riis, *Sukas I* (1970) and G. Ploug, *Sukas II* (1973) (Tell Sukas) and also P. Courbin, *AAS* (1972, 1973, 1975, 1976 and 1977-8) (Ras el Bassit). Also P. Courbin, "Ras el Bassit, Al Mina et Tell Sukas", *Revue Archéologique* (1974) 174-178, for a more general discussion of the relationship between the three sites.

2. L.H. Jeffery, *The Local scripts of archaic Greece* (Oxford 1961) 5-12; L.H. Jeffery, "Greek alphabetic writing". *CAH* III, Pt.1 (Cambridge 1982) 827-830. but see M. Guarducci, "Appunti di epigrafia greca arcaica (leggendo il libro di Lilian H. Jeffery)", *Archeologia Classica* 16 (1964) 124-127; M. Burzachechi, "L'adozione dell'alfabeto nel mondo greco", *Parola del Passato* 31 (1976) 87-89, and Chapter 8 n. 36 below.

3. C.L. Woolley, "Excavations near Antioch in 1936", *AJ* 17 (1937) 1-15; C.L. Woolley, "Excavations at Al Mina, Suedia I - II", *JHS* 58 (1938) 1-30; 133-170. The Early Greek Pottery: M. Robertson, "The Excavations at Al Mina, Suedia IV. The Early Greek Vases", *JHS* 60 (1940) 2-21. The Cypriot-Syrian pottery: J.du Plat Taylor, "The Cypriot and Syrian Pottery from Al Mina, Syria", *Iraq* 21 (1959) 62-92 and E. Gjerstad, "The Stratification at Al Mina (Syria) and its Chronological Evidence", *Acta Archaeologica* 45 (1974) 107-123. Also C. Clairmont, "Greek Pottery from the Near East", *Berytus* 11 (1954-55) index 141; J. Boardman, "Early Euboean Pottery and History", *BSA* 52 (1957) 5-8; J. Boardman, "Greek Potters at Al Mina?" *Anatolian Studies* 9 (1959) 163-9; J.N. Coldstream, *Greek Geometric Pottery* (London 1968) 312-316; E.J. Peltenburg, "Al Mina Glazed Pottery and its Relations", *Levant* 1 (1969) 73-96; J.-P. Descoeudres, "Euboeans in Australia. Some Observations on the Imitations of Corinthian Kotylai made in Eretria and found in Al Mina", *Eretria VI* (Bern 1978) 7-19; M.R. Popham, H. Hatcher and A.M. Pollard, "Al Mina and Euboea", *BSA* 75 (1980) 151-161; J.-P. Descoeudres and R. Kearsley, "Greek Pottery at Veii: Another Look," *BSA* 78 (1983) 9-53. No material from level X has yet been published.

4. Compare Boardman (n. 3, 1957) 8 n. 45 with *GGP* 314 for an example of the confusion surrounding the stratification of even the published pottery. Also *Eretria VI* 17-18, n. 91.

5. Woolley (n. 3, 1938) 16-18.

6.   J. Boardman, *The Greeks Overseas,* (London 1980) 39; D. Ridgway, "The First Western Greeks: Campanian Coasts and Southern Etruria" in *Greeks, Celts and Romans*, eds. C. and S. Hawkes (London 1973) 9. Coldstream *GGP* 385 also makes a break after level VII on architectural grounds, although in his consideration of the pottery he makes the break after VIII (312-6). In contrast to this view are T.J. Dunbabin, *The Greeks and their Eastern Neighbours* (London 1957) 28 and Descoeudres, *Eretria VI* 18, both of whom maintain Woolley's original scheme.

7.   Woolley (n. 3, 1938) 16-17 felt that the marked changes in architecture and pottery in level VIII were a result of foreign conquest. Such an event was subsequently connected with the campaign of Sargon II during 709 (E. Gjerstad, *The Swedish Cyprus Expedition*, Vol IV, part 2 [Stockholm 1948] 462.) The higher chronology proposed by Taylor in 1959 (n. 3) 91-2 has been adopted by Boardman (n. 6) 43-44, Coldstream *GGP* 313 and Ridgway (n. 6) 10. But a more recent assessment of the Cypriot and Syrian pottery by Gjerstad (n. 3) 121-2 lowers Miss Taylor's dates by about 50 years and again brings into question the wisdom of relying on the Near Eastern dates. (The insecurity of Iron Age chronology in the Near East is acknowledged even by those Classical scholars prepared to place their faith in it; compare Coldstream *GGP* 313 with his comments on 305, and see also the comments of Boardman [n. 6] 43.) The problems in Cypriot Iron Age chronology are further demonstrated by attempts to date the local pottery by Greek geometric imports in the island: see A. Demetriou, "Die Datierung der Periode Cypro-Archaisch I", *AA* 93 (1978) 12-25. Furthermore the high chronology is partly dependent on the assumption that Cypriot-Syrian pottery occurs in similar quantity to the Greek pottery in level IX (Boardman [n. 6] 43; Braun [n. 1] 9). This is explicitly stated not to be the case by Woolley (n. 3, 1938) 16-17 and reiterated by Gjerstad (n. 3) 108, 118. Woolley's chronology was not universally discarded, however, see Robertson (n. 3) 21; C. Roebuck, *Ionian trade and colonization* (New York 1959) 61-4; *Eretria VI* 16-17 (where there is also a summary of the various opinions in tabulated form [Table 3]).

8.   Robertson (n. 3) 20.

9.   *GGP* 312-316 and *Eretria VI* 18 on more precise identifications of Cycladic and East Greek fabrics.

10.   The great uncertainty in our knowledge of the pendent semicircle skyphos class, and the need for a re-examination, has been pointed out by Descoeudres, *Eretria VI* 18. As an example of the different attributions of the psc skyphos fragments at Al Mina, compare Boardman (n. 3, 1957) 7 with Coldstream, *Geometric Greece* (London 1977) 93-4, 103.

11. Robertson (n. 3) 2; Coldstream (n. 10) 93; Ridgway (n. 6) 8; Boardman (n. 6) 41.

12. On the date of pottery from Levels IX and VIII: Robertson (n. 3) 21; Coldstream *GGP* 312-6 and (n. 10) 93; *Eretria VI* 17-19. (No doubt because of the scarcity of the earliest material, it has also been proposed that there was a period of purely Asiatic occupation at Al Mina before the Greeks arrived [Boardman (n. 6) 43-44] but the excavation report is in total disagreement with this [Woolley (n. 3, 1937) 10; (n. 3, 1938) 16] and this is re-emphasised in the most recent study of the Near Eastern pottery by Gjerstad [n. 3] 117.)

13. S.C. Bakhuizen, *Chalcis-in-Euboea, Iron and Chalcidians Abroad* (Chalcidian Studies III, Leiden 1976) 27 n. 110; *Eretria VI* 18 (see also the various attempts to provide parallels for the Tell Abu Hawam fragment and the Hama skyphoi: Coldstream *GGP* 152[i] and [n. 10] 66; *Sukas I* 152; *Sukas II* 12-13).

14. V.R. Desborough, *Protogeometric Pottery* (Oxford 1952) 169, 180-194. Two less comprehensive surveys accompanied by distribution maps appeared somewhat later: H.-G. Buchholz, "Tell Halaf IV - Zu den Kleinfunden von Tell Halaf", *Berliner Jahrbuch für Vor- und Früh-geschichte* 5 (1965) 224-229; Riis, *Sukas I* 142-159.

15. V.R. Desborough, "The Low-Footed Skyphoi with pendent semi-circles", in P. Dikaios, "A 'Royal' Tomb at Salamis", Appendix II, *AA* 78 (1963) 204-6.

16. *GGP* 151-157.

17. M.R. Popham and L.H. Sackett (eds.), *Lefkandi I: The Iron Age. Text and Plates* (London 1979, 1980) 300.

18. Boardman (n. 3, 1957) 7-8. And more recently, Braun (n. 1) 9.

19. Lefkandi: *Lefkandi I* 367-8; *Lefkandi 1968* 33; L.H. Sackett and M.R. Popham, "Lefkandi: A Euboean Town of the Bronze Age and the Early Iron Age (2100-700 BC)", *Archaeology* 25 (1972) 16-19. Eretria: C. Bérard, *Eretria. Fouilles et recherches, III: L'Héróon à la porte de l'ouest* (Berne 1970) 25-27. Pithecusae: G. Buchner, "Pithekoussai, Oldest Greek Colony in the West", *Expedition* 8, 4 (1966) 4-12; G. Buchner, "Recent Work at Pithekoussai (Ischia), 1965-71", *ArchRep* (1970-71) 63-67; D. Ridgway, *The Etruscans* (University of Edinburgh, Department of Archaeology, Occasional Paper no. 6, 1981) 21-22. General: Ridgway (n. 6) 6-28; V.R. Desborough, "The Background to Euboean Participation in Early Greek Maritime Enterprise", *Tribute to an Antiquary: Essays Presented to Marc Fitch* (London 1976) 27-40.

20. For a full report on the site, see *Lefkandi I,* together with the comprehensive bibliographies supplied on 4 n. 9 and 355 n. 1.

21. The only specific attempt to establish this connection, by means of atomic absorption spectrometry, failed to achieve the desired result: M.R. Popnam *et al.* (chapter 1 n. 3) 151-161. See more complete discussion of this study in chapter 2 below.

22. *Eretria VI* 18.

23. Desborough's observation (n. 15) has subsequently received wide support as a number of Late Geometric contexts for pendent semicircle skyphoi in the Near East are indisputable. Buchholz (n. 14) 225; E.Walter-Karydi, "Geometrische Keramik aus Naxos" *AA* 87 (1972) 387; A.J. Graham, "The Foundation of Thasos", *BSA* 73 (1978) 69-70; O.T.P.K. Dickinson, Review of *Eretria VI, JHS* 101 (1981) 208.

24. *Eretria VI* 19; *Lefkandi I* 367.

25. Time and financial considerations imposed limitations, however, because the skyphoi are scattered in many parts of Europe, North America and the Middle East. Even the pottery from Al Mina is not found in one place. Much is in England, with collections held by the British Museum, the Ashmolean Museum, the Museum of Classical Archaeology at Cambridge, the Institute of Archaeology and University College London, as well as in the museum of Eton School. Material has also travelled further afield: there is, for example, a collection of sherds in the Nicholson Museum in Sydney (Descoeudres, *Eretria VI*). The pottery that was not taken to England by Woolley lies in the Antakya Museum in Turkey, and it is there that the material from the earliest level (X) is to be found (Robertson [n. 3] 2). This is so far completely unpublished and I was unfortunately not able to include it.

     Thanks to the very generous assistance of the late Mr V.R. Desborough, Mr M.R. Popham and Dr H.W. Catling, I was given access to results of the excavations at Lefkandi in December 1976 and February 1977. Drawings, photographs and descriptions of pendent semicircle skyphoi, which were then unpublished, were made available and many comments in the text are based on these and on discussions with Mr Desborough himself. There was a little pottery from Lefkandi in the Collection at the British School at Athens, which is also discussed, but with the exception of one skyphos (Skoubris T.59:2 *112*) it was not possible to study at first hand the bulk of the Lefkandi material before its publication.

26. *Revised Soil Color Charts,*[2] (Tokyo 1970). The Japanese *Soil Color Charts* have some extra colour chips to suit the requirements of local soils. In the ranges where these charts and the Munsell *Soil Colour Charts* coincide, the notation is identical.

NOTES TO CHAPTER 2

1. It has been accepted in the past that the characteristic circles and semicircles of the Protogeometric style were accomplished with a multiple brush compass (*PGP* 124). However, convincing arguments have been advanced recently against this assumption on purely technical grounds, especially where the semicircles are of varied length, as in the case of a skyphos. It is suggested that it is more likely that groups of individual compasses were used, each with a fixed radius (H. Eiteljorg II, "The Fast Wheel, the Multiple-Brush Compass and Athens as Home of the Protogeometric Style", *AJA* 84 [1980] 450-451).

   The conclusions of Eiteljorg appear to be supported by one of the two pendent semicircle skyphoi from Kalamaria, Thessaloniki 4714 *85*. On one side of this skyphos the two sets of pendent semicircles comprise different numbers of arcs: one has six, the other seven. The most likely explanation is that each arc was painted separately and that the potter simply miscounted in one case. On the other side of the vessel, each set of semicircles has seven arcs.

2. Probably from the same pot as *13*a. Although the fragments do not join exactly, there is similarity in the quality of the clay, an identical profile, and a very characteristic brush-stroke in the semicircles.

3. It is probable from the similarity in the clay and profile that this and the following fragment are from the same skyphos. Popham *et al.* (Chapter 1 n. 3) 154 draw the same conclusion.

4. Fragments *25-27* are from boxes labelled "Chalcis" in the sherd room at the British School.

5. Although this skyphos, as restored, was almost complete when it was published in 1972, only the large rim fragment (ht 5.5) on the left of the photograph could be found in the Chalcis Museum on my visit in January 1978.

6. The published information for this and the following skyphos *36* is supplemented by observation of the skyphoi on display in New York. Unfortunately there was not sufficient time to draw and photograph the pots.

7. Thanks are due to Mrs I.K. Raubitschek for information about this skyphos.

8. I wish to thank Dr A.W. Johnston and Ms E.L. Watts for assistance in obtaining details. The Wellcome Institute Collection was dispersed in 1981.

9. I wish to thank Dr C. Krause for permission to publish *68-74* and Dr J.-P. Descoeudres for descriptions and profile drawings of the fragments.

10. The details of the pottery in this bothros and FK 3038 *74* will appear in a forthcoming volume on the archaic pottery from Eretria by Dr J.-P. Descoeudres. The description and profile of this and the following fragment are his.

11. Thanks are due to Dr J.-P. Descoeudres for drawings of this and *78-79*.

12. Verdelis lists a skyphos from Kapakli which I was not able to find in the museum at Volos in February 1977 (*PGRT* 27 no. 55).

13. This skyphos could not be found on my visit to the Tenos Museum in January 1978.

14. This skyphos could not be found when I visited the museum in February 1977.

15. I am grateful to Professor J.N. Coldstream and the Managing Committee of the British School at Athens for allowing me to include the as yet unpublished material from Teke. Professor Coldstream informs me that it will appear in a *BSA Supplement* in the near future, together with all the rest of the material from the large cemetery.

16. This pot is very misshapen and the drawing published by Verdelis is misleading because the widely-outswinging body profile represents only the distorted part of the pot.

17. These measurements are from copies of the original drawings before they were reduced for publication.

18. *Lefkandi I* 37 n. 18 states that all the profiles on pl.33 come from one small area and that none is illustrated on pl.18. However the caption for pl.33 states that pl.33,1 = pl.18,276; pl.33,2 = pl.18, 277 and pl.33,3 = pl.18,286.

19. From a box labelled "Lefkandi" in the sherd room at the British School.

20. The description and profile are those of Dr J.-P. Descoeudres.

21. The skyphos in Mykonos Museum which bears the number A1467 is different from that published by Coldstream, *GGP*, pl.32,h. That skyphos has ten semicircles in each set and is in fact A1466 (Mykonos 20).

152

22. This fragment was on display at the Thessaloniki Museum during my visit there in February 1977 but could not be removed from the case for study.

23. The context for this and the following three fragments is painted on the sherd but provides no information without a full publication of the site. I am advised by Dr S. Wolff of the Oriental Institute that Dr R. Dornemann, of Milwaukee Public Museum, will be publishing the material.

24. At the time of my visit there, August 1977, the skyphos was on display and it was not possible to make a detailed study.

25. It is possible that either this skyphos, or *224* following, is that referred to in *PGRT* 27 no. 54. However, as the dimensions differ from both it is more likely that it is a third skyphos from Thessaly of which the provenance is unknown and which I did not see.

26. Drawing and description are by Dr J.-P. Descoeudres. Although inventoried as belonging to the National Museum of the Villa Giulia at Rome, it is now stored in the Forte Sangallo at Cività Castellana, together with most of the finds from the Quattro Fontanili Cemetery at Veii.

27. Unfortunately this skyphos could not be located by Dr J.-P. Descoeudres either at Cività Castellana or in the Villa Giulia in November 1979. The description is that of Fabricotti.

28. At the time of my visit to Thessaloniki Museum, skyphoi *231-233* and *235-236* were still stored in boxes with other material from Vergina. *234* could not be found.

29. Description by Dr J.-P. Descoeudres. He identifies the clay as being of Eretrian type. Unfortunately it has not been possible to publish his profile drawing here, but the shape of the skyphos is extremely similar to Veii *229*.

30. The skyphos was on display in the Museum during my visit in February 1977, but it was not possible to study it.

31. I wish to thank Professor A. Cambitoglou for permission to publish *240-242* and Associate Professor J.R. Green for description and drawings of the fragments.

32. My thanks are due to Professor A. Cambitoglou for permission to include this skyphos. In the History Teaching Collection at Macquarie University, Sydney, there is a skyphos (inv. 389) which bears only one set of semicircles on each side. Ht 8.0 cm; **diam of lip** 13.0 cm. Flaring offset **lip**; low ring **foot**. Clay, slipped with some small inclusions but no mica. One set of eight semicircles on each side. Provenance unknown.

33. I wish to thank Mr D. Ridgway for information about this skyphos.

34. My thanks are due to Dr A.W. Johnston for information about this fragment.

35. On his distribution maps of the pendent semicircle skyphos which are published in (Chapter 1 n.14) 227 and *82* 91, Fig. 26, Buchholz lists several sites not included here. Unfortunately no bibliographical details are given for the new sites listed in 1975 and I have been unable to find references to pendent semicircle skyphoi there. It seems possible that the sites do not strictly belong with this catalogue, as, for example:

(a) Vrokastro: E.H. Hall, *Excavations in Eastern Crete: Vrokastro* (Philadelphia 1914) 164, Fig. 99d. A kalathos rather than a skyphos. See *PGP* 262.

(b) Samos: Two fragments with pendent semicircle decoration are published in H. Walter, *Samos V: Frühe samische Gefässe* (Bonn 1968) 92, pl. 6, 27 and 97, pl. 19, 109. However, the shape of both is described as a small krater. No rim diameter is given.

(c) Camirus: G. Jacopi, "Esplorazione archelogica di Camiro II", *Clara Rhodos* 6-7 (1932-33) 189 f., Figs. 223, 227. These are not skyphoi and bear only one set of pendent semicircles on each side. See *PGP* 185.

Similarly Buchholz identifies a pendent semicircle skyphos fragment at Scoglio del Tonno: "Ägäische Funde in Randgebieten des Mittelmeers", *AA* 89 (1974) 340 but the comparative material to which F. Biancofiore, *La Civiltà Micenea nell'Italia Meridionale I* (Rome 1963) 97 refers includes two closed vases as well as an open one and it is impossible to be sure which shape he considers the fragment to belong to.

Other distribution maps of pendent semicircle skyphoi, in the Near East only, are to be found in J. Bouzek, *Homerisches Griechenland* (Prague 1969) 144, Fig. 55; *Sukas I* 165, Fig. 58; Saidah (Chapter 2 *99*) 198.

154

NOTES TO CHAPTER 3

1. *PGP* 183-4.

2. Compare Robertson (Chapter 1 n.3) 2 and *Délos XV* 52-54 with the more precise descriptions provided by J.B. Pritchard (Chapter 2 [199]) 96 and P.M. Bikai (Chapter 2 [227]) pl. XXII, 4.

3. H.W. Catling *et al.* "Correlations between Composition and Provenance of Mycenaean and Minoan Pottery", *BSA* 58 (1963) 94-115; J. Boardman and F. Schweitzer, "Clay Analyses of Archaic Greek Pottery", *BSA* 68 (1973) 267-83; W.B. Stern and J-P. Descoeudres, "X-Ray Fluorescence Analysis of Archaic Greek Pottery", *Archaeometry* 19 (1977) 73-86; A.P. Grimanis *et al.*, "Neutron Activation and X-Ray Analysis of 'Thapsos Class' Vases. An Attempt to Identify their Origin", *Journal of Archaeological Science* 7 (1980) 227-239; and see too A.L. Wilson, "Elemental Analysis of Pottery in the Study of its Provenance: A Review", *Journal of Archaeological Science* 5 (1978) 219-236 for a review of the methodology of elemental analysis of pottery and experimental procedures.

4. See Stern/Descoeudres (n.3) 74, 78, 82 and Boardman/Schweitzer (n.3) 267-9 for some of the archaeological problems involved.

5. Catling (n.3) 94-101.

6. Catling (n.3) 111-112.

7. Catling (n.3) 110 and Table 7.

8. D. Ridgway, "Composition and Provenance of Western Geometric Pottery: A Prospectus", *British Archaeological Reports Supplementary Series* 41 (1978) 121-123.

9. Ridgway (n.8) 123.

10. Popham *et al.* (Chapter 1 n.3) 151-2.

11. Popham *et al.* (Chapter 1 n.3) 153-6.

12. Popham *et al.* (Chapter 1 n.3) 156-7.

13. Stern/Descoeudres (n.3) 78-82; Popham *et al.* (Chapter 1 n.3) 152. See, for example, Grimanis (n.3) 237 where, despite the good match in the composition of the four groups of Corinthian Geometric pottery being tested, results were given only in terms of probability and further avenues for investigation of the same problem proposed.

14. As already pointed out (Chapter 1 n.10 above) the fragments from Al Mina have confidently been attributed both to Euboea and the Northern Cyclades. Euboea: Boardman (Chapter 1 n.3 1957) 7 (although see *Eretria VI* 19 for a different opinion on the relationship of the Al Mina fragments to Euboea). Cyclades: Coldstream (Chapter 1 n.10) 93; Hanfmann (Chapter 2 34) 173.

15. *73* and *74* are not included here because they are considered imports and not local products. See Chapter 8 n.20 below.

16. This sort of problem is not restricted to visual analyses of clay. See Stern/Descoeudres (n.3) 78.

17. *PGP* 185; *Eretria VI* 18.

NOTES TO CHAPTER 4

I.   For the criteria used in defining the Types, see Chapter 5, n.1.

2.   The published photograph of the Kardiani skyphos is rather unclear.

3.   The three elements selected for use (diameter of lip, diameter of
     foot and height) are those felt to be most influential in determining
     the total profile of the vase.   To these must obviously be added
     a description of individual features, such as lip or foot.   The
     definition of shape by ratio rather than simply by terms such as
     "tall" or "squat" is designed to improve objectivity in description
     and general clarity, in the same way that standard soil colour
     charts are now applied to the description of fabric colour,
     Descoeudres/Kearsley (Chapter 1 n.3) 13 n. 23.   See Appendix 2
     for an explanation of the effect of an error margin of 3mm in
     measurement on these figures.

4.   This fragment is identified (Lefkandi I 28-9) as a skyphos fragment
     with uncarinated profile.   The large diameter of lip (20cm), together
     with the angle at which the profile is published, suggest it may
     rather be a fragment from a small krater.   It is not included among
     the fragments identified as skyphoi on the caption for *Lefkandi I*
     Pl.30.

5.   Marmariani 118 - 140:100:51, Marmariani 122 - 168:100:73.

6.   This ratio is only an approximation because a small portion of the
     rim alone was preserved, and thus there is some uncertainty as to
     the lip diameter.

7.   Another apparent example of this sort of lip at Lefkandi occurred
     in the latest deposit in Xeropolis Area 3 (South).   No profile is
     published.   *Lefkandi I* 44 no. 515. Pl.23.

8.   It is possible that the rim fragment Amathous *17/2* also belongs here,
     but certainty is impossible from the published photograph.   There
     are also three further possible fragments from Eretria - See Chapter
     2 *72*.

NOTES TO CHAPTER 5

1. See I. Rouse, "The Classification of Artifacts in Archaeology,"
   AmAnt 25 (1960) 316-7; J.H. Rowe, "Stratigraphy and Seriation",
   AmAnt 26 (1961) 324-330 (reprinted in B.M. Fagan [ed]), *Intro-*
   ductory Readings in Archaeology, (Boston 1970) 65-68 for method-
   ological considerations underpinning the present typology.
   The use of the terms "class" and "group" follows that of J.D. Beazley,
   Attic Red-Figured Vase-Painters Vol. I (Oxford 1942) xliii.

2. See Desborough's comments in *PGP* 187. By contrast, only a ring
   foot has been found on skyphoi in Lefkandi (*Lefkandi I* 300), but
   the presence of many conical feet in the Moulds deposit is noted and
   it is felt that some of these may come from skyphoi (of which the
   pendent semicircle variety is the most frequent) *Lefkandi I* 27. Of
   the cemetery skyphoi, it appears that S.T59,2 comes closest to having
   a low conical foot (Fig. 23(a) above).

3. Vases from the same burial at Lefkandi are generally presumed to be
   roughly contemporary (*Lefkandi I* 282 n.5).

4. See *Lefkandi I* 301 for a similar conclusion on the value of subsidiary
   decorative features.

5. *Lefkandi I* 27-44; *Lefkandi 1968* 26-28. Xeropolis Area 3 South also
   provided a stratified sequence in three stages (*Lefkandi I* 44-45).
   The earliest, the fill under the yard floor, is said to be comparable
   to the Moulds deposit and also perhaps to the lower fill of the North
   Channel (*Lefkandi I* 47). It would have been helpful to have profiles of the pendent semicircle fragments from Area 3 South, as
   this would have amplified the relatively sparse psc material from
   the Moulds and North Channel deposits.

6. Moulds deposit (*Lefkandi I* 28-29; 299). There are 18 rims of pendent semicircle skyphoi and only one is less than 1.5cm in height
   127. Lips: (a) Offset – *125; 127-129;* (b) Everted – *126*. Also possibly *124* – see Chapter 4 n.4 above. Foot: *129*. Decoration: *129*

7. *Lefkandi I* 32. Lips: (a) Tall *130-135;* (b) Short *136*.

8. *Lefkandi I* 37 and n.19, 293 and n.87. Lips: Pl. 33, 1-28. (The
   profiles on Pl. 33 all come from one small area, *Lefkandi I* 37 n. 18).
   Foot: none. The lower part of Pl. 33, 1 is a hypothetical recon-
   struction (*ibid*).

9. See especially the rim fragment with uncarinated lip *126*. Another
   such rim comes from the North Channel Lower Fill *122*, which consists mainly of LPG pottery (*Lefkandi I* 282). Yet a further uncarinated lip (context unknown) has been found at Xeropolis
   (*Lefkandi I* 52 n. 64). The solitary fragmentary example from the
   cemetery is P.T27,2 *119*. Decoration: *Lefkandi I* 299 n. 129.

10. *Lefkandi I* 301.

11. Since the Type 3 lip does not exceed 1.4cm this class falls into the category of medium at Lefkandi (*Lefkandi I* 28 n. 3). There is one example on *Lefkandi I* Pl. 31 from the Pit fill at Xeropolis *136* and possibly a second on Pl. 15, 121. There are also two skyphoi from the Palia Perivolia cemetery, *118* and *120*.

12. *Type 4: Lefkandi I* Pl. 33:1, 2, 7-14, 16, 18-26 (= *137, 138, 143-150, 152, 154-162.*). *Type 5:* Pl. 33, 3, 17 (= *139, 153*). *Lefkandi I* 36 n. 19 includes pl 33, 28 instead of Pl. 33, 17 in this class). *Type 6:* Pl. 33, 15, 27, 28 (= *151, 163, 164*). Although no fragments of Type 6 are identified by Desborough in the initial publication of the material, see Popham *et al.* (Chapter 1 n. 3) 151, where attention is drawn to the presence of "Al Mina type" profiles among the Levelling material.

13. *PGP* 125-6, 291-2; V.R. d'A Desborough, *The Last Mycenaeans and Their Successors* (Oxford 1964) 260-2.

14. *PGP* 188-9, 192-3. However, if Eiteljorg's argument (Chapter 2 n. 1) against the use of the multiple brush for Protogeometric decoration on skyphoi is correct, as seems likely, then the theory of a chronological relationship between these two vases based only on the decoration is difficult to maintain. In the *Andros Museum Guide* (Chapter 2 *239*) 101 nos. 339-341, these three vases have the following inventory numbers: No. 45 = C2; No. 145 = C67; No. 146 = C68.

15. *PGRT* 50-70.

16. D. Theocharis, "Iolkos", *Ergon* (1960) 55-61 and *Ergon* (1961) 51-60. The transition from a Sub-Mycenaean to a Protogeometric style independently of Athens has now been claimed for other areas and would appear to support Verdelis' hypothesis - Samos: J. Ducat, "La céramique de Samos et les ceramiques de la Grèce de l'Est du Xe au VIIe siècle," *Revue Archeologique* (1971) 81; Kalapodhi: R.C. Felsch and H.J. Kienast, "Ein Heiligtum in Phokis", *AAA* 8 (1975) 18.

17. Desborough (n. 13) 262; A.M. Snodgrass, *The Dark Age of Greece* (Edinburgh 1971) 61 supports Desborough's opinion.

18. PGP 162; V.R. d'A Desborough, "A Group of Vases from Amathus", *JHS* 77 (1957) 215.

19. Desborough (n. 18 1957) 214-5. *GGAPC* 23 no. 1, Pl. 1,1. Two skyphos fragments found subsequently at Xeropolis have, in Desborough's opinion, provided the closest parallels to the Amathous skyphos (*Lefkandi I* 52, Pl. 34,3). The Amathous skyphos, together with the cup found with it, are the earliest post-Mycenaean imports known so far from Cyprus (Desborough [Chapter 2 *32*] 196).

20. Desborough (n. 18 1957) 215.

21. For instance, the pedestal skyphoi in Thessaly: Heurtley and Skeat (Chapter 2 *166*) Pl. VII, 123 and 124. Desborough (*PGP* 84) notes the general lack of imitations of the Attic skyphos in the Cycladic area.

22. Thessaloniki 4709: Ht 14.5cm, diam. lip 17.7-18.5, diam. base 8.4, ht of lip 1.4, ht of foot 3.3   Ext.: two sets of eight semicircles. On one side of the pot they are only partly visible, but on the other they do not intersect. The clay is very micaceous and rather coarse and friable: core 7.5YR 6/6 (yellowish brown); surface un-slipped. Probably from one of 12 cist graves (N.G.L. Hammond, "Illyris, Epirus and Macedonia in the Early Iron Age", *CAH* III, 1 [Cambridge 1982] 650).

23. W.A. Heurtley, "Early Iron Age Pottery from Macedonia" *AJ* 7 (1927) 49, 54; Heurtley (Chapter 2 *84*) 106.

24. *PGRT* 55-6, 83-4.

25. It is significant that in the publication of the pottery from Lefkandi the shape is now specifically called a bowl in LPG and a skyphos thereafter (*Lefkandi I* 297 n. 112). Furthermore, there is no doubt that the Sub-Mycenaean pottery at Lefkandi is rooted in the true Mycenaean style (*Lefkandi I* 284-5). Whether the producers of the Sub-Mycenaean pottery at Lefkandi were newcomers cannot be determined at this stage (*Lefkandi I* 356), but makes no difference to the strong connections of the skyphos with the Mycenaean deep bowl. The sub-Mycenaean, Early and Middle Protogeometric styles exhibit a consistent development and a number of shapes are common to the whole period, including the deep bowl (*Lefkandi I* 283 and 297-8).

26. Mycenaean IIIC: M.R. Popham and E. Milburn, "The Late Helladic IIIC Pottery of Xeropolis (Lefkandi): Summary", *BSA* 66 (1971) Figs. 4, 7. Sub-Mycenaean: *Lefkandi I* 297-8.

27. *Delphi inv. 7697*: Ht 14.2cm, diam. lip 16.1-16.7, diam. base 6.7, ht. of lip 2.0, ht. of foot 0.9.

28. In the case of all the vases, except that from Delphi where measurements were taken at the museum, the ratios were obtained from published photographs or drawings such as those referred to in n. 26 above.

29. Compare this with the deep bowl from Lefkandi (Popham/Milburn [n. 26] pl. 57, 2) or another from Athens (Desborough [n. 13 1964] pl. 14, d).

30. Compare the shape of this skyphos particularly with the two deep bowls from Lefkandi - *Lefkandi 1968*, Figs. 27, 47.

31. Desborough (n. 13 1964) 11; Desborough (Chapter 2 *32*) 39; Popham/Milburn (n. 26) 340; *Lefkandi I* 297 and, for example, Pl. 106, S.T51, 3.

32. H.W. Catling, "Archaeology in Greece, 1981-82", *ArchRep* (1981-82) 16-17, Fig. 34.

33. *Lefkandi I* 299.

34. *Lefkandi I* 359 and n.23 on the development of the psc skyphos from the Mycenaean deep bowl.

35. Compare this particularly with the deep bowl from Lefkandi - *Lefkandi I 1968*, Fig. 53.

36. *Lefkandi I* Pl. 99: S.T20,4.

37. *IIIC:* Popham/Milburn (n. 26) Pl. 57, 1 and 2; *Sub-Mycenaean:* S.T3,2 (*Lefkandi I,* Pl. 92); *EPG:* S.T20,4 (n. 36); *MPG:* Toumba grave (n. 32 above). It has now been established at Lefkandi that the shape also continued to exist right down to the time when the psc skyphos was being produced (Popham *et al.*, [Chapter 2 *123/2*] 230).

38. The jug with cutaway neck and the kantharos with high-swung handles are two other local shapes revitalised by the impact of the Protogeometric style. (See Snodgrass [n. 17] 61-2).

39. P. Courbin, "Argos", *BCH* 77 (1953) 262, Fig. 55; G. Roux, "Argos" *BCH* 81 (1957) 664, Fig. 55. See also Desborough (Chapter 2 *32*) 166 and *Lefkandi I* 285.

40. Kraiker/Kübler (Chapter 2 *24*) Pl. 30 no. 525; also *PGP* 78.

41. Desborough (n. 13 1964) 261-2.

42. *PGP* 84.

43. S.T18,2 and T20,4 *Lefkandi I* Pll. 97,99.

44. Desborough (Chapter 2 *32*) 348; Desborough (Chapter 1 n. 19) 34-5; *Lefkandi I* 356 f.

45. Sackett and Popham (Chapter 1, n. 19) 16-17; Desborough (Chapter 2 *32*) 45, 54, 57; Coldstream (Chapter 1 n. 10) 41; Popham *et al.*, (Chapter 2 *123/2*) 237 and 247.

46. J. Boardman, "The Multiple Brush", *Antiquity* 34 (1960) 86-7; Desborough (n. 13 1964) 262.

47. This is also the conclusion of the excavators (*Lefkandi I* 285-6; P. G. Themelis, *Frühgriechische Grabbauten* [Mainz 1976] 72). See, however, Eiteljorg (Chapter 2 n. 1) 452 on the unlikelihood of an overwhelming influence from a single centre as far as the technical aspects of the Protogeometric style are concerned.

48. *PGP* 194-5. He gives seven skyphoi: one each from Cyprus, Tenos, Thebes, Phthiotic Thebes and Skyros, and two from Delos. To this list must now be added a skyphos from Vergina, E26 (*Vergina I* 169, Fig. 23); a wall fragment from Al Mina (unpublished, Cambridge AG26), Cyprus B1889 (*GGAPC* 24 no. 4, Pl. 1, 4) and those fragments from Lefkandi given in n. 49 below. A circles skyphos from Rome is reported by E. La Rocca (Chapter 2 *230*) 91 no. 1. But this is reconstructed from a solitary wall fragment which could equally well belong to a pendent semicircle skyphos. The same uncertainty applies to a fragment from Kition (*Kition IV* 18 no. 4, 20; *GGAPC* 62, Pl. 1, 5). There are also some unpublished examples from Smyrna (*Lefkandi I* 301 n. 141).

49. *Lefkandi I* 28, 32, 37-8, 266, 292 n. 85, 300-301 and n. 141. Moulds deposit: Pl. 14, 33 = Pl. 30, 15; Pit fill deposit: Pl. 15, 95-97, 104-107, 111-113, 116-118 and Pl. 31, 11, 12, 14-16; Levelling material: Pl. 18, 297-312 (with the probable exception of 307).

50. Desborough (*PGP* 194-5) had already noted differences in lip and body profile without attempting any typological classification. While it is still not possible to make an independent typology of the class, there are indications that the concentric circle skyphoi will by-and-large fall into the Types defined for the pendent semicircle skyphos in Chapter 4. For example, see Desborough's comments on the skyphos from Thebes (*PGP* 195) for a possible candidate for Type 1, and also a fragment in the Moulds deposit at Xeropolis which has simple flaring lip, deep body and decoration of reserved bands beneath the concentric circles (*Lefkandi I* Pl. 14, 33 = Pl. 30, 15). Similarly the skyphos from Skyros, according to Desborough's description (*PGP* 195), is similar to Type 3, and that from Cyprus (*PGP* 194) to Type 4. Another fragment from Xeropolis (*Lefkandi I* Pl. 25,667, with profile Pl. 34,7) looks very like a Type 2 skyphos. The Xeropolis stratification indicates, however, that there are some differences, in particular the tendency for the lip of the concentric circle skyphos at all stages to have a smooth transition to the body and not to be offset.

NOTES TO CHAPTER 6

1.   See, for example, Rowe (Chapter 5, n. 1) 58-69; D.J. Tugby,
      "Archaeology and Statistics" in D. Brothwell and E. Higgs (eds.),
      Science in Archaeology (New York 1970) 635 and A.C. Spaulding,
      "Some Elements of Quantitative Archaeology", in F.R. Hodson *et al.*,
      (eds.), *Mathematics in the Archaeological and Historical Sciences,*
      (Edinburgh 1971) 11.

2.   W.S Robinson, "A Method for Chronologically Ordering Archaeological
      Deposits", *AmAnt* 16 (1951) 293-301 and G.W. Brainerd, "The Place
      of Chronological Ordering in Archaeological Analysis", *AmAnt* 16
      (1951) 301-313. The method was developed further by F. Hole and
      M. Shaw, "Computer Analysis of Chronological Seriation", *Rice
      University Studies* 53 (1967) 1-166.

3.   See, for example, D.L. Clarke, "Matrix Analysis and Archaeology
      with Particular Reference to British Beaker Pottery", *PPS* 28 (1962)
      371-83 (and, more fully, D.L. Clarke, *Beaker Pottery of Great
      Britain and Ireland*, Vols.I and II [Cambridge 1970]). For criticism
      of the methodology, see J. Matthews, "Application of Matrix Analysis
      to Archaeological Problems", *Nature* 198 (1963) 930-34 and J.E. Doran
      and F.R Hodson, *Mathematics and Computers in Archaeology* (Boston
      1975) 149, 169-70, and 275-6. In reply to Matthews, see D.L. Clarke,
      "Matrix Analysis and Archaeology", *Nature* 199 (1963) 790-92.

4.   See, for example, F.R. Hodson *et al.*, "Some Experiments in the
      Numerical Analysis of Archaeological Data", *Biometrika* 53 (1966)
      311-324; G.L. Cowgill, "Archaeological Applications of Factor, Cluster
      and Proximity Analysis", *AmAnt* 33 (1968) 373-4; Spaulding (n.1)
      14; Doran and Hodson (n. 3) 272; and the review article by A.M.
      Bieber *et al.*, "Application of Multivariate Techniques to Analytical
      Data on Aegean Ceramics", *Archeometry* 18 (1976) 59-74.

5.   See J.H. Rowe, "Archaeological Dating and Culture Process", *South-
      western Journal of Anthropology* 15 (1959) 319-22 for a description
      of the advantages of similarity seriation of individual units. A
      basic weakness of the Robinson/Brainerd method, apart from its
      limited applicability, is that it forces the material into a pattern of
      unlineal development, even when this causes great distortion in the
      data (C. Renfrew and G. Sterud, "Close Proximity Analysis: A
      Rapid Method for the Ordering of Archaeological Materials", *AmAnt*
      34 (1969) 276). By contrast, the multidimensional techniques allow
      both inherent clustering and linear ordering to become apparent
      (see Hodson *et al.* [n.4] 313-4 on the advantages of multivariate
      techniques in this respect).

6.   A brief summary is found in Doran and Hodson (n. 3) 280-1.

7.   Renfrew/Sterud (n. 5) 265-77.

8.   C. Renfrew, *The Emergence of Civilization* (London 1972) 142-147; D. Frankel, *Middle Cypriot White Painted Pottery: An Analytical Study of the Decoration*, Vols. I and II (M.A. thesis, University of Sydney 1973) 115 and 123-4; Frankel, "Intersite Relationships in the Middle Bronze Age of Cyprus", *World Archaeology* 6 (1974) 202-3.

9.   Certain weaknesses in the method, however, have been acknowledged by the authors. Firstly, the strongest links are emphasised at the expense of the weaker (Renfrew/Sterud [n. 5] 276); and second, there is the problem common to all proximity analysis, that artificial clustering may occur because of discontinuity in the features due to uneven sampling (Renfrew/Sterud [n.5] 268).

10. An exception was made in the case of Lefkandi because the site is so important for tracing the development of the psc skyphos. Furthermore, access to drawings at a scale of 1:1 for all skyphoi included here ensured that measurements would be reliable. See Chapter 1, n. 25.

11. At the time the programme for analysis of the skyphoi was developed (during the course of my M.A. Hons degree) no first-hand information for the four skyphoi of Type 6 was available. Since then, however, Dr J.-P. Descoeudres has studied Veii *229* and the Villasmundo skyphos. It is hoped to include in future analyses these and any other skyphoi for which information has subsequently become available.

12. Where a unit has two different catalogue measurements for the diameter of rim, the mean has been used.

13. The method of coding is far less cumbersome than that used by Hodson *et al.* (n. 4) 316-7.

14. See Appendix 2 for a description of the influence on the ratios of a 0.3cm error margin.

15. It is noted that the ranges for high, medium and low lips at Lefkandi (*Lefkandi I* 300) differ from those used here. This is because two different bodies of material are being analysed: histograms plotted for the 55 units in this study suggest that the divisions used here are the most natural for the skyphoi from the various sites involved.

16. See A.C. Spaulding, "The Dimensions of Archaeology" in B.M. Fagan (ed.), *Introductory Readings in Archaeology*, (Boston 1970) 205 on the selection of attributes for proximity analysis. Attribute 3, on the other hand, has a wide spread because the range is produced by the larger range in the height of the pots.

17. Contrast this with the coding procedure adopted by *Hodson et al.* (n. 4), 316-7 and see the comments on inadvertent weighting in Doran/Hodson (n. 3) 141.

18. See the discussion at the beginning of Chapter 5, p. 105.

19. This coefficient was used by Hodson *et al.* (n. 4) 317, 323 and proved suitable for both seriation and cluster techniques. (The Simple Matching Coefficient is found in P.H.A. Sneath and R.R. Sokal, *Principles of Numerical Taxonomy* [San Francisco 1973] 132-3).

20. The exception is the pair no. 1 (Delphi 5909) and no. 9 (Lefkandi S.T56,3) of Types 1 and 2, where the correlation is at the level of 2.8. The result comes as a surprise because Delphi 5909 has its highest coefficient (8.0) with another skyphos of Type 2 from Lefkandi (no. 6, Lefkandi P.T3,14).

21. The occurrence of 11 semicircles on both nos. 38 and 39 – a number found only three times out of the possible 55 – is enough to outweigh other similarities which archaeological judgement suggests are more significant for classification.

22. It is suggested by Renfrew and Sterud (n. 5) 268 that when ambiguity occurs because too many coefficients are of the same value, only fairly strongly-linked units should be considered and an arbitrary cut-off level of correlation drawn. This suggestion was carried out, with 9.0 arbitrarily being chosen as the cut-off point.

NOTES TO CHAPTER 7

1. *PGP* 193.

2. See, for example, *PGP* 187, 193.

3. *Lefkandi 1968* 27-8; *Lefkandi* (Chapter 2) where the absolute chronology of the site is set out.

4. *Lefkandi 1968* 27; *Lefkandi I* 36 and n. 16; 43-44.

5. Overlapping appears most likely in all stages of the pit. The distinction between the Moulds and Pit fill deposit is somewhat blurred by admixture. Similarly, some material in the Pit could belong to early SPG III, thus possibly, overlapping with the Levelling material at least a little (*Lefkandi I* 42-3).

6. *Lefkandi I* 299 n. 128 also dates the other Type 1 fragment *122* which does not come from the pit in Area 2, to the LPG period.

7. See n. 4 above.

8. On the date of these Attic pyxides see *Lefkandi I* 290 n. 61, 351 and n. 507, 353. S.T59 is placed as the earliest tomb in SPG III while P.T21 is said to be the latest of SPG II (*Lefkandi I* 292). A certain amount of imprecision is inevitable as the borders between the phases are not clearly defined, especially between SPG II and III (*Lefkandi I* 363). The present typology differs from the Lefkandi report in placing S.T45 in SPG III rather than SPG II. Such differences are not surprising in the light of some uncertainty in the attribution of material to the various phases (Lefkandi I 288, 293 n. 88). Thus at one point S.T45 is said by the excavators to belong to the late SPG phase, together with S.T59, which is turn is placed in SPG III (*Lefkandi I* 52, 206). On this, see too, Popham *et al.*, (Chapter 2 *123/2*) 245.

9. *Lefkandi I* 44, Pl. 20, 446-450 and Pl. 43, 61-2. The excavators are reluctant to recognize a date lower than 750 for the Levelling material (*Lefkandi I* 44). However not all the Late Geometric pottery is accounted for by the two pits dug down from above (*Lefkandi I* 58): for example, nos. 62 and 447. Nos. 425, 434 and 444 on Pl. 20 also appear to be Late Geometric, and there are several unillustrated sherds referred to in the text which could also well be LG (*Lefkandi I* 41 (v), (vi)). Considering the stylistic overlapping observed in the earlier stages of the pit (see n. 5 above) it would be surprising indeed if the break between MG II and Late Geometric was absolutely clean-cut unless there had been a change of population; something that has never been suggested. See n. 34 below and Chapter 8 n. 21 for other Late Geometric fragments in the Levelling material.

10. The detailed reports of these excavations are not yet published and this information has been supplied by Dr. J.-P. Descoeudres.

11. A personal communication from Associate Professor J.R. Green. It has been suggested that the Atticising Early Geometric skyphos found at the same time as Chalcis *30* of Type 4 may be an indication of the date of that skyphos (*GGP* 152-4, 303; *Lefkandi I* 291 n. 69). But the two skyphoi are now known merely to be chance finds and there are no grounds for supposing that the Early Geometric skyphos was actually associated with the pendent semicircle skyphos. See Andreiomenou, (Chapter 2 *30* 1972) 182.

    The contexts of the skyphoi from Delos and Rheneia are un-helpful. The Delos skyphoi came from the Purification Trench which contained a large amount of pottery from mixed sources so the date of the deposit can be given only in very broad terms. The situation is the same for the skyphoi from Rheneia, which are some of the offerings from several tombs of uncertain date (*PGP* 153-8, 187).

12. On the Thucydidean dates see *Eretria V* 50-1 and A.J. Graham "The colonial expansion of Greece", *CAH* III, 3 (Cambridge 1982) 89.

13. J. Close-Brooks, "Considerazioni sulla cronologia delle facies arcaiche dell' Etruria", *Studi Etruschi* 35 (1967) 323-329 (original English text in D. and F.R. Ridgway [eds.], *Italy Before the Romans* [London 1979] 107 ff); *GGP* 355.

14. Descoeudres/Kearsley (Chapter 1 n. 3) 28; C.W. Neeft, "Corinthian Fragments from Argos at Utrecht and the Corinthian Late Geometric Kotyle", *BABesch* 50 (1975) 121.

15. Descoeudres/Kearsley (Chapter 1 n. 3) 33-34.

16. Descoeudres/Kearsley (Chapter 1 n. 3) 52.

17. Karageorghis, (Chapter 2 *17/1*) 692-4, Fig. 25. Note, however, that this tomb was used over a considerable length of time and there is no certainty that the two Greek vases were actually associated.

18. Coldstream and Desborough in Dikaios (Chapter 2 *195*) 199-206; *Lefkandi I* 39. A pendent semicircle plate, with single rather than double handles, has recently been found in an earlier context in the Toumba cemetery at Lefkandi. It is possibly an earlier variety, Popham *et al.*, (Chapter 2 *123/2*) 232.

19. Fugmann (Chapter 2 *76*) 269; *Sukas I* 148-152. Cypriot chronology is still debated, but in one scholar's view at least a skyphos of this kind from Soli belongs right at the end of the eighth century (Karageorghis [Chapter 2 *203*] 280). See Gjerstad (Chapter 1 n. 3) 120-1 for a different opinion. Unfortunately, the two Tarsus

166

fragments *206* and *207* are of no assistance in dating Type 5 as they belong to the early part of the Middle Iron period there, and the date for its beginning is tentative (*Tarsus III* 20).

20. Nos. *139* and *153*. See n. 9 above.

21. Karageorghis and Kahil (Chapter 2 *105*) 133. (Note also that the base fragment of a possible pendent semicircle skyphos from Kition also occurs in a Late Geometric context, *Kition IV* 17-18.)

22. The combination of an up-to-date potter with a rather old-fashioned painter has already been observed on Corinthian kotylai imitations at Eretria (*Eretria VI* 14).

23. Eretria: *Eretria V* 45 and n. 152; A. Andreiomenou, "Geometrike kai Upogeometrike Kerameike ex Eretrias", *AE* (1975-76) 210, Fig. 1, 18; A. Andreiomenou, "Ausgewählte geometrische Keramik aus Eretria" in *Tainia. Roland Hampe zum 70. Geburtstag am 2. Dezember 1978 dargebracht* (Mainz 1980) 28 nos. 36-38, Fig. I, 23-25.

    Lefkandi: *Lefkandi 1968* 33; Chalcis and Al Mina: Boardman (Chapter 1 n. 3 1957) 5. The similarity in shape between the Hawam fragment and fragments from Al Mina has already been pointed out in Popham *et al.* (Chapter 1 n. 3) 151.

24. *GGP* 192.

25. Andreiomenou (n. 23 1980) 33.

26. D. Ridgway, "The Foundation of Pithekoussai" in *Nouvelle contribution à l'étude de la société et de la colonisation eubéenne* (Naples 1981) 50, no. 1, pl. ii.

27. Neeft (n. 14) 121 Table V; Descoeudres/Kearsley (Chapter 1 n. 3) 17-18, Cor. IV. See also Ridgway (n. 26) 50.

28. Cambitoglou *et al.*, *Zagora I* (Sydney 1971) 58. Fig. 44. But on the date see Descoeudres/Kearsley (Chapter 1 n. 3) 17 n.31.

29. Descoeudres/Kearsley (Chapter 1 n. 3) 20-23.

30. Descoeudres/Kearsley (Chapter 1 n. 3) 24.

31. Veii: Descoeudres/Kearsley (Chapter 1 n. 3) 36, Fig. 27; Eretria: see n. 23 above.

32. The stratification of the pendent semicircle fragments at Al Mina is in agreement with this interpretation. The fragment which most clearly imitates the slip-filled skyphos, *1*, was the only one that clearly belonged to level IX, while three others are marked VIII,

and the rest IX-VIII. Another imitation of the same shape as the majority of Al Mina psc skyphos fragments has also been found at the site. It belongs to the bichrome skyphos class and is also marked IX-VIII. (*Eretria VI*, Fig. 1:7 and see also discussion on p. 12).

33. Lefkandi : n. 18 above; Salamis: J.N. Coldstream, "The Chronology of the Attic Geometric Vases", in Dikaios (Chapter 2 *195* Appendix 1) 199-204.

34. Coldstream *GGP* 191-3; *Eretria V* 44. For shape of *26* see Descoeudres/ Kearsley (Chapter 1 n. 3) 31, Fig. 34 and Andreiomenou (n. 23 1975-76) 217, Fig. 1, 22; Andreiomenou (n. 23 1980) 24 no. 13, Fig. 1, 11.

35. Shape of Chalcis *29*, Lefkandi *142* - Eretria V 28 FK 434/1330/1.5, Beil. 6; Andreiomenou (n. 23 1975-76) 216, Fig. 1, 21; Andreiomenou (n. 23 1980) 27 no. 31, Fig. 1, 18. The cross-hatched lozenge motif is popular on skyphoi in Late Geometric at Lefkandi (*Lefkandi 1968* 31-2. It is also found at Chalcis (Boardman [Chapter 1 n. 3 1957] 3, pl. 1[b] 7; 18) and Eretria (Andreiomenou [n. 23 1980] 23 no. 5, pl. 3, 5a).

36. Zagora: see *Eretria V* 22, FK 195.6 and 195.5 respectively, Beil. 8.

37. Soli: see *Eretria V* 26, FK 420/22.2 Beil. 7; Delphi: Boardman (Chapter 2, following *74*) Fig. 3, 10; Veii *230* - Eretria V 25, FK 418.2. Beil. 7.

38. Al Mina *6* and *10* - Eretria V 25, FK 418.2, Beil. 7; Al Mina *16* finds its best parallel in a locally-made skyphos from Capua which itself imitates a Euboean Late Geometric shape (W. Johannowsky, "Scambi tra ambiente greco e ambiente italico nel periodo precoloniale e protocoloniale e loro conseguenze", *Dialoghi di Archeologia* 3 [1969] appendix 219 and Fig. 13, a).

39. Oxford 1954.271/7: Ht 1.5; diam lip ?; ht of lip 0.5. Ext.: seven arcs of one set preserved. Int.: painted, except for a reserved band with groups of strokes painted across it. Light pinkish brown clay (5YR 7/3) no mica. Brown slip (5YR 6/4). Context: level VIII. Gjerstad (Chapter 1 n. 3) 116; Descoeudres/Kearsley (Chapter 1 n. 3) 52 n. 144. Here Fig. 44, Pl. 9(c).

40. For an earlier example, see *Eretria V* 41 n. 102, and for the later type at Tarsus: *Tarsus III* 307-8 nos. 1517-18; *Eretria V* 52.

41. This discontinuity in the development of the pendent semicircle sky-phos at the beginning of the Late Geometric period is similar to

that observed generally in the transition from the Middle Geometric to Late Geometric style at Lefkandi (*Lefkandi I* 367-8). Given the source of the new influences, Athens and Corinth, one must attribute the ceramic changes to a marked increase in contact between these areas (which were previously only rarely in touch with each other, if ceramic styles are any guide).

42. *Eretria VI* 12 for the date of the bichrome skyphos fragment from Al Mina, which follows the same Euboean model as the majority of the Type 6 psc skyphoi.

43. On the identification of the destruction level at Tarsus, see *Tarsus III* 19-20. On Greek pottery belonging to the destruction level, see J. Boardman, "Tarsus, Al Mina and Greek Chronology", *JHS* 85 (1965) 10 and *Eretria* V 52.

44. From the fill: *209* and *211*. Boardman (n. 43) 10.

45. On the identification of Middle Iron floors in complexes P, J, K and the floor at 14.50 in the area under H as part of the destruction level, see Boardman (n. 43) 10. Cycladic cups were found in complex P associated with the reflooring at *ca.* 14.50 (*Tarsus III* 113); also in the area under H (*Tarsus III* 128 and 305). Nos. 1506 and 1507 are also said to be from the destruction level (*Tarsus III* 306-7).

46. An indication of the shape of such fragments, however, is provided by the observation of the excavators that there is a resemblance between one of them and some fragments from Al Mina.

47. Khaldeh: R. Saidah, "Fouilles de Khaldé: Rapport préliminaire sur la première et deuxième campagne (1961-62) *BMB* 19 (1966) 90; Tyre: P.M. Bikai (Chapter 2 *227*) 64-67. The problems in constructing a relative chronological framework are mainly due to the apparently long life of many of the common shapes of the Iron Age and also to regional variations within the Bichrome, Red-Slip and Black-on-Red fabrics which make reliable ceramic comparisons between sites much more difficult. See S.V. Chapman, "A Catalogue of Iron Age Pottery", *Berytus 21* (1972) 181-2; R. Amiran, *Ancient Pottery of the Holy Land* (New Jersey 1970) 191-2; Gjerstad, (Chapter 1 n. 3) 115, 117; *Tarsus III* 38, 52; J. Birmingham, "The Chronology of Some Early and Middle Iron Age Cypriot Sites", *AJA* 64 (1963) 27. The view that Phoenician shapes had a long lifetime has recently been questioned (P.M. Bikai, "The Late Phoenician Pottery Complex and Chronology", *BASOR* 229 [1978] 47) but see n. 69 below.

48. Y. Aharoni and R. Amiran, "A New Scheme for the Sub-division of the Iron Age in Palestine", *IEJ* 8 (1958) 171-184; K.M. Kenyon, "Megiddo, Hazor, Samaria and Chronology ", *Bulletin of the Institute of Archaeology, London* 4 (1964) 143-152.

49. In addition, there is an indirect effect on Greek chronology for the period between the tenth and seventh centuries – *GGP* 302-309.

50. *PGP* 294; Boardman (Chapter 1 n. 3 1957) 8; *GGP* 305; Snodgrass (Chapter 5 n. 17) 113 f; *Tarsus III* 305.

51. R.W. Hamilton (Chapter 2 *23*) 5; B. Maisler, "The Stratification of Tell Abu Hawam on the Bay of Acre", *BASOR* 124 (1951) 25; L.H. Vincent, "Tell Abou Hawam, Origines de Haifa", *RBibl* 44 (1935) 434; Aharoni/Amiran (n. 48) 178.

52. Hamilton (Chapter 2, 23) 5-7 and Fig. 8.

53. R.S. Lamon and G.M. Shipton, *Megiddo I* (Chicago 1939) pl. 29: 107.

54. Both systems are conveniently set out in *GGP* 306 and 308. According to Miss Birmingham, who published an extensive revision of Cypriot chronology, these bowls are found in mainland contexts right to the end of the eighth century at least (Birmingham [n. 47] 32).

55. Hamilton (Chapter 2, 23) 7 and Fig. 9.

56. See, for further details, Gjerstad (Chapter 1 n. 3) 119; Amiran (n. 47) 207 f; J. Briend and J.-B. Humbert (eds.), *Tell Keisan (1971-1976): une cité phénicienne en Galilée* (Orbis Biblicus et Orientalis, Series Archaeologica I, Paris 1980) 170-1.

57. Megiddo: Lamon/Shipton (n. 53) Pl. 25:57; Samaria: J.W. Crowfoot *et al.*, *Samaria III* (London 1957) 154, Figs. 9, 2 and 18, 6; Ashdod: M. Dothan, "Ashdod II-III, The Second and Third Seasons of Excavations, 1963, 1965", *Atiquot* (Eng. Ser.) Supplement Volume 9-10 (1971) 21 and 95, Figs. 37 no. 17 and 59 no. 10.

58. Briend/Humbert (n. 56) 26.

59. Hamilton (Chapter 2 *23*) 67.

60. Hamilton (Chapter 2 *23*) 68; Maisler (n. 51) 24; Aharoni/Amiran (n. 48) 172, 178.

61. Vincent (n. 51) 434. Although Albright dismissed this suggestion soon after its publication – see, for example, W.F. Albright, "The excavation of Tell Beit Mirsim, The Iron Age", *AASOR* 21-22 (1941-3) 6 n. 2 – on the grounds that Hawam III pottery paralleled only levels VI-V, this is now acknowledged to be incorrect and the correlation is extended to include levels V, IV and III. (See n.48 above, and also Chapman [n. 47] 180 and Maisler [n. 51] 25.)

62. See n. 48 above. In her study of Phoenican pottery from Tyre, Bikai (n. 47) 53-54 has also suggested that occupation of Hawam could possibly cover the late eighth or early seventh century. It is surprising to note that the illustrated plate from Hawam III is identified with the earlier Class I bowls at Tyre (pp. 52-3). As the profile of the Hawam plate is slightly carinated (Hamilton [Chapter 2 *23*] Fig. 9) and not hemispherical, it belongs to the late Class 2, Type 1 (Bikai Fig. 3, 9).

63. Hamilton (Chapter 2 *23*) 67.

64. Vincent (n. 51) 430.

65. Chapman (n. 47) 177; W. Culican, *The First Merchant Venturers* (London 1966) 97-100; Briend/Humbert (n. 56) 176.

66. G.W. Van Beek, "The Date of Tell Abu Hawam, Stratum III", *BASOR* 138 (1955) 36.

67. It is used by Taylor in her discussion of the chronology of Al Mina, for example (Chapter 1 n. 3) 77-8.

68. *Ashdod*: Dothan (n. 57) 113; *Tarsus: Tarsus III* 31 and 104. In fact, however, Hamilton's catalogue of the pottery from level III describes the Red-Slip bowls as being "horizontally burnished". He does not state whether by hand or on the wheel, so no firm conclusion can be drawn, but the fact that the very similar bowls at Samaria are wheel-burnished would suggest the horizontal burnishing of the Hawam examples is also done on the wheel.

69. The situation is clearly reflected in the study of Iron Age pottery from three sites by Miss Chapman (n. 47) 180. The degree of precision she was able to give to subdivisions in the Iron Age is about 400 years, with the Middle Iron period which includes Megiddo V and later; Tell Qasile VIII and later; Tell Abu Hawam III and Khaldeh III, extending from 900-550 BC.

70. Hamilton (Chapter 2 *23*) 23-4, nos. 95-6; Vincent (n. 51) 429; Maisler, (n. 51) 24; Van Beek (n. 66) 36.

71. Heurtley, (Chapter 2 *212*) 181. But see now J. Balensi, "Revising Tell Abu Hawam", *BASOR* 257 (1985) 69 for another Greek fragment.

72. Desborough (Chapter 5 n. 18) 217-8; *GGP* 302-3; Van Beek (n. 66) 37-8; and Courbin (Chapter 2 *212*) 157 n. 54.

73. The identification of the cup has also become better defined since the excavation of Lefkandi - Coldstream (Chapter 1 n. 10) 66 - but as the two Greek imported fragments were not found in the same context (Hamilton [Chapter 2, *23*] 24), the chronology of one fragment is not necessarily an indication of the date of the other.

74. See *166-174*.

75. *GGP* 303 compares it with Chalcis *30* and Coldstream (Chapter 1 n.10) 66, 93, with one of the skyphoi from S.T59 at Lefkandi *112*.

NOTES TO CHAPTER 8

1. The absolute chronology for the Protogeometric style at Lefkandi is uncertain, but it seems likely to be roughly contemporary with that of Athens and to date between 1050 – 900 (*Lefkandi I* 285-6, 300).

2. See *Lefkandi 1968* 26 on the quality of pendent semicircle skyphos fragments from the pit.

3. There are one or two very competent skyphoi from Thessaly, such as those from Sesklo *200* and Argyropouli Tirnavou *22*.

4. *Lefkandi I* 301.

5. *Lefkandi I* 299.

6. The impression that Lefkandi may have led the way in the development of the pendent semicircle skyphos is reinforced by several other Type 2 skyphoi from Lefkandi which retain Late Helladic decorative features: *111, 129, 130*. Such features occur on Type 2 skyphoi more commonly there than elsewhere.

7. *Lefkandi I* 286-8, 299.

8. See Chapter 5 n. 25 above.

9. It is not impossible, however, in view of the strength of the Protogeometric settlement and the possibility of continuity of occupation there from Mycenaean times, that a claim will be made for Iolkos when more is known of the site. See the summary of evidence in Desborough (Chapter 5 n. 13) 135-6 and Desborough (Chapter 2 *32*) 208-12. Also P.G. Themelis (Chapter 2 following *74*) 318 and Popham and Milburn (Chapter 5 n. 26) 349 for the possible Thessalian origin of Lefkandi's Protogeometric style.

10. Lefkandi I 362; Desborough (Chapter 1 n. 19) 35; Coldstream, (Chapter 1 n. 10) 64, 90.

11. The skyphoi from Amathous *17/1* and Kition *100*. Perhaps some second-hand evidence of pendent semicircle skyphoi in Cyprus at a relatively early stage may be provided by two Cypriot imitations, nos. *19* from Amathous and *182* from Palekythro. Although the Palekythro skyphos was not identified as a Cypriot product by Catling in 1973 (Chapter 2 *182*) there are peculiarities of both shape (the high foot and profile of the bowl) and decoration (reserved band on the exterior lip and large reserved area inside) when compared with the Greek series. See J.N. Coldstream, "Geometric Skyphoi in Cyprus", *RDAC* (1979) 256-7, and especially 259, no. 5, Fig. 1c, Pl. XXIX, 4 for a Cypriot stemmed bowl from Ayios Iakovos which combines local shape with Middle Geometric decoration.

12. The occurrence in Crete of the two Type 4 skyphoi, which appear to be of Euboean fabric, is especially interesting in light of the solitary pendent semicircle skyphos previously known from Knossos. Although the published photograph does not allow certain classification, that skyphos appears to belong to Type 1 and its isolation until the discovery of the many psc fragments at the Teke cemetery was rather a mystery. It is now clear that the producers of these skyphoi, probably Euboeans, had an early and continuing link with Knossos.

13. See Desborough (Chapter 1 n. 19) 34-6 where very similar interconnections between the regions of the Central and North Aegean have already been delineated on more general grounds.

14. The excavators' comments on the type of lip most common in the sanctuary at Kalapodhi suggest the same may be true in certain parts of Central Greece (Felsch [Chapter 2 *86*] 48).

15. See n. 3 above.

16. Coldstream (Chapter 1 n. 10) 90 emphasizes the difference in lip-type between the two areas at this stage. Since Delos was such an important sanctuary at this time, it would not be surprising to find some pendent semicircle skyphoi whose shape is typical of other areas, for example, the Type 4 skyphoi, Delos *42, 46, 48, 54*. Unfortunately it is not possible to say whether or not these are imports, but they certainly form a minority when compared to the number of Type 5 skyphoi there. The exact place of manufacture of the Type 5 skyphoi must also remain uncertain, but the island of Naxos, where psc skyphos fragments have already been found, had important connections with the sanctuary at Delos during the late eighth century and possibly earlier (L.H. Jeffery, *Archaic Greece: the city-states c.700-500 BC* [London 1976] 179; W.G.G. Forrest, "Euboea and the islands" *CAH* III, Pt. 3 [Cambridge 1982] 258). This makes it a likely leader in the ceramic style of the surrounding islands, where Type 5 skyphoi mainly occur. It is surprising to discover, however, that none of the Type 5 skyphoi from the Aegean is made of clay containing a lot of mica, for it is usually to be found in quantity in Naxian clay (J.N. Coldstream, "The Cesnola Painter: A Change of Address", *BICS* 18 [1971] 4). But it has been observed by Walter-Karydi that this is not a decisive argument against attributing wares to Naxos, as there is considerable variation in mica content among Naxian geometric sherds (Chapter 2 *177*) 416.

17. *PGP* 192-3.

18. It is noteworthy that both *229,* from Veii, and *230* date to the Late Geometric period. For the conclusions to be drawn from this see Descoeudres/Kearsley (Chapter 1 n. 3) 52.

19. The withdrawal of Central Greece from the ceramic koine after 750 has been observed both at Delphi (W.G.G. Forrest, "Central Greece and Thessaly", *CAH* III, Pt. 3 [Cambridge 1982] 308) and Kalapodhi (Catling [Chapter 5 n. 32] 29).

20. Eight of the nine Type 6 Eretrian fragments are of local fabric, but *73* is probably an import. So is fragment *74*, which appears to imitate a slightly later Euboean shape. The fragments at Lefkandi are of local clay (*Lefkandi I* 36).

21. For the Late Geometric house constructed above the pit, see *Lefkandi I* 15-16. For Late Geometric pottery in the Levelling material, see Chapter 7 n. 9. (Two other pendent semicircle skyphos fragments in the Levelling material, *140* and *141* may also be of Late Geometric date.)

22. P. Auberson and K. Schefold, *Führer durch Eretria* (Bern 1972) 18-19; P. Auberson, "Chalcis, Lefkandi, Erétrie au VIIIe siècle", *Contribution à l'étude de la société et de la colonisation eubéenes* (Cahiers du Centre Jean Bérard II 1975) 13-14; *Eretria V* 37 n. 45; Coldstream (Chapter 1 n. 10) 88-90; A. Altherr-Charon and C. Bérard, "Erétrie: l'organisation de l'espace et la formation d'une cité grecque" in *L'archéologie aujourd'hui* (Paris 1978) 237-38.

    For a different view of the relationship between Lefkandi and Eretria, see Bakhuizen (Chapter 1 n. 13) 7-9 and *Lefkandi I* 423-26. It has also been pointed out recently, however, that the foundation date of Eretria may now need to be modified because of the amount of earlier pottery appearing (L. Kahil, "Contribution a l'étude de l'Erétria géométrique", *Stele N. Kontoleontos* [Athens 1980] 527).

23. Themelis comments that fragments found by him at Eretria (see Chapter 2, following *74* 315), resemble skyphoi from Cyprus and Near Eastern sites. Full publication of this material would be extremely useful in determining even more closely Eretria's involvement in the production of the pendent semicircle skyphos during the ninth and eighth centuries.

24. Cambitoglou *et al.* (Chapter 7 n. 28) 58; J.-P. Descoeudres, "Zagora auf der Insel Andros - eine eretrische Kolonie?" *AntK* 16 (1973) 88. Professor J.R. Green, of the Zagora excavation team, speaks in terms of 60 per cent.

25. This possibility was suggested some years ago by Graham (Chapter 1 n. 23) 70. But it is not always easy to distinguish Greek geometric imports from local imitations because of the high-quality technique of some of the latter. See Coldstream (n. 11) 259.

26. Of the 25 fragments examined from Al Mina, the clay of about half had small white and dark-coloured grits. Mica was occasionally

present, although always in small quantities. In contrast, none of the eight pendent semicircle fragments from Eretria, which are Type 6 and occur in clear Late Geometric contexts, had either grits or mica. Furthermore, none of the nine psc fragments has a slip, while all but two at Al Mina have. It is also interesting to recall the results of the analysis by Popham *et al.*, where the clay of psc skyphos sherds from Lefkandi and Al Mina were found to be chemically distinct and that from Chalcis inconclusive in its connections (Chapter 1 n. 3) 156, 159. See n. 29 below, however, for a possible comparison with the fabric of local Al Mina bichrome skyphoi, especially as regards the presence of small white inclusions.

27. Al Mina: Woolley (Chapter 1 n. 3 1937) 9-10; J. Boardman (Chapter 1 n. 3) 163-9, who suggests that the bichrome skyphoi were made by Greeks living at Al Mina. Descoeudres (*Eretria VI* 12) points out, however, that the skyphoi could equally well be the work of Levantine potters at the site, as does Coldstream (n. 11) 269.

28. *Tarsus III* 118-120, 128 (Tarsus); Pritchard (Chapter 2 *199* 95) (Sarepta). At Tarsus, some psc skyphoi are described as being "smaller than the standard Cycladic cup" (*Tarsus III* 306). Al Mina *6* would appear to fall into the same category. Perhaps all of these belong to the class of miniature imitations made in the area during the eighth century (Birmingham [Chapter 7 n. 47] 35). See Coldstream (n. 11) 255-269 for a discussion of 26 Cypriot imitations of Middle and Late Geometric skyphoi. See also n. 11 above for two psc skyphos imitations from Cyprus.

29. *Eretria VI* 11-12 no. 7 and n. 17. See also Chapter 7 n. 32 above. As 12 of the 35 pieces of Type 6 are found at Al Mina itself, it seems that these pendent semicircle skyphoi were probably being made there. The fabric of the following local bichrome skyphos fragments was examined: Oxford 1954.387/2 (levels VIII-IX), no mica, core 5YR 8/2 with greyish centre and small white inclusions; Oxford 1954.382/9 (no level), no mica, core 5YR 7/4 with very small white inclusions; Oxford 1954.379/5 (level IX), no mica, core 5YR 8/2 with very small white inclusions; Oxford 1954.379/4 (level 7), no mica, core 5YR 8/4 with very small dark and white inclusions; Oxford 1954.379/1 (no level), no mica, core 5YR 8/4 with small white inclusions; Oxford 1954.375 (no level), no mica, core 5YR 8/4; Cambridge AL 123 (no level), core 5YR 7/4; slipped, one or two specks of mica, small white inclusions. A comparison of these fragments (and those published by Boardman (Chapter 1 n. 3 1959) 168-9 and Descoeudres (*Eretria VI* 8 nos. 4, 7) with the description of the Al Mina fragments *1-16* above will show that there is nothing to exclude their emanating from the same source. The strong reservations expressed in Chapter 2 on the validity of visual description of fabric should be borne in mind, however. Production of similar skyphoi at other Near Eastern sites should not be exluded: at Tarsus, for example, the same shape is found in a fragmentary local skyphos from the kiln area (*Tarsus III* 201 no. 504, Fig. 123) and two pendent semicircle skyphoi were found in the kiln area (*Tarsus III* 118).

30. See for general comments: Desborough (Chapter 1 n. 19) 38; Coldstream (Chapter 1 n. 10) 95. For Tarsus, see *Tarsus III* 111, and for Salamis, Coldstream in Dikaios (Chapter 2 *195*) 199-203. In addition to the many skyphoi, fragments from two large vases, probably either dinoi or kraters analogous to others found in Euboea, are also found at Al Mina: Oxford 1954.346/2 (no level), decorated with a large cross-hatched lozenge flanked by groups of vertical lines; Oxford, no number (level VIII), decorated with concentric pendent semicircles. These may be compared with Boardman (Chapter 1 n. 3 1957) 4 no. 43 (Chalcis), and Boardman (Chapter 2 following *74*) 15, Fig. 9 (Eretria).

31. See Chapter 4, p.95ff.

32. For a similar view see *Lefkandi I* 368. Despite the lack of conclusive evidence, however, strong cases have been put forward for a predominant role by both Eretria (Jeffery [n. 16] 63) and Chalcis (S. C. Bakhuizen, "Greek Steel", *World Archaeology* 9 [1977] 227-8) at Al Mina. Boardman (Chapter 1 n. 3 1957) 23-24 and Bakhuizen (Chapter 1 n. 3) 79-82 stress the probable importance of Amarynthos.

33. *Eretria V* 37, n. 45; *Eretria VI* 13.

34. *Eretria VI* 14 and nos. 20-24. Nos. 2, 17 and possibly 32, are also Eretrian.

35. *GGP* 312 and *Eretria VI* 17 (including nn. 82 and 83) for lists of the pottery other than pendent semicircle skyphoi that may be of pre-750 date. At most ten fragments, and as Coldstream has pointed out with regard to Tell Sukas, a handful of sherds (nine in the case of Sukas) hardly supports the hypothesis that Greeks were resident at that time (J.N. Coldstream, Review of *Sukas I* and *Sukas II*, *AJA* 79 [1975] 156).

36. Thus, from the purely Greek point of view, the grounds for raising Woolley's and Robertson's date for the beginning of the actual occupation of the site beyond *ca.*750 are much less now than 20 years ago. In addition, Gjerstad's study of the Cypriot and Syrian pottery at Al Mina indicates that Taylor's earlier dates, on which classical archaeologists have relied, are too high (Chapter 1 n. 3 118). He emphasizes strongly (p.121) a fact sometimes ignored in the past, that virtually no Asiatic pottery occurs in level IX. Thus it cannot be used to date the foundation of the site in any case. As Dr J.-P. Descoeudres has pointed out to me, this chronology for the early levels of Al Mina also has an important bearing on the debate about the way in which the Phoenician alphabet was transmitted to the Greeks. Now it has been established that the level of Greek activity at Al Mina in the first half of the eighth century was so small, arguments in favour of an alternative location, such as Crete, for the initial contact with the Phoenicians, are strengthened. See,

for example, Coldstream (Chapter 1 n. 10) 269-301; Guarducci (Chapter 1 n. 2) 129-131; Burzachechi (Chapter 1 n. 2) 90-92.

37. Woolley (Chapter 1 n. 3 1938) 16, followed by Robertson (Chapter 1 n. 3) 21.

38. Three skyphos rim fragments: Oxford 1954.271/5 *12*; Oxford 1954. 271/12-13 (*14a,b*); one wall fragment: Oxford 1954.271/9, and the lekanis rim fragment Oxford 1954.271/7 (see Chapter 7 n. 39).

39. Although the proportion of Greek pottery in level VIII is small compared to the Asiatic (Woolley [Chapter 1 n. 3 1937] 9 and [Chapter 1 n. 3 1938] 16, those fragments – apart from the psc skyphos fragments – from this context are the same sort of Late Geometric skyphoi found in level IX. For example, among pottery from level VIII now in England are four rim fragments of skyphoi with cross-hatched lozenges flanked by vertical lines (Oxford 1954.385/4; Oxford 1954.385/5; Oxford 1954.385/9; London 1968.3-25.150. The last two are marked as coming from Room 8 of level √III). As Miss Taylor has pointed out (Chapter 1 n. 3) 63, this was one of the very clear contexts from level VIII. There is also one rim fragment of a kotyle with cross-hatched lozenge decoration (Cambridge AL.74), a shoulder fragment of a large open vase with dotted lozenge decoration (Oxford 1954.335/5), at least five rim fragments of skyphoi with a row of concentric circles on the rim (Cambridge AL.6; Oxford 1954.368/6; Oxford 1954.368/8; Oxford 1954.370; Oxford 1954.368/3), the rim of a chevron skyphos (Cambridge AL. 34), and several other Late Geometric fragments such as Oxford 1954.396/1; Oxford 1954.394; Oxford 1954.345; Oxford 1954.335/3; Oxford 1954.396/1; Oxford 1954.387/7; Oxford 1954.384/10; Oxford 1954.368/1; Cambridge AL. 73, and three unnumbered wall fragments from the Ashmolean Museum. The similarity of the Greek material in levels IX and VIII is underlined by Gjerstad (Chapter 1 n. 3) 121-2.

BIBLIOGRAPHY

Y. Aharoni and R. Amiran, "A New Scheme for the Sub-Division of the Iron Age in Palestine", *IEJ* 8 (1958) 171–184.

C. Albizzati, *Vasi antichi dipinti del Vaticano, Fasc. i* (Rome 1925).

W.F. Albright, "The Excavation of Tell Beit Mirsim, The Iron Age", *AASOR* 21–22 (1941–1943).

A. Altherr-Charon and C. Bérard, "Erétrie: l'organisation de l' espace et la formation d'une cité grecque" in *L'archéologie aujourd'hui* (Paris 1978) 229–249.

R. Amiran, *Ancient Pottery of the Holy Land* (New Jersey 1970).

A. Andreiomenou, "Nea Lampsakos", *ADeltChr* 16 (1960) 150.

A. Andreiomenou, "Ereunai kai Tychaia Heuremata en te Polei kai te Eparchia, Chalkidos", *ADeltChr* 27 (1972) 170–184.

A. Andreiomenou, "Geometrike kai Hupogeometrike Kerameike ex Eretrias", *AE* (1975) 206–229.

A. Andreiomenou, "Ausgewählte geometrische Keramik aus Eretria" in *Tainia. Roland Hampe zum 70. Geburtstag am 2. Dezember 1978 dargebracht* (Mainz 1980) 21–34.

M. Andronikos, Vergina, The Prehistoric Necropolis and the Hellenistic Palace (*Studies in Mediterranean Archaeology* 13, London 1964) 3–11.

M. Andronikos, *Vergina I. To Nekrotapheion ton Tumbon* (Athens 1969).

P. Auberson, "Chalcis, Lefkandi, Erétrie au VIIIe siècle" in *Contribution a l'étude de la société et de la colonisation eubéenes* (Cahiers du Centre Jean Bérard II, Naples 1975) 9–14.

P. Auberson and K. Schefold, *Führer durch Eretria* (Bern 1972).

P. Aupert, "Rapport sur les travaux de la mission de l'école française à Amathonte en 1977", *BCH* 102 (1978) 939–975.

S.C. Bakhuizen, *Chalcis-in-Euboea, Iron and Chalcidians Abroad* (Chalcidian Studies III, Leiden 1976).

S.C. Bakhuizen, "Greek Steel", *World Archaeology* 9 (1977) 220–234.

G. Bakalakis, "Aus den Grotten in Antiparos und Paros", *AA* 84 (1969) 125–132.

J.D. Beazley, *Attic Red-Figure Vase-Painters Vol. 1* (Oxford 1942).

C. Berard, *Eretria. Fouilles et recherches III: L'Héröon à la porte de l'ouest* (Berne 1970).

P. Bernard, "Céramiques de la première moitié du VIIe siècle à Thasos", *BCH* 88 (1964) 77-146.

F. Biancofiore, *La Civiltà Micenea nell'Italia Meridionale I*: La Ceramica (Rome 1963).

A.M. Bieber Jr., D.W. Brooks, G. Harbottle and E.V. Sayre, "Application of Multivariate Techniques to Analytical Data on Aegean Ceramics", *Archaeometry 18* (1976) 59-74.

P.M. Bikai, *The Pottery of Tyre* (Warminster 1978).

P.M. Bikai, "The Late Phoenician Pottery Complex and Chronology", *BASOR* 229 (1978) 47-56.

J. Birmingham, "The Chronology of Some Early and Middle Iron Age Cypriot Sites", *AJA* 64 (1963) 15-42.

C.W. Blegen, C.G. Boulter, J.L. Caskey, M. Rawson, *Troy IV* (Princeton 1958).

J. Boardman, "Pottery from Eretria", *BSA* 47 (1952) 1-48.

J. Boardman, "Early Euboean Pottery and History", *BSA* 52 (1957) 1-29.

J. Boardman, "Greek Potters at Al Mina?" *Anatolian Studies* 9 (1959) 163-169.

J. Boardman, "The Multiple Brush", *Antiquity* 34 (1960) 85-89.

J. Boardman, "Tarsus, Al Mina and Greek Chronology", *JHS* 85 (1965) 5-15.

J. Boardman, *Excavations in Chios, 1952-55, Greek Emporio* (London 1967).

J. Boardman, *The Greek Overseas*: their early colonies and trade [3] (London 1980).

J. Boardman and F. Schweitzer, "Clay Analyses of Archaic Greek Pottery", *BSA* 68 (1973) 267-283.

J. Boehlau and K. Schefold (edd.), *Larisa am Hermos III* Die klein Funde (Berlin 1942).

A. Bounni, E. and J. Lagarce and N. Saliby, "Rapport préliminaire sur la deuxième campagne de fouilles (1976) à Ibn Hani (Syrie)", *Syria* 55 (1978) 233-301.

J. Bouzek, *Homerisches Griechenland* in Lichte der archaologischen Quellen (Prague 1969).

R.J. Braidwood, "Report on Two Sondages on the Coast of Syria, South of Tartous", *Syria* 21 (1940) 183-221.

G.W. Brainerd, "The Place of Chronological Ordering in Archaeological Analysis", *AmAnt* 16 (1951) 301-313.

T.F.R.G. Braun, "The Greeks in the Near East", *CAH III Pt.3: The Expansion of the Greek World, Eighth to Sixth Centuries BC* (Cambridge 1982) 1-31.

J. Briend and J.-B. Humbert (eds.), *Tell Keisan (1971-1976): une cité phénicienne en Galilée* (Paris 1980).

H.-G. Buchholz, "Tell Halaf IV - Zu den Kleinfunden von Tell Halaf", *Berliner Jahrbuch für Vor- und Frühgeschichte* 5 (1965) 215-231.

H.-G. Buchholz, *Methymna* (Mainz 1975).

H.-G. Buchholz, "Ägäische Funde in Randgebieten des Mittelmeers", *AA* 89 (1974) 325-462.

G. Buchner, "Pithekoussai, Oldest Greek Colony in the West", *Expedition* 8, 4 (1966) 4-12.

G. Buchner, "Recent Work at Pithekoussai (Ischia), 1965-71", *ArchRep* (1970-71) 63-67.

M. Burzachechi, "L'adozione dell'alfabeto nel mondo greco", *Parola del Passato* 31 (1976) 82-102.

R. Campbell Thompson and R.W. Hutchinson, "The Excavations on the Temple of Nabu at Nineveh", *Archaeologia* 79 (1929) 103-148.

A. Cambitoglou, *Archaeological Museum of Andros, Guide to the finds from the excavations of the Geometric town at Zagora* (Athens 1981).

A. Cambitoglou, J.J. Coulton, J. Birmingham and J.R. Green, *Zagora I* (Sydney 1971).

S. Casson, "Excavations in Macedonia - II", *BSA* 26 (1923-4, 1924-5) 1-29.

Cambridge Ancient History [2] *Vol.III Part 1.* The Prehistory of the Balkans; and the Middle East and the Aegean World, tenth to eighth centuries BC (Cambridge 1982).

Cambridge Ancient History [2] *Vol.III Part 3.* The Expansion of the Greek World, Eighth to Sixth Centuries BC (Cambridge 1982).

H.W. Catling, "A Pendent Semicircle Skyphos from Cyprus and a Cypriot Imitation", *RDAC* (1973) 179-185.

H.W. Catling, "The Knossos Area, 1974-1976", *ArchRep* (1976-77) 3-23.

H.W. Catling, "Archaeology in Greece, 1981-82", *ArchRep* (1981-82) 3-62.

H.W. Catling, E.E. Richards and A.E. Blin-Stoyle, "Correlations between composition and provenance of Mycenaean and Minoan pottery", *BSA* 58 (1963) 94-115.

S.V. Chapman, "A Catalogue of Iron Age Pottery from the Cemeteries of Khirbet Silm, Joya, Qrayé and Qasmieh of South Lebanon", *Berytus* 21 (1972) 55-194.

D. Chrestou, "Archaiotetes kai Mnemeia Kyprou 1971-1974", *ADeltChr* 29 (1973-74) 1011-1026.

C. Clairmont, "Greek Pottery from the Near East", *Berytus* 11 (1954-1955) 85-141.

D.L. Clarke, "Matrix Analysis and Archaeology with Particular Reference to British Beaker Pottery", *PPS* 28 (1962) 371-83.

D.L. Clarke, "Matrix Analysis and Archaeology", *Nature* 199 (1963) 790-792.

D.L. Clarke, *Beaker Pottery of Great Britain and Ireland, Vols. I and II* (Cambridge 1970).

J. Close-Brooks, "Considerazioni sulla cronologia delle facies arcaiche dell' Etruria", *Studi Etruschi* 35 (1967) 323-329.

J.N. Coldstream, "The Chronology of the Attic Geometric Vases", in P. Dikaios, "A 'Royal' Tomb at Salamis, Cyprus", *AA* 78 (1963) 199-204.

J.N. Coldstream, *Greek Geometric Pottery* (London 1968).

J.N. Coldstream, "The Cesnola Painter: A Change of Address", *BICS* 18 (1971) 1-15.

J.N. Coldstream, "Cypro-Aegean Exchanges in the 9th and 8th Centuries BC", *Praktika tou Protou Diethnous Kyprologikou Synedriou A* (Nicosia 1972) 15-22.

J.N. Coldstream, Review of P.J. Riis, *Sukas I* and G. Ploug, *Sukas II*, *AJA* 79 (1975) 155-156.

J.N. Coldstream, *Geometric Greece* (London 1977).

J.N. Coldstream, "Geometric Skyphoi in Cyprus", *RDAC* (1979) 255-269.

J.N. Coldstream, "The Greek Geometric and Plain Archaic Imports", in *Excavations at Kition IV. The Non-Cypriote Pottery* (Nicosia 1981) 17-22.

Corpus Vasorum Antiquorum, Denmark 2, Copenhagen National Museum 2 (Paris, no date).

P. Courbin, "Argos. Nécropole géométrique", *BCH* 77 (1953) 258-263.

P. Courbin, "Rapport sur la fouille de Ras el Bassit 1971", *AAS* 22 (1972) 45-61.

P. Courbin, "Ras el Bassit: Rapport sur la campagne de 1972", *AAS* 23 (1973) 25-37.

P. Courbin, "Ras el Bassit, Al Mina et Tell Sukas" *Revue Archéologique* (1974) 174-178.

P. Courbin, "Rapport sur la 4ème campagne de fouilles (1974) à Ras el Bassit", *AAS* 25 (1975) 59-71.

P. Courbin, "Rapport sur la 5eme campagne de fouilles à Ras el Bassit", *AAS* 26, (1976) 63-69.

P. Courbin, "Une Pyxis Géométrique Argienne (?) au Liban", *Berytus* 25 (1977) 147-157.

P. Courbin, "Rapport sur la sixième campagne de fouilles à Ras Bassit (Syrie)", *AAS* 27-28 (1977-1978) 29-40.

P. Courbin, "A-t'on retrouvé l'antique Posideion à Ras el-Bassit? *Archéologia* 116 (1978) 48-62.

G.L. Cowgill, "Archaeological Applications of Factor, Cluster and Proximity Analysis", *AmAnt* 33 (1968) 367-375.

J.W. Crowfoot, G.M. Crowfoot and K.M. Kenyon, *Samaria-Sebaste III*: The Objects from Samaria (London 1957).

W. Culican, *The First Merchant Venturers:* The ancient Levant in history and commerce (London 1966).

A. de Agostino, J.B. Ward-Perkins, R.A. Staccioli, A.P. Vianello, D. Ridgway, J. Close-Brooks, M.T. Amorelli Falconi, G.C. Alciati and R. Passarello, "Veio (Isola Farnese). Scavi in una necropoli villanoviana in località "Quattro Fontanili", *NSc* 17 (1963) 77-278.

A. Demetriou, "Die Datierung der Periode Cypro-Archaisch I nach Fund-zusammenhängen mit griechischer Keramik", *AA* 93 (1978) 12-25.

V.R. d'A. Desborough, *Protogeometric Pottery* (Oxford 1952).

V.R. d'A. Desborough, "A Group of Vases from Amathus", *JHS* 77 (1957) 212-219.

182

V.R. d'A. Desborough, "The Low-footed Skyphoi with pendent semicircles" in P. Dikaios, "A 'Royal' Tomb at Salamis, Cyprus", *AA* 78 (1963) 204-206.

V.R. d'A. Desborough, *The Last Mycenaeans and Their Successors: an archaeological survey ca. 1200-ca.1000 BC* (Oxford 1964).

V.R. d'A. Desborough, *The Greek Dark Ages* (London 1972).

V.R. d'A. Desborough, "The Background to Euboean Participation in Early Greek Maritime Enterprise" in *Tribute to an Antiquary: Essays Presented to Marc Fitch* (London 1976) 27-40.

V.R. d'A. Desborough, "A Group of Vases from Skyros" in *Stele N. Kontoleontos* (Athens 1980) 55-58.

J.-P. Descoeudres, "Zagora auf der Insel Andros - eine eretrische Kolonie? *AntK* 16 (1973) 87-88.

J.-P. Descoeudres, "Die vorklassische Keramik aus dem Gebiet des Westtors", in *Eretria V* (Bern 1976) 13-58.

J.-P. Descoeudres, "Euboeans in Australia. Some Observations on the Imitations of Corinthian Kotylai Made in Eretria and Found in Al Mina" in *Eretria VI* (Bern 1978) 7-19.

J.-P. Descoeudres and R. Kearsley, "Greek Pottery at Veii: Another Look", *BSA* 78 (1983) 9-53.

L.P. di Cesnola, *Descriptive Atlas of the Cesnola Collection of Cypriote Antiquities, in the Metropolitan Museum of Art, Vol.II* (New York 1894).

O.T.P.K. Dickinson, Review of *Eretria VI*, *JHS* 101 (1981) 207-208.

P. Dikaios, "A 'Royal' Tomb at Salamis, Cyprus", *AA* 78 (1963) 126-198.

J.E. Doran and F.R. Hodson, *Mathematics and Computers in Archaeology* (Boston 1975).

J. Dörig, *Art Antique. Collections Privées de Suisse Romande* (Geneva 1975).

M. Dothan, "Ashdod II-III, The Second and Third Seasons of Excavations, 1963, 1965", *Atiquot* (Eng.Ser.) Suppl. Vol.9-10 (1971).

J. Ducat, "La céramique de Samos et les céramiques de la Grèce de l'Est du Xe au VIIe siècle," *Revue Archéologique* (1971) 81-92.

C. Dugas and C. Rhomaios, "Les vases de Délos 1. Les vases préhelleniques et géométriques", (Exploration archéologique de Délos, Paris 1934).

T.J. Dunbabin, *The Greeks and their Eastern Neighbours* (London 1957).

H. Eiteljorg II, "The Fast Wheel, the Multiple-Brush Compass and Athens as Home of the Protogeometric Style", *AJA* 84 (1980) 445-452.

E. Fabbricotti, "Veio (Isola Farnese). Continuazione degli scavi nella necropoli villanoviana in località "Quattro Fontanili", *NSc* 26 (1972) 242-272.

A. Fairbanks, *Museum of Fine Arts, Catalogue of Greek and Etruscan Vases, I,* (Cambridge, Mass. 1928).

R.C.S. Felsch and H.J. Kienast, "Ein Heiligtum in Phokis", *AAA* 8 (1975) 1-24.

R.C.S. Felsch, H.J. Kienast, H. Schuler, "Apollon und Artemis oder Artemis und Apollon? Bericht von den Grabungen im neu entdeckten Heiligtum bei Kalapodi 1973-1977", *AA* 95 (1980) 38-123.

W.G.G. Forrest, "Euboea and the islands", *CAH III Pt.3: The Expansion of the Greek World, Eighth to Sixth Centuries BC* (Cambridge 1982) 249-260.

W.G.G. Forrest, "Central Greece and Thessaly", *CAH III Pt.3: The Expansion of the Greek World, Eighth to Sixth Centuries BC* (Cambridge 1982) 286-320.

D. Frankel, *Middle Cypriot White Painted Pottery: An Analytical Study of the Decoration, Vols.I and II,* unpublished M.A. thesis (University of Sydney 1973).

D. Frankel, "Intersite Relationships in the Middle Bronze Age of Cyprus", *World Archaeology* 6 (1974) 190-208.

E. Fugmann, *Hama. Fouilles et recherches 1931-38, Vol.II, 1. L'architecture des périodes pré-hеllénistiques* (Copenhagen 1958).

H. Gallet de Santerre, *Délos primitive et archaique* (Paris 1958).

H. Gallet de Santerre and J. Tréheux, "Rapport sur le dépôt égéen et géométrique de l'Artémision à Délos", *BCH* 71-72 (1947-1948) 148-254.

J. Garstang, "Explorations in Cilicia, Excavations at Mersin 1938-9. The Historic Periods, Pts. III and IV", *Liverpool Annals of Archaeology and Anthropology* 26 (1940) 89-158.

E. Gjerstad, *The Swedish Cyprus Expedition, Vol.IV, Pt.2. The Cyprogeometric, Cypro-archaic and Cypro-classical periods* (Stockholm 1948).

E. Gjerstad, "The Stratification at Al Mina (Syria) and its Chronological Evidence", *Acta Archaeologica* 45 (1974) 107-123.

E. Gjerstad, *Greek geometric and archaic pottery found in Cyprus* (Stockholm 1977).

H. Goldman, *Excavations at Gözlü Kule, Tarsus. III: The Iron Age* (Princeton 1963).

A.J. Graham, "The foundation of Thasos", *BSA* 73 (1978) 61-98.

A.J. Graham, "The colonial expansion of Greece", *CAH III Pt.3: The Expansion of the Greek World, Eighth to Sixth Centuries BC* (Cambridge 1982) 83-162.

A.P. Grimanis, S.E. Filippakis, B. Perdikatsis, M. Vassilaki-Grimani, N. Bosana-Kourou and N. Yalouris, "Neutron Activation and X-ray Analysis of 'Thapsos Class' Vases. An Attempt to Identify their Origin", *Journal of Archaeological Science* 7 (1980) 227-239.

M. Guarducci, "Appunti di epigrafia greca arcaica (leggendo il libro di Lilian H. Jeffery)", *Archeologia Classica* 16 (1964) 122-153.

E.H. Hall, *Excavations in Eastern Crete: Vrokastro* (Philadelphia 1914).

R.W. Hamilton, "Excavations at Tell Abu Hawam", *QDAP* 4 (1934-5) 1-69.

N.G.L. Hammond, "Illyris, Epirus and Macedonia in the Early Iron Age", *CAH III Pt.1: The Prehistory of the Balkans; and the Middle East and the Aegean World, tenth to eighth centuries BC* (Cambridge 1982) 619-656.

G.M.A. Hanfmann, "On some Eastern Greek wares found at Tarsus" in S.Weinberg (ed.), *Studies Presented to Hetty Goldman* (New York 1956) 165-184.

G.M.A. Hanfmann, "The Ninth Campaign at Sardis (1966)", *BASOR* 186 (1967) 17-52.

M. Hartley, "Early Greek Vases from Crete", *BSA* 31 (1930-31) 56-114.

W.A. Heurtley, "Early Iron Age Pottery from Macedonia", *AJ* 7 (1927) 44-59.

W.A. Heurtley, "Note on Fragments of Two Thessalian Proto-geometric Vases found at Tell Abu Hawam", *QDAP* 4 (1934-1935) 181.

W.A. Heurtley, *Prehistoric Macedonia* (Cambridge 1939).

W.A. Heurtley and C. Ralegh Radford, "Report on Excavations at the Toumba of Saratsé, Macedonia, 1929" *BSA* 30 (1928-29, 1929-30) 113-150.

W.A. Heurtley and T.C. Skeat, "The Tholos Tombs of Marmáriane", *BSA* 31 (1930-1931) 1-55.

F.R. Hodson, P.H.A. Sneath and J.E. Doran, "Some Experiments in the Numerical Analysis of Archaeological Data", *Biometrika* 53 (1966) 311-324.

F. Hole and M. Shaw, "Computer Analysis of Chronological Seriation", *Rice University Studies* 53 (1967) 1-166.

B. Hrouda, *Tell Halaf IV*. Kleinfunde aus historicher Zeit (Berlin 1962).

G. Jacopi, "Parte 1: Esplorazione archeologica di Camiro - II", *Clara Rhodos* 6-7 (1932).

L.H. Jeffery, *The Local Scripts of Archaic Greece* (Oxford 1961).

L.H. Jeffery, *Archaic Greece: the city-states ca.700-500 BC* (London 1976).

L.H. Jeffrey, "Greek alphabetic writing", *CAH III Pt.1: The Prehistory of the Balkans; and the Middle East and the Aegean World, tenth to eighth centuries BC* (Cambridge 1982) 819-833.

W. Johannowsky, "Scambi tra ambiente greco e ambiente italico nel periodo precoloniale e protocoloniale e loro consequenze", *Dialoghi di Archeologia* 3 (1969) 31-43 and appendix 213-219.

L. Kahil, "Contribution à l'étude de l'Érétrie géométrique", *Stele N. Kontoleontos* (Athens 1980) 525-531.

V. Karageorghis, "Chronique des fouilles à Chypre en 1960", *BCH* 85 (1961) 277-280.

V. Karageorghis, "Chronique des fouilles et découvertes archéologiques à Chypre en 1961", *BCH* 86 (1962) 327-414.

V. Karageorghis, "Une tombe de guerrier à Palaepaphos", *BCH* 87 (1963) 265-300.

V. Karageorghis, "Chronique de fouilles et découvertes archéologiques à Chypre en 1972", *BCH* 97 (1973) 601-689.

V. Karageorghis, "Chronique des fouilles et découvertes archéologiques à Chypre en 1979. 1. Musée de Chypre (Nicosie)", *BCH* 104 (1980) 761-769.

V. Karageorghis, "Chronique des fouilles et découvertes archéologiques à Chypre en 1980. 19. Fouilles de sauvetage dans la nécropole d'Amathonte", *BCH* 105 (1981) 1007-1021.

V. Karageorghis, "Chronique des fouilles et découvertes archéologiques à Chypre en 1981", *BCH* 106 (1982) 685-744.

V. Karageorghis, "Cyprus", *CAH III Pt.1: The Prehistory of the Balkans; and the Middle East and the Aegean World, tenth to eighth centuries BC* (Cambridge 1982) 511-533.

V. Karageorghis and L. Kahil, "Témoignages eubéens à Chypre et chypriotes à Erétrie", *AntK* 10 (1967) 133-135.

K.M. Kenyon, "Megiddo, Hazor, Samaria and Chronology", *Bulletin of the
   Institute of Archaeology, London 4* (1964) 143-152.

W. Kraiker and K. Kübler, *Kerameikos, Ergebnisse der Ausgrabungen I,*
   Die Nekropolen des 12 bis 10 Jahrhunderts (Berlin 1939).

W. Lamb, "Antissa", *BSA* 32 (1931-32) 41-67.

R.S. Lamon and G.M. Shipton, *Megiddo I.* Seasons of 1925-34. Strata I-V
   (Chicago 1939).

E. La Rocca, "Due tombe dell'Esquilino", *Dialoghi di Archeologia* 8 (1974-
   1975) 86-103.

E. La Rocca, "Ceramica d'importazione a Roma" in *Civiltà del Lazio Primitivo*
   (Rome 1976).

E. La Rocca, "Note sulle importazioni greche in territorio Laziale nell'VIII
   secolo A.C." *Parola del Passato* 32 (1977) 375-397.

L. Lerat, "Fouilles à Delphes, à l'est du grand sanctuaire", *BCH* 85 (1961)
   316-366.

D. Levi, "La Necropoli geometrica di Kardiani a Tinos", *ASAtene* 8-9
   (1925-1926) 203-234.

D. Levi, "Gli scavi a Festòs nel 1956 e 1957", *ASAtene* 35-36 (1957-1958)
   193-361.

D. Levi, "Le campagne 1962-1964 a Iasos", *ASAtene* 43-44 (1965-1966)
   401-546.

B. Maisler, "The Stratification of Tell Abu Hawam on the Bay of Acre",
   BASOR 124 (1951) 21-25.

J. Matthews, "Application of Matrix Analysis to Archaeological Problems",
   Nature 198 (1963) 930-934.

J.-P. Michaud, "Chronique des fouilles et découvertes archéologiques
   en Grèce en 1973", *BCH* 98 (1974) 579-722.

J.L. Myres, *The Metropolitan Museum of Art. Handbook of the Cesnola
   Collection of Antiquities from Cyprus* (New York 1914).

C.W. Neeft, "Corinthian Fragments from Argos at Utrecht and the Corinthian
   Late Geometric Kotyle", *BABesch* 50 (1975) 97-134.

K. Nicolaou, "Archaeology in Cyprus, 1976-80", *ArchRep* (1980-81) 49-72.

I.Ch. Papachristodoulou, "Geometrikos Taphos eis Vati, Rodou", *AAA* 8 (1975) 223-226.

H.G.G. Payne, "Early Greek Vases from Knossos", *BSA* 29 (1927-1928) 224-298.

E.J. Peltenburg, "Al Mina Glazed Pottery and its Relations", *Levant* 1 (1969) 73-96.

P. Perdrizet, *Fouilles de Delphes. V,* Monuments figurés: petits bronzes, terres-cuites, antiquités diverses (Paris 1908).

G. Ploug, *Sukas II. The Aegean, Corinthian and Eastern Greek Pottery and Terracottas* (Copenhagen 1973).

M.R. Popham, H. Hatcher and A.M. Pollard, "Al Mina and Euboea", *BSA* 75 (1980) 151-161.

M.R. Popham and E. Milburn, "The Late Helladic IIIC Pottery of Xeropolis (Lefkandi): a Summary", *BSA* 66 (1971) 333-352.

M.R. Popham and L.H. Sackett, *Excavations at Lefkandi, Euboea, 1964-66: a preliminary report* (London 1968).

M.R. Popham and L.H. Sackett (eds.), *Lefkandi I. The Iron Age: The Settlement and the cemeteries* Text and Plates (Oxford 1979, 1980).

M.R. Popham, E. Touloupa and L.H. Sackett, "Further Excavation of the Toumba Cemetery at Lefkandi, 1981", *BSA* 77 (1982) 213-248.

F. Poulsen and C. Dugas, "Vases archaiques de Délos", *BCH* 35 (1911) 350-422.

J.B. Pritchard, *Sarepta: a preliminary report on the Iron Age* (Philadelphia 1975).

C. Renfrew, *The emergence of civilization:* The Cyclades and the Aegean in the third millennium BC (London 1972).

C. Renfrew and G. Sterud, "Close Proximity Analysis: A Rapid Method for the Ordering of Archaeological Materials", *AmAnt* 34 (1969) 265-277.

C.A. Rhomasios, "Anaskaphe sto Karabournaki tes Thessalonikes" in *Epitumbion Chr. Tsountas* (Athens 1941) 358-387.

G.M.A. Richter, *The Metropolitan Museum of Art. Handbook of the Greek collection* (Cambridge, Mass. 1953).

D. Ridgway, "The First Western Greeks: Campanian Coasts and Southern Etruria" in C. and S. Hawkes, eds., *Greeks, Celts and Romans* (London 1973) 5-38.

D. Ridgway, "Composition and Provenance of Western Geometric Pottery: A Prospectus", *British Archaeological Reports Supplementary Series* 41 (1978), 121-128.

D. Ridgway, "The Foundation of Pithekoussai" in *Nouvelle contribution à l'étude de la société et de la colonisation eubéenes* (Naples 1981) 45-56.

D. Ridgway, *The Etruscans* (University of Edinburgh, Department of Archaeology, Occasional Paper no. 6 1981).

D. Ridgway and O.T.P.K. Dickinson, "Pendent Semicircles at Veii: a Glimpse", *BSA* 68 (1973) 191-192.

D. Ridgway and F.R. Ridgway (eds.), *Italy before the Romans: the Iron Age. Orientalizing and Etruscan periods* (London 1979).

P.J. Riis, "L'activité de la mission archéologique danoise sur la côte phenicienne en 1959", *AAS* 10 (1960) 111-132.

P.J. Riis, *Hama: fouilles et recherches, 1931-1938. Vol.2 Pt.3. Les cimetières a crémation* (Copenhagen 1948).

P.J. Riis, *Sukas I. The North-East sanctuary and the First Settling of Greeks in Syria and Palestine* (Copenhagen 1970).

G. Rizza and V. Santa Maria Scrinari, *Il santuario sull'acropoli di Gortina I* (Rome 1968).

M. Robertson, "The Excavations at Al Mina, Suedia.IV. The Early Greek Vases", *JHS* 60 (1940) 2-21.

W.S. Robinson, "A Method for Chronologically Ordering Archaeological Deposits", *AmAnt* 16 (1951) 293-301.

L. Rocchetti, "La ceramica dell'abitato geometrico di Festos a occidente del palazzo minoico", *ASAtene* 52-53 (1974-1975) 169-300.

C. Roebuck, *Ionian trade and colonization* (New York 1959).

R. Romeo (ed.), *Storia della Sicilia I* (1979).

I. Rouse, "The Classification of Artifacts in Archaeology", *AmAnt* 25 (1960) 313-323.

G. Roux, "Argos. La rotonde", *BCH* 81 (1957) 663-665.

J.H. Rowe, "Archaeological Dating and Culture Process", *Southwestern Journal of Anthropology* 15 (1959) 317-324.

J.H. Rowe, "Stratigraphy and Seriation" *AmAnt* 26 (1961) 324-330. (Reprinted in B.M. Fagan (ed.), *Introductory Readings in Archaeology* (Boston 1970) 58-69.

L.H. Sackett and M.R. Popham, "Lefkandi: A Euboean Town of the Bronze Age and the Early Iron Age (2100-700 BC)", *Archaeology* 25 (1972) 8-19.

R. Saidah, "Fouilles de Khaldé: Rapport préliminaire sur la première et deuxième campagnes (1961-1962)", *BMB* 19 (1966) 51-90.

R. Saidah, "Objets grecs d'époque géométrique découverts récemment sur le littoral libanais (à Khaldé près de Beyrouth)", *AAS* 21 (1971) 193-198.

D.U. Schilardi, "The Decline of the Geometric Settlement of Koukounaries at Paros" in R. Hägg (ed.) *The Greek Renaissance*, (Monograph XIV, Institute of Archaeology, University of Los Angeles 1983) 175-183.

S. Smith, "The Greek Trade at Al Mina: A Footnote to Oriental History", *AJ* 22 (1942) 87-112.

P.H.A. Sneath and R.R. Sokal, *Numerical Taxonomy the principles and practice of numerical classification* (San Francisco 1973).

A.M. Snodgrass, *The Dark Age of Greece: an archaological survey of the eleventh to the eighth centuries* (Edinburgh 1971).

A.C. Spaulding, "The Dimensions of Archaeology" in B.M. Fagan (ed.), *Introductory Readings in Archaeology* (Boston 1970) 201-218.

A.C. Spaulding, "Some Elements of Quantitative Archaeology" in *Mathematics in the Archaeological and Historical Sciences*, F.R. Hodson *et al.*, eds. (Edinburgh 1971).

W.B. Stern and J.-P. Descoeudres, "X-Ray Fluorescence Analysis of Archaic Greek Pottery", *Archaeometry* 19 (1977) 73-86.

J. du Plat Taylor, "The Cypriot and Syrian Pottery from Al Mina, Syria", *Iraq* 21 (1959) 62-92.

P.G. Themelis, "Eretria" *AAA* 3 (1970) 314-319.

P.G. Themelis, *Frühgriechische Grabbauten* (Mainz 1976).

D.R. Theocharis, "Iolkos, whence sailed the Argonauts", *Archaeology* 11 (1958) 13-18.

D.R. Theocharis, "Iolkos", *Ergon* (1960) 55-61.

D.R. Theocharis, "Iolkos", *Ergon* (1961) 51-60.

D.R. Theocharis, "Protogeometrikoi Taphoi N.Ionias Volou", *Thessalika E* (1966) 47-53.

K. Tuchelt, "Didyma. Bericht über die Arbeiten 1969-70", *Ist.Mitt* 21 (1971) 45-108.

D.J. Tugby, "Archaeology and Statistics" in D. Brothwell and E. Higgs, eds., *Science in Archaeology,* (New York 1970) 634-648.

G.W. Van Beek, "The Date of Tell Abu Hawam, Stratum III", *BASOR* 138 (1955) 34-38.

N.M. Verdelis, *Ho Protogeometrikos Rhythmos tes Thessalias* (Athens 1958).

L.H. Vincent, "Tell Abou Hawam. Origines de Haifa", *RBibl* 44 (1935) 416-437.

G. Voza, "L'attività della Soprintendenza alle Antichità della Sicilia Orientale, Parte II," *Kokalos* 22-23 (1976-77) 551-586.

G. Voza, "La necropoli della valle del Marcellino presso Villasmundo", in "Insediamenti coloniali greci in Sicilia nell'VIII e VII secolo A.C.," *Cronache di Archeologia* 17 (1978) 104-110.

H. Walter, *Samos V: Frühe samische Gefässe* (Bonn 1968).

E. Walter-Karydi, "Geometrische Keramik aus Naxos", *AA* 87 (1972) 386-421.

A.L. Wilson, "Elemental Analysis of Pottery in the Study of its Provenance: A Review", *Journal of Archaeological Science* 5 (1978) 219-236.

C.L. Woolley, "Excavations near Antioch in 1936", *AJ* 17 (1937) 1-15.

C.L. Woolley, "Excavations at Al Mina, Suedia. I=II", *JHS* 58 (1938) 1-30 and 133-170.

Ph. Zapheiropoulou, "Apo ton Geometrikon Synoikismon tes Donouses", *AAA* 6 (1973) 256-259.

Ph. Zapheiropoulou, "Donousa", *ADeltChr* 28 (1973) 544-547

APPENDIX TO TEXT

Since the manuscript was submitted, certain bibliographical items of relevance have appeared and, although it is not possible at this late stage to incorporate them into the body of the text, a list with brief comments is given below together with an indication of where related matters are discussed in the body of the work.

CHAPTER 1: INTRODUCTION

n.2:   An inscribed sherd from levels VII-VI at Al Mina (J. Boardman, "An Inscribed Sherd from Al Mina", *Oxford Journal of Archaeology* 1 (1982) 365-67).

n.4:   A.J. Graham, "The historical interpretation of Al Mina", *Dialogues d'histoire ancienne* 12 (1986) 51-65.

n.25:   A new pendent semicircle skyphos fragment from Al Mina has been found in Oxford recently (E.D. Francis and Michael Vickers, "Greek Geometric Pottery at Hama and its Implications for Near Eastern Chronology", *Levant* 17 (1985) 132 n. 5).

CHAPTER 2: CATALOGUE

New finds have been published from the following sites:-

A1. ASINE

Rim fragment

Ht 5.0; **diam lip** 14.0; **th** 0.5.   Brownish grey to greenish clay, local.   **Lip**, offset, ht (1.8-2.0).   **Ext:**   nine arcs of one set.   **int:** painted, except for reserved band on lip.   Blackish-brown paint.   **Context:** uncertain, either phase 1 or phase 4 (*ca.*1075 – into the ninth century).

B. Wells, *Asine II. Fasicle 4: The Protogeometric Period. Part 2: An Analysis of the Settlement* (Acta Instituti Atheniensis Regni Sueciae, Series in 4°, XXIV 4:2, Stockholm 1983) 58-60 and 204 nr.271, figs. 146 and 147:271.

This fragment appears to belong to Type 2.   There is also a skyphos rim fragment decorated with pendent semicircles from a clear phase 1 context (*ibid* 58 and 204 nr. 270, fig. 146:270).   This appears to have been decorated with at least three sets of semicircles on each side and to have had a high conical foot.   A second such fragment is to be found in Box AS1079 of the material from the Swedish excavations at the site in the 1920s:[1] **Ht** 4.5; **w** 4.0; **diam lip** ? (only 0.3 cm of rim preserved.) Clay 7.5YR 7/6 (reddish-yellow), fine and well-levigated. No inclusions and no slip. **Lip**, not offset, ht 1.5. **Ext**: nine arcs of one set, and above reserved band on painted lip. **Int**: painted, except for reserved band on lip. **Context**: mixed deposit from the lower city.[2] These two fragments are probably from skyphoi comparable to that from Heroôn at Lefkandi.[3]

A2. CHALCIS

A. Andriomenou, "Skyphos de l'atelier de Chalcis (fin Xe – fin VIIIe s. av. J.-C.) II", *BCH* 109 (1985) 51-55, nrs. 10-23. (The profiles of the rim fragments published in Fig. 1 suggest that the material contains a mixture of Type 2 (nrs. 10,11) and Type 5 skyphoi (nrs. 12, 15, 16), with perhaps one example of Type 6 (nr. 23) also.)

A3. CLAZOMENAE

Two rim fragments which appear to be from pendent semicircle skyphoi have been reported from a mixed deposit.

J. de la Genière, "Recherches récentes à Clazomènes", *Revue des Archéologues et Historiens d'Art de Louvain* 15 (1982) 87-88, Fig. 8 and 9.

A4. COS

The skyphos from Serraglio is now published: *Serraglio Grave 27:16 (inv.767).*

Ht 6.5; **diam lip** 11.7. Yellow-reddish clay, well-levigated, not local. **Lip**, offset, slightly flaring. Ring **foot**. **Ext**: two sets of nine semicircles, intersecting. **Int**: entirely painted. Brown paint. **Context**: tomb containing pottery in the style of early Middle Geometric.

L. Morricone, "Sepolture della prima Età del Ferro a Coo". *ASAtene* 56, N.S. 40 (1978) 202, fig. 394. Chronology discussed on pp. 29-30.

A5. CYPRUS

Private Collection of A. Mourtouvanis

One complete skyphos with two sets of 12 semicircles which intersect. **Lip**, short, offset.

M. Popham, A.M. Pollard and H. Hatcher, "Euboean Exports to Al Mina, Cyprus, and Crete: a Reassessment", *BSA* 78 (1983) pl.33(b).

A6. KNOSSOS

Local imitations of pendent semicircle skyphoi are reported to be among
the finds from the North Cemetery (H.W. Catling, "Archaeology in Greece
1982-83", *ArchRep* (1982-83) 52).

A7. LEFKANDI

Fourteen new skyphoi are reported from excavations in the Toumba
cemetery (H.W. Catling, "Archaeology in Greece 1984-85", *ArchRep*
(1984-85) 15-16).

A8. NAXOS

In the Atti del Convegno Internazionale Grecia, Italia e Sicilia nell'VIII
e VII secolo a C., Atene 15-20 ottobre 1979, vol. 3, *ASAtene* N.S. 45
(1983) 1984, photographs of four rim fragments of pendent semicircle
skyphoi from a geometric and archaic necropolis are published by V.K.
Lambrinoudakis, "Nea Stoicheia gia te gnose tes Naxiakes geometrikes
kai proimes archaikes kerameikes", 110, Fig. 1 and also a photograph
of two complete skyphoi by F. Zaphiropoulou, "Geometrika aggeia apo
te Naxo" 126, Fig. 12.

A9. PONTECAGNANO

B. d'Agostino reported the discovery of an almost completely preserved
skyphos from T. 4697 in the necropolis at Pontecagnano at the First
Australian Congress of Classical Archaeology, Greek Colonists and Native
Populations (University of Sydney, 9-14 July, 1985). It is a flat-based
skyphos which appears to belong to Type 6. The decoration of two sets
of intersecting semicircles was partly obscured in antiquity by black
paint.

A10. SARDINIA

A wall fragment without context (THT 81/6/6), which is possibly from
a pendent semicircle skyphos, is published in E. Acquaro, "Tharros
VIII. Lo Scavo del 1981", *Rivista di Studi Fenici* 10 (1982) 51, pl.26,2
and 33.   The fragment is identified in F. Boitani and David Ridgway,
"Provenance and Firing Techniques of Geometric Pottery from Veii: A
Mössbauer Investigation", *BSA* 80 (1985) 148.   See also David Ridgway,
"The First Western Greeks and Their Neighbours 1935-85", *Ancient
Hellenism: Greek Colonists and Native Populations. Proceedings of the
First Australian Congress of Classical Archaeology,* (ed.) J.-P.
Descoeudres (Oxford, forthcoming).

A11. SAREPTA

Robert B. Koehl, *Sarepta III. The Imported Bronze and Iron Age Wares from Area II, X* (Beirut 1985) p.136 nos. 248 (= *199*), 249.

A12. TORONE

Fragments of two locally-made skyphoi were reported from the University of Sydney excavations by Mr J. Papadopoulos at a seminar in the Institutionen för antikens kultur och samhallsliv, University of Stockholm, in May 1984. One was found in a grave of the Protogeometric cemetery, the other in a mixed deposit on the lekythos.

Additional Bibilographical References:

HAMA

Francis and Vickers, (Appendix, Ch.1 n.25 above) 131-32 and Fig. 1 (= 7B23 *76*; 8A189 *79*).

TELL ABU HAWAM

J. Balensi, "Revising Tell Abu Hawam", *BASOR* 257 (1985) 69; J. Balensi and M.-D. Herrera, "Tell Abou Hawam 1983-84, rapport preliminaire", *RBibl* 92 (1985) 103; M.D. Herrera and J. Balensi "More about the Greek Geometric Pottery at Tell Abu Hawam", *Levant* 18 (1986) 169-71.

VATI

I. Papchristodoulou, "Geometrika heuremata sto Vati Rodou" in Atti del Convegno Internazionale Grecia, italia e Sicilia nell'VIII et VII secolo a. C., Atene 15-20 ottobre 1979, vol.3, *ASAtene* N.S. 45 (1983) 1984, 14, Fig. 4.

CHAPTER 3: FABRIC

Two more reports of analyses have appeared: M. Popham, A.M. Pollard and H. Hatcher, "Euboean Exports to Al Mina, Cyprus, and Crete: A Reassessment", *BSA* 78 (1983) 281-90; F. Boitani and David Ridgway, (A*10*), 139-50. The reliability of the results in absolute terms, however, continues to be limited by the lack of comparative analyses from all other possible alternative sources of manufacture (Popham *et al* (1983) 289; Boitani and Ridgway (1985) 150).

CHAPTER 5: RELATIVE CHRONOLOGY

n.32:   A further prototype of the pendent semicircle skyphos has been found at Toumba, Lefkandi (H.W. Catling, "Archaeology in Greek, 1982-83", *ArchRep* (1982-83), 112, Fig. 19).

CHAPTER 7: ABSOLUTE CHRONOLOGY

n.19; 48:   On the chronology of the pendent semicircle skyphoi from Hama and also problems of Near Eastern chronology in the Iron Age, see Francis and Vickers, (Appendix Ch. 1 n. 25 above), 131-38.

nn.50f: On the date of the skyphos fragments from Tell Abu Hawam III to the Late Geometric period: Balensi and Herrera, (Tell Abu Hawam above) 103; R.A. Kearsley, "The Redating of Tell Abu Hawam III and the Greek Pendant Semicircle Skyphos", *BASOR* 263 (1986), pp.85-6.

NOTES TO APPENDIX

1.   This is stored in Uppsala (B. Wells, A*1*, 122 n. 678).

2.   My thanks are due to Professor Tullia Linders of the Institutionen för antikens kultur och samhallsliv, University of Uppsala for permission to include details of this fragment, and to Mrs Yvonne Backe-Forsberg for her generous assistance during my visits to the Collection in March-April 1984.

3.   H.W. Catling, "Archaeology in Greece 1981-82", *ArchReps* 1981-82, 17, Fig. 34 top right. A third published skyphos fragment is decorated with either concentric circles or pendent semicircles. If there are indeed semicircles, since they are not compass-drawn the fragment does not belong to the pendent semicircle skyphos class. (B. Wells, A*1*, Fig. 201:823).

September 1986
Macquarie University, Sydney

APPENDIX 1

TABLE 3: TABULATION OF ATTRIBUTES

1	12.0	16.0	1.3	3	1	1	4	3	3	2	2	1	2	D 5909 (*58*)
2	10.5	14.0	1.3	2	2	1	3	3	2	2	2	2	2	VER AΓ24 (*235*)
3	10.9	15.0	1.4	2	2	1	3	3	3	2	2	2	2	MAR 121 (*172*)
4	10.0	13.0	1.3	4	2	1	4	3	2	2	1	2	1	CHAU. (*31*)
5	15.6	17.5	1.1	2	2	1	4	13	4	1	2	2	1	LEF 2:1 (*116*)
6	9.6	12.8	1.3	3	2	2	4	3	2	1	2	1	2	LEF 3:14 (*117*)
7	12.5	16.5	1.3	3	2	1	4	13	4	1	1	2	2	LEF 33:1 (*108*)
8	9.4	12.4	1.3	3	2	2	3	6	2	1	1	2	2	LEF 33:2 (*109*)
9	9.6	14.3	1.5	2	2	1	3	14	2	1	1	2	1	LEF 56:3 (*111*)
10	9.3	13.1	1.4	3	2	1	3	3	2	1	1	2	2	KAR B79 (*95*)
11	9.9	14.1	1.4	3	2	1	4	6	2	1	1	2	2	VER Δ15 (*231*)
12	10.9	15.6	1.4	2	2	1	4	5	3	1	1	2	1	VER P21 (*233*)
13	11.9	16.5	1.4	2	1	1	3	5	3	1	2	2	2	VER P1 (*232*)
14	11.5	16.1	1.4	3	2	2	4	5	3	1	1	2	2	MAR 119 (*170*)
15	10.1	16.5	1.6	3	2	2	4	5	2	1	1	2	2	KAP 57 (*88*)
16	9.9	15.1	1.5	3	2	2	3	5	2	1	1	2	2	KAP 56 (*87*)
17	10.5	16.6	1.6	3	1	1	4	4	3	1	1	2	2	DEL 19 (*57*)
18	9.9	13.4	1.4	3	2	1	3	4	2	1	1	2	2	NI K2237(*179*)
19	11.1	15.8	1.4	2	1	1	3	5	3	1	2	2	2	KAP 58 (*89*)
20	9.7	15.1	1.6	3	2	1	4	8	2	1	1	2	2	ARG TIRN (*22*)
21	9.9	16.1	1.6	3	2	1	3	6	2	1	1	2	2	LARISA (*106*)
22	10.9	16.0	1.5	3	2	1	4	1	3	1	1	2	2	MAR 120 (*171*)
23	10.7	15.9	1.5	3	2	1	4	7	3	1	1	2	2	SESKLO (*200*)
24	8.2	12.3	1.5	4	1	1	4	12	1	1	1	2	2	VER AZ16 (*236*)
25	6.7	11.0	1.6	3	4	1	2	6	1	1	1	2	2	LEF 59:2 (*112*)
26	7.1	10.0	1.4	3	3	2	2	5	1	1	1	2	2	LEF 59A:3 (*113*)
27	10.0	14.8	1.5	2	2	1	2	13	2	1	1	2	2	LEF 59A:4 (*114*)
28	5.7	8.8	1.5	2	2	1	1	1	1	2	3	2	2	LEF 21:10 (*118*)
29	7.2	10.3	1.4	2	2	1	1	5	1	2	1	2	2	LEF 39B:5 (*120*)
30	9.7	13.9	1.4	2	2	1	3	5	2	1	3	2	2	NI K2235 (*178*)
31	10.3	15.2	1.5	2	2	1	2	4	3	1	3	2	2	KAP 59 (*90*)
32	11.0	15.8	1.4	2	2	1	2	5	3	1	2	2	2	KAP 60 (*91*)
33	11.0	16.5	1.5	1	2	1	2	5	3	1	2	2	2	KAP 61 (*92*)
34	10.5	15.7	1.5	1	2	1	2	5	3	1	3	2	2	VOLOS K1117 (*224*)
35	10.5	15.6	1.5	1	1	1	1	5	3	1	2	2	2	VOLOS K1144 (*223*)
36	12.0	18.2	1.5	1	1	1	2	6	3	1	1	2	2	KAL 5710 (*84*)
37	10.1	14.8	1.5	2	2	1	2	4	2	2	3	2	2	MAR 116 (*167*)
38	8.9	12.8	1.4	1	2	1	2	7	2	2	1	2	2	MAR 115 (*166*)
39	8.8	15.1	1.7	1	2	1	1	7	2	1	1	2	2	SYD 73.03 (*244*)
40	6.9	10.4	1.5	2	3	1	2	6	1	1	1	2	2	LEF 45:3 (*110*)
41	9.8	16.8	1.7	2	3	1	2	6	2	1	1	2	2	DEL 16 (*54*)
42	8.4	13.0	1.5	2	3	1	2	6	2	1	1	2	2	DEL 8 (*46*)
43	7.9	13.4	1.7	2	3	1	2	3	1	1	2	2	2	DEL 4 (*42*)
44	7.3	13.0	1.8	1	3	1	1	4	1	1	1	2	2	DEL 10 (*48*)
45	9.0	13.7	1.5	2	3	3	2	3	2	1	1	2	2	BOS 72.76 (*33*)
46	7.4	12.5	1.7	2	2	3	2	6	1	1	1	2	2	RH A1463 (*189*)
47	7.9	12.6	1.6	2	3	3	2	5	1	1	1	2	2	RH A1464 (*190*)
48	8.0	12.5	1.6	3	3	3	3	9	1	1	1	2	2	RH A1465 (*191*)
49	7.9	12.4	1.6	3	3	3	3	6	1	1	1	2	2	RH A1466 (*192*)
50	7.7	13.0	1.7	2	2	3	2	5	1	1	1	2	2	RH A1467 (*193*)
51	7.5	10.5	1.4	2	3	3	2	4	1	1	1	2	2	DEL 5 (*43*)
52	7.8	12.5	1.6	2	3	3	2	5	1	1	1	2	2	DEL 6 (*44*)
53	7.5	12.6	1.7	1	3	3	1	6	1	1	1	2	2	DEL 7 (*45*)
54	7.5	13.5	1.8	2	3	3	1	6	1	1	1	2	2	DEL 11 (*49*)
55	8.0	11.9	1.5	1	2	3	1	5	1	1	1	2	2	FOGG 116 (*31*)

```
   28   29   30   31   32   33   34   35   36   37   38   39   40   41   42   43   44   45    46   47   48   49   50   51   52   53   54   55
.7  4.9  3.9  4.8  5.9  5.8  4.8  6.8  5.8  4.8  4.9  3.6  3.8  3.6  3.7  5.6  3.5  3.8   2.6  2.7  3.7  3.7  2.6  2.9  2.7  2.6  2.5  2.8
.7  7.9  8.9  6.8  7.9  6.8  5.8  5.8  4.8  8.8  7.9  6.6  5.8  6.6  6.7  7.6  4.5  6.8   5.6  4.7  4.7  4.7  5.6  4.9  4.7  3.6  4.5  4.8
.8  7.9  7.9  7.9  8.9  7.8  6.8  6.9  5.8  7.9  6.9  5.6  5.8  5.6  5.8  7.6  4.5  5.8   5.6  4.7  4.8  4.8  5.6  5.0  4.7  3.6  4.5  4.9
.7  6.8  5.8  4.8  4.8  4.7  4.7  3.8  4.7  6.8  7.8  6.5  4.7  5.5  5.7  4.5  4.5  5.7   4.5  3.6  3.7  3.7  4.5  3.9  3.6  3.5  3.4  4.7
.5  5.6  6.6  6.5  7.6  6.5  5.5  5.5  4.5  5.5  4.6  5.3  5.5  5.3  5.5  6.3  4.3  4.5   5.3  4.4  3.4  3.4  5.3  4.6  4.4  3.3  4.2  4.5
.7  3.9  5.9  4.8  5.9  5.8  4.8  4.8  3.8  4.8  4.9  5.6  3.8  4.6  4.7  5.6  3.5  5.8   4.6  3.7  4.7  4.7  4.6  3.9  3.7  3.6  3.5  4.8
.7  6.8  6.8  6.8  6.8  6.8  6.8  6.8  5.8  6.7  5.8  6.8  7.5  6.8  6.5  6.7  5.6  6.5   6.6  5.7  6.7  6.7  6.6  5.9  5.6  5.6  5.5  6.8
.7  5.8  7.8  5.8  5.8  5.8  5.8  4.8  6.7  5.8  6.8  7.5  6.8  7.5  7.7  4.6  5.5  6.7   7.6  5.7  7.7  8.7  6.6  5.9  5.6  6.6  6.5  6.8
.9  6.9  8.9  7.0  6.9  6.0  6.0  5.0  6.0  7.0  6.9  7.7  7.0  7.7  7.9  5.8  5.7  7.0   6.8  5.9  5.9  5.9  6.8  5.9  5.9  4.8  5.7  6.0
.8  7.0  9.0  6.9  7.0  6.9  6.9  5.9  7.9  6.9  8.0  8.7  7.9  8.8  6.7  6.6  6.9  7.5   5.8  7.8  7.8  6.7  6.0  5.8  6.7  6.6  6.9
.8  7.0  8.0  6.9  7.0  6.9  6.9  5.9  7.9  6.9  8.0  8.7  7.8  8.7  7.8  5.7  6.6  6.9   7.5  5.8  6.8  7.6  6.7  6.0  5.8  6.7  6.6  6.9
.9  8.0  8.0  7.9  9.0  7.9  7.9  6.9  6.9  6.0  6.0  6.7  6.9  6.7  6.9  5.7  6.6  5.9   6.7  6.8  4.8  4.8  7.7  6.0  6.8  4.7  5.6  6.9
.8  6.9  8.9  7.9  9.9  8.8  7.9  9.7  7.8  5.9  4.9  5.6  6.8  6.6  6.8  7.6  5.6  5.8   5.6  6.7  5.8  5.8  6.6  6.0  6.7  4.7  5.5  5.9
.8  7.0  7.0  6.9  8.0  7.9  7.9  6.9  6.8  4.9  5.9  6.6  5.9  5.6  5.8  4.7  5.6  5.8   6.9  6.8  6.7  5.7  5.9  5.8
.9  6.8  7.8  5.8  6.8  6.8  6.8  6.8  5.8  5.9  5.8  6.8  7.9  5.8  6.9  6.9  4.9  5.8   6.9  6.9  7.0  6.9  6.9  7.9  5.7  7.0  5.9  5.8  7.8
.0  6.9  8.9  5.9  6.9  7.0  7.0  5.9  6.0  5.9  6.9  7.8  6.0  6.8  7.0  4.8  5.7  7.0   6.8  6.9  8.0  7.9  7.8  5.8  6.9  5.8  5.7  8.0
.0  5.8  5.8  7.9  6.8  6.9  7.9  8.5  9.5  5.8  6.8  6.9  6.8  7.0  5.9  7.8  5.9  7.8   5.9  5.9  6.0  7.0  7.0  5.9  6.8  6.0  5.9  5.8  5.8
.8  6.9  8.9  7.8  6.9  6.8  6.8  5.9  6.9  6.9  7.8  7.9  7.9  8.6  6.8  7.6  7.5  6.8   6.6  5.7  7.7  7.6  6.6  5.9  5.7  5.6  5.5  6.8
.7  7.0  9.0  7.9  10.0  8.9  7.9  9.9  7.9  5.9  5.0  5.7  6.9  6.7  6.8  7.5  5.6  5.9   5.7  6.8  5.8  5.8  6.7  6.0  6.8  4.7  5.6  5.9
.0  6.8  7.8  6.9  6.8  6.9  6.9  5.9  6.9  6.9  7.8  8.6  6.9  7.8  8.0  5.8  6.7  7.0   6.8  6.0  7.0  7.0  6.8  5.8  5.9  5.9  5.7  6.9
.9  6.8  8.8  6.8  6.8  6.8  6.8  5.8  7.9  6.9  7.8  8.9  7.9  8.9  8.5  5.9  6.8  6.9   7.9  6.0  7.9  8.9  6.5  7.6  6.0  6.9  6.8  6.8
.9  7.0  7.0  8.0  8.0  8.0  8.0  7.0  7.9  6.0  7.0  7.6  7.0  7.0  7.7  6.9  6.7  6.5   6.7  5.8  6.9  6.9  6.7  5.9  5.8  5.7  5.6  7.0
.9  6.9  6.9  8.0  7.9  8.0  8.0  7.0  8.0  6.0  7.9  8.7  7.0  6.7  6.9  5.8  6.7  6.0   6.8  5.9  6.9  6.9  6.8  5.9  5.9  5.8  5.7  7.0
.9  6.5  5.9  6.0  5.9  6.0  7.0  8.0  5.0  5.9  6.7  8.0  6.6  8.7  8.7  7.7  7.6  6.9   6.8  6.9  6.9  6.8  6.8  6.8  6.7  7.0
.6  6.7  5.7  6.8  6.8  6.8  6.8  5.8  8.5  5.8  6.8  6.9  9.8  8.9  8.9  7.9  7.8  6.9   8.9  7.9  7.9  8.9  7.9  7.8  8.0  8.0  7.8  6.8
.8  7.0  6.0  5.9  7.0  6.9  6.9  5.9  6.9  4.9  6.0  5.6  8.9  7.6  7.8  7.7  7.6  7.9   7.7  9.8  8.8  8.8  8.7  9.0  9.8  7.7  7.6  7.9
.9  7.9  8.9  9.0  8.9  8.0  8.0  6.0  8.0  9.0  8.9  8.7  9.0  9.7  9.7  7.6  6.7  8.9   8.8  7.9  5.9  5.9  8.7  7.9  7.8  5.8  6.6  7.0
.0  9.9  7.9  9.6  5.9  9.5  5.9  5.0  8.9  6.6  9.6  9.7  6.8  7.0  5.8  6.6  6.8  6.7   5.0  6.8  5.8  5.9  6.8  5.8  6.7  6.0
.912.0  8.0  6.9  8.0  6.9  6.9  5.9  8.0  8.7  7.7  7.5  6.7  6.9  7.7  7.6  5.9  7.7   7.8  5.8  5.8  8.7  7.0  7.8  6.7  7.6  8.9
.9  8.012.0  8.9  9.0  7.9  8.9  6.9  5.9  9.0  7.0  7.7  6.9  7.7  7.9  6.7  5.6  6.9   6.7  6.8  5.8  5.8  7.7  6.0  6.8  4.7  5.6  6.9
.9  6.9  8.912.0  9.9  9.0  10.0  7.0  7.910.0  7.0  6.7  8.0  7.7  7.9  7.7  6.7  6.9   7.6  6.9  4.9  4.9  7.7  7.9  6.8  4.8  5.6  6.9
.9  8.0  9.0  9.9  12.0  10.0  9.9  8.9  7.9  8.0  7.0  6.7  6.7  7.7  7.7  9.8  7.5  5.6   6.9  7.7  7.8  4.8  8.7  7.0  7.8  4.7  5.6  6.9
.9  6.9  7.9  9.0  10.9  12.0  11.0  10.0  9.0  7.0  7.9  7.7  7.0  6.8  6.9  7.8  6.7  6.0   6.8  6.9  4.9  4.9  7.8  5.9  6.9  5.8  4.7  8.0
.9  6.9  8.910.0  9.911.0  12.0  9.0  9.0  8.0  7.9  7.7  7.0  6.7  6.9  6.8  6.7  6.0   6.8  6.9  4.9  4.9  5.8  4.9  5.9  6.8  5.7  8.0
.9  6.9  6.9  7.0  8.910.0  9.012.0  10.0  5.9  7.7  6.5  7.5  6.8  7.7  5.0  4.8  5.9   4.9  4.9  5.8  4.9  5.9  6.8  5.7  8.0
.0  5.9  5.9  7.9  7.9  9.0  9.0  9.012.0  5.9  7.9  7.8  9.0  8.8  9.0  6.8  7.7  7.0   7.8  6.5  9.6  6.8  6.8  6.9  7.8  6.7  7.0
.9  8.0  9.010.0  8.0  7.0  8.0  5.0  5.912.0  9.0  6.7  6.9  7.7  7.9  6.7  5.6  6.9   6.7  5.8  3.9  3.9  6.7  6.9  5.8  3.7  4.6  5.0
.9  8.0  7.0  7.0  7.0  7.9  7.9  5.9  7.9  9.012.0  9.7  6.9  7.7  7.9  5.6  6.6  6.9   6.7  5.8  4.8  4.8  6.7  5.9  5.8  5.7  4.6  6.9
.8  7.7  7.7  6.7  6.7  7.7  7.7  7.7  7.8  6.7  9.712.0  6.8  8.0  7.8  6.0  8.9  6.8   7.0  5.9  5.8  5.7  7.0  5.6  5.9  8.0  6.9  8.7
.0  7.9  6.9  8.0  7.9  7.0  7.0  6.0  9.0  6.9  6.9  6.812.010.812.0  10.9  9.8  8.7  9.0   9.8  9.9  7.9  8.9  8.8  9.9  9.9  8.8  9.7  7.0
.8  6.7  7.7  7.7  7.6  6.8  6.7  5.7  8.8  7.7  7.7  8.010.812.011.8  9.0  7.9  9.8   9.0  8.9  6.8  7.8  8.0  8.6  8.9  8.0  8.9  5.7
.6  6.8  7.7  9.7  7.9  6.9  6.9  5.9  9.0  7.9  7.810.911.012.0  8.7  7.710.0  8.8   8.7  7.0  8.0  7.0  8.8  8.8  8.9  7.8  8.7  5.8
.8  6.7  6.7  7.7  8.7  7.6  6.8  6.8  6.7  5.7  6.0  9.8  9.0  8.812.0  7.9  8.8  8.0   8.9  6.8  6.9  8.8  8.7  8.9  7.0  7.9  5.8
.7  7.6  5.6  6.7  5.6  6.7  6.7  7.7  7.5  5.6  6.6  8.9  8.7  7.9  7.7  7.912.0  6.7   6.9  7.8  7.8  7.6  6.9  8.6  7.8  9.9  9.0  8.7
.0  5.9  6.9  6.9  6.0  6.0  5.0  7.0  6.9  6.9  8.0  9.810.0  8.8  6.712.0  8.8  8.9   7.9  7.9  8.9  8.9  9.7  8.9  9.7  8.8  8.7  7.0
.8  7.7  6.7  7.7  7.6  6.8  6.8  4.8  7.8  6.7  6.7  7.0  9.9  8.0  8.8  8.0  6.8  12.0   7.9  8.911.0  9.7  9.9  9.0  9.9  8.8
.9  7.8  6.8  6.9  7.8  6.9  6.9  5.9  6.9  5.8  5.8  5.9  9.9  8.9  8.9  8.9  7.8  9.9   9.912.0  9.0  9.010.910.812.0  8.9  9.8  8.9
.0  5.8  5.8  4.9  4.8  4.9  4.9  4.9  5.9  3.9  4.8  5.8  7.9  6.8  7.0  6.8  7.8  7.9   7.9  9.012.011.0  7.9  8.9  9.0  8.9  8.7  7.9
.0  5.8  5.8  4.9  4.8  4.9  4.9  4.9  5.9  3.9  4.8  5.8  8.7  7.8  8.0  6.9  7.8  7.9   7.9  9.011.0  12.0  7.9  8.9  9.9  9.9  7.7  7.9
.8  8.7  7.7  7.7  8.7  7.8  7.5  5.8  6.8  6.7  6.7  7.0  8.8  8.0  7.8  8.0  6.9  8.811.010.7  9.7  7.912.0  9.710.9  8.0  8.9  9.8
.8  7.0  6.0  7.9  7.0  5.9  5.9  4.9  6.8  6.9  5.9  5.6  9.9  8.6  8.8  8.7  8.6  9.8   9.710.8  8.8  8.8  9.712.010.7  8.7  9.6  7.9
.9  7.8  6.8  6.7  7.8  6.9  6.9  5.9  9.8  8.9  8.9  8.9  8.7  7.8  9.9  9.912.0  9.0   9.0  9.010.910.712.0  8.9  9.8  8.9
.8  6.7  4.7  4.8  4.7  5.8  5.8  6.8  7.8  3.7  5.7  8.0  8.8  8.0  7.8  7.0  9.7  7.8   9.0  8.9  9.9  9.9  8.0  8.7  8.912.010.9  9.8
.7  7.6  5.6  5.6  5.6  4.7  4.7  5.7  6.7  4.6  4.6  6.9  9.7  8.9  8.7  7.9  9.0  8.7   9.9  9.8  8.7  9.7  8.9  9.6  9.810.912.0  8.7
.9  8.9  6.9  6.0  6.9  8.0  8.0  8.0  7.0  5.0  6.9  8.7  7.0  5.7  5.9  5.8  8.7  7.0   8.8  8.9  7.9  7.9  9.8  7.9  8.9  9.8  8.712.0
```

MATRIX OF CORRELATION COEFFICIENTS

```
      1    2    3    4    5    6    7    8    9   10   11   12   13   14   15    16   17   18   19   20   21   22   23   24   25   26   27
 1 12.0  7.0  7.9  6.0  4.7  8.0  6.0  4.0  2.8  5.9  5.9  4.9  6.9  5.9  4.6   3.7  7.5  5.0  6.9  5.7  4.6  6.8  6.8  5.8  4.6  3.9  3.8  4
 2  7.0 12.0 10.9  8.0  6.7  7.0  6.0  7.0  7.8  8.9  6.9  5.9  7.9  4.9  5.6   6.7  4.7  8.0  7.9  6.7  7.6  5.8  5.8  4.8  4.6  3.9  7.8  7
 3  7.9 10.9 12.0  6.9  6.6  5.9  5.9  5.9  6.8  8.0  5.9  6.9  9.0  6.0  4.7   5.8  5.7  7.0  8.9  5.8  6.7  6.9  6.9  4.8  4.7  4.0  6.9  7
 4  6.0  8.0  6.9 12.0  6.7  6.0  7.0  6.0  7.7  7.8  7.8  7.3  3.9  5.9  6.6   5.7  5.6  6.9  3.8  7.7  6.6  6.8  6.8  6.7  6.4  6.3  6.8  5
 5  4.7  6.7  6.6  6.7 12.0  5.7  8.7  4.7  7.5  5.6  6.6  8.6  6.6  5.6  5.4   4.5  5.4  5.7  6.6  6.4  5.4  6.5  6.5  5.5  4.4  3.6  7.5  5
 6  8.0  7.0  5.9  6.0  5.7 12.0  7.0  8.0  4.8  7.9  7.9  4.9  4.9  7.9  8.6   7.7  5.7  7.0  4.9  7.7  6.6  6.8  6.8  4.8  4.6  5.9  5.8  3
 7  6.0  6.0  5.9  7.0  8.7  7.0 12.0  8.0  6.8  8.9  9.9  7.8  5.9  8.9  8.6   7.8  8.7  9.0  5.9  9.7  8.6  9.8  9.7  7.6  6.9  8.8  5
 8  4.0  7.0  5.9  6.0  4.7  8.0  8.0 12.0  7.8  9.9  9.5  5.8  5.9  8.9  9.6  10.7  6.7 10.9  5.9  8.7 10.6  7.8  7.5  5.8  7.6  7.9  7.8  4
 9  2.8  7.8  6.8  7.7  7.5  4.8  6.8  7.8 12.0  8.9  7.9  8.9  6.9  5.9  6.8   8.0  5.9  8.8  6.9  7.9  8.8  7.0  7.0  6.0  5.8  4.9  9.0  5
10  5.9  8.9  8.0  7.8  5.6  7.9  8.9  9.9  8.9 12.0 10.0  7.0  7.0  8.0  8.7   9.8  7.8 10.9  7.0  9.8 10.7  8.9  8.9  6.9  7.7  7.0  8.9  5
11  5.9  6.9  5.9  7.8  6.6  7.9  9.9  9.5  7.9 10.0 12.0  8.0  5.9  9.0  9.7   8.9  8.8  9.9  6.0 10.8 10.9  9.9  9.7  9.8  8.7  7.0  8.9  5
12  4.9  5.9  6.9  8.6  4.9  7.8  5.8  5.8  8.9  7.0  8.0 12.0  7.9  7.9  7.8   6.9  7.8  6.9  8.0  7.8  6.9  9.0  8.9  6.9  5.7  6.0  7.9  5
13  6.9  7.9  9.0  3.9  6.6  4.9  5.9  5.9  6.9  7.0  5.9  7.9 12.0  7.0  5.7   6.8  7.8  7.0 11.9  5.8  6.7  6.9  6.9  6.8  5.7  6.0  6.9  5
14  5.9  4.9  6.0  5.9  5.6  7.9  8.9  8.9  5.9  8.0  9.0  7.9  7.0 12.0 10.7   9.8  8.9  7.9  7.0  8.7  7.9  9.9  9.6  6.9  6.9  6.9  4
15  4.6  5.6  4.7  6.6  5.4  8.6  8.6  9.6  6.8  8.7  9.7  7.8  5.7 10.7 12.0  10.9  7.9  8.7  5.7  9.9  9.0  8.8  8.6  8.7  7.0  8.7  7.8  4
16  3.7  6.7  5.8  5.7  4.5  7.7  7.7 10.7  8.0  9.8  8.9  6.9  6.8  9.8 10.9  12.0  6.9  9.8  6.9  9.0  9.9  7.9  7.9  6.0  6.9  8.8  7.9  5
17  7.7  4.7  5.7  5.6  5.4  5.7  8.7  6.7  5.9  7.8  8.8  7.8  7.8  8.7  7.9   6.9 12.0  8.7  7.8  9.0  7.9  9.9  9.9  9.8  9.7  9.6  8.6  6.9  5
18  5.0  8.0  7.0  6.9  5.7  7.0  9.0 10.0  8.8 10.9  9.6  6.7  7.0  7.9  8.7   9.8  8.7 12.0  6.9  9.7 10.7  8.8  8.8  6.8  7.6  6.9  8.8  5
19  6.9  7.9  8.9  3.8  6.4  4.9  5.9  5.9  6.9  7.0  6.0  8.0 11.9  7.0  5.7   6.9  7.8  6.9 12.0  5.8  6.8  6.9  6.9  6.9  5.7  6.0  6.9  5
20  5.7  6.7  5.8  7.7  6.4  7.9  9.7  8.7  7.9  9.8 10.8  7.8  5.8  8.9  9.9   9.0  9.0  9.7  5.8 12.0  9.9  9.9  9.7  7.9  7.9  6.8  8.9  6
21  4.6  7.6  6.7  6.6  5.4  6.6  8.6 10.6  8.8 10.7 10.8  6.8  6.7  7.7  9.0   9.7  9.9 10.7  6.8  9.9 12.0  8.8  8.6  8.9  9.0  6.7  8.8  5
22  6.8  5.8  6.9  6.8  6.5  6.8  9.7  8.7  7.0  8.9  9.9  9.0  6.9  9.9  9.8   7.9  9.9  8.8  6.9  9.9  8.8 12.0 11.0  8.0  7.8  6.9  8.0  5
23  6.8  5.8  6.9  6.8  6.5  6.8  9.7  7.8  7.0  8.9  9.7  8.9  6.9  9.6  8.6   7.9  9.9  8.8  6.9  9.7  8.6 11.0 12.0  8.0  7.8  6.9  8.0  5
24  5.8  4.8  4.8  6.7  5.5  4.8  7.8  5.8  6.0  6.9  7.9  6.9  6.8  6.9  6.8   6.0  8.9  6.8  6.9  7.9  6.8  8.0  8.0 12.0  7.8  6.9  7.0  5
25  4.6  4.6  4.7  4.6  4.4  4.6  7.6  7.5  5.8  7.7  8.7  5.7  5.7  6.7  7.0   6.9  9.7  6.5  5.7  7.9  9.0  7.8  7.8 12.0  8.7  7.8  5
26  3.9  3.9  4.0  3.8  3.6  5.9  6.9  7.9  4.9  7.0  7.0  6.0  6.0  9.0  8.7   8.8  6.8  6.9  6.0  6.7  6.9  6.9  9.8 12.0  6.9  4
27  3.8  7.8  6.9  6.8  7.5  5.8  8.8  7.8  9.0  8.9  8.9  7.9  6.9  6.9  7.8   7.9  6.9  8.8  6.9  8.9  8.8  8.0  8.0  7.0  7.8  6.9 12.0  6
28  4.7  7.7  7.8  5.7  5.5  3.7  5.7  4.7  5.9  5.8  5.8  5.9  5.8  4.8  4.9   5.0  5.0  5.8  5.8  6.0  5.9  6.9  5.9  5.9  5.9  5.4  4.8  6.9 12
29  4.7  9.7  9.8  6.8  5.6  3.9  6.8  5.5  8.6  7.0  7.0  6.8  6.9  5.8  6.8   6.9  5.9  7.0  6.8  6.9  6.9  5.9  5.7  7.0  7.9  9
30  3.9  8.9  7.9  5.8  6.6  5.9  6.8  7.8  8.9  9.0  8.0  8.0  6.9  7.8  8.8   7.0  8.8  7.0  6.9  6.9  5.9  5.7  6.0  8.9  7
31  4.8  6.8  7.9  4.8  6.5  4.8  6.8  5.8  7.0  6.9  6.9  7.9  7.9  6.9  5.8   5.9  7.9  7.8  7.9  6.9  6.8  8.0  8.0  6.0  6.8  5.9  9.0  7
32  5.9  7.8  8.9  4.8  7.6  5.9  6.8  5.8  6.9  7.0  7.0  9.0  9.9  8.0  6.8   6.9  6.9 10.0  6.8  6.8  8.0  7.9  5.9  6.8  7.0  8.9  6
33  5.8  6.8  7.8  4.7  6.5  5.8  6.8  6.0  6.9  6.9  7.9  8.8  7.9  6.8  7.0   6.9  6.8  7.9  6.9  6.8  8.0  8.0  6.0  6.8  6.9  8.05
34  4.8  5.8  6.8  4.7  5.5  4.8  6.8  5.8  6.0  6.9  6.9  7.9  7.9  7.9  6.8   7.0  6.9  6.8  7.9  6.9  6.8  8.0  8.0  6.0  6.8  6.9  8.06
35  6.8  5.8  6.9  3.8  5.5  4.8  5.8  4.8  5.0  5.9  5.9  5.6  9.9  6.5  5.8   5.9  7.9  5.8  9.9  5.5  5.8  7.0  7.0  5.8  6.0  6.05
36  5.8  4.8  5.8  4.7  4.5  3.8  6.7  6.7  6.9  6.6  6.8  7.9  6.9  7.0  6.8   5.9  6.0  8.9  6.9  6.9  7.9  8.0  8.0  8.6  6.9  8.05
37  4.8  8.7  7.9  6.7  5.5  4.8  5.8  5.7  7.0  6.9  6.9  6.0  5.9  4.9  5.8   5.9  5.9  7.8  5.9  6.9  6.8  6.0  6.0  5.0  5.8  4.9  9.08
38  4.9  7.9  6.9  7.8  4.6  4.9  6.8  6.8  6.9  8.0  8.0  6.0  4.9  5.9  6.8   6.9  5.8  7.9  5.0  7.8  7.8  7.0  7.9  5.9  6.8  6.0  8.96
39  3.6  6.6  5.6  6.5  5.3  5.6  7.5  7.5  7.7  8.6  8.7  6.5  5.6  6.6  7.9   7.8  6.8  8.6  5.7  8.8  8.9  8.7  8.7  6.7  6.9  5.6  8.76
40  3.8  5.8  5.8  4.7  5.5  3.8  6.8  6.8  7.0  7.9  7.9  6.6  5.9  5.9  6.0   6.8  6.8  6.9  7.9  9.6  6.9  7.0  8.0  9.8  8.9  9.07
41  3.6  6.6  5.6  5.5  5.3  4.6  6.5  7.5  7.7  7.6  8.7  6.7  6.6  5.6  6.9   6.8  6.8  7.6  6.7  7.8  8.9  6.7  6.7  6.8  8.9  7.6  9.75
42  3.7  6.7  5.8  5.7  5.5  4.7  6.7  7.7  7.9  7.8  8.8  6.9  6.9  5.7  7.6   7.0  7.0  6.8  8.0  8.9  6.9  6.9  6.9  8.9  7.6  7.6
43  5.6  7.6  7.6  4.6  4.5  3.5  5.6  5.4  5.8  6.7  5.7  5.7  7.6  4.7  4.9   4.8  5.9  5.6  7.7  5.8  5.9  5.7  5.8  6.7  7.9  7.7  7.76
44  3.5  4.5  4.5  4.3  4.3  3.5  6.5  5.5  6.6  6.6  6.5  5.6  5.6  5.6  5.8   5.7  7.8  7.5  5.6  6.7  6.8  6.6  6.7  7.7  7.8  7.6  6.76
45  3.8  6.8  5.8  5.7  4.5  5.8  5.7  6.7  7.0  7.9  6.9  5.9  5.8  5.8  6.9   7.0  5.9  6.8  5.9  7.0  6.9  5.9  6.0  6.0  6.9  7.9  8.95
46  2.6  5.6  5.6  4.5  5.3  4.6  6.7  7.6  6.8  6.7  7.6  6.5  6.6  6.9  6.8   6.5  8.6  5.7  6.8  6.0  6.0  5.8  5.9  6.7  9.9  8.9  7.86
47  2.7  4.7  4.7  3.6  3.4  3.7  5.7  5.7  5.8  5.8  6.8  6.7  6.8  7.0  6.9   6.0  5.7  6.8  6.0  6.0  5.8  5.9  6.7  9.9  9.8  7.95
48  3.7  4.7  4.8  3.7  3.4  4.7  6.7  7.7  5.9  7.8  6.4  4.8  5.8  6.8  6.9   8.0  7.0  7.7  5.8  7.0  7.9  6.9  6.9  6.9  7.9  8.5  5.9
49  3.7  4.7  4.8  3.7  3.4  4.7  6.7  8.7  5.9  7.8  7.4  4.8  5.8  6.8  6.9   7.9  7.0  7.5  5.8  7.0  8.9  6.9  6.9  6.9  8.9  8.85
50  2.6  5.6  5.6  4.5  5.3  4.6  6.6  6.6  6.8  6.7  7.6  6.7  7.6  6.6  7.7   7.9  7.8  5.9  6.6  6.7  6.8  6.9  6.7  6.8  7.9  8.7  8.86
51  2.9  4.9  5.0  3.9  4.6  3.9  5.9  5.9  5.9  6.0  6.0  6.0  6.0  6.0  5.7   5.8  6.8  6.9  6.0  5.8  5.7  5.9  5.9  6.9  7.9  9.0  7.95
52  2.7  4.7  4.7  3.6  4.4  3.7  5.6  5.6  5.9  5.8  5.8  6.8  6.7  6.7  7.0   6.9  6.0  5.7  6.8  5.9  6.0  5.8  5.9  6.9  8.0  9.8  7.85
53  2.6  3.6  3.6  3.5  3.3  3.6  5.6  6.6  4.8  5.7  6.7  4.7  4.7  5.7  5.9   5.8  5.9  5.6  4.7  5.9  6.9  5.7  5.8  6.8  8.0  7.7  5.8
54  2.5  4.5  4.5  3.4  4.2  3.5  5.5  6.5  5.7  5.6  6.5  5.6  5.5  5.6  5.8   5.7  5.8  5.5  5.6  5.7  6.8  5.6  5.7  6.7  7.8  7.6  6.6
55  2.8  4.8  4.9  4.7  4.5  4.8  6.8  6.8  6.0  6.9  6.9  6.9  5.9  7.9  7.8   8.0  5.9  6.8  5.9  6.9  6.8  7.0  7.0  7.0  6.8  7.9  7.0
```

APPENDIX 2

It may appear that there are wide differences between the ratios of sky-phoi in any single Type. For this reason the following aims to demonstrate how even such a small error in measurement as 0.3cm can have a great effect on the resulting ratio:

(a) **Delphi 5909** *58:* Ht 12.0cm; Diameter of rim 16.0cm .

The maximum ratio can be found by adding 0.3 to the diameter of rim and subtracting 0.3 from the height, thus

16.3 ÷ 11.7 = 1.39 (the maximum ratio assuming a measuring error of 0.3cm).

The minimum ratio is similarly found: subtract 0.3 from the diameter of rim and add 0.3 to the height, hence

15.7 ÷ 12.3 = 1.27.

So a 10 percent change in the ratios results from a 0.3 error in any measurement among the larger skyphoi. And the change resulting from the same error margin in smaller skyphoi is approximately double.

(b) **Chalcis 1385** *30:* Ht 6.7cm; diameter of rim 11.0cm.

Maximum ratio 11.3 ÷ 6.4 = 1.77

Minimum ratio 10.7 ÷ 7.0 = 1.53

A 20 percent change in the ratio results from a 0.3cm error in any measurement among the smaller skyphoi.

(A measuring error of only 0.2cm results in a change of 8 percent in the ratios of large skyphoi and 15 percent in smaller ones).

Therefore a 20 percent change in the ratios of skyphoi of any given Type may be due to measuring error of these orders.

200

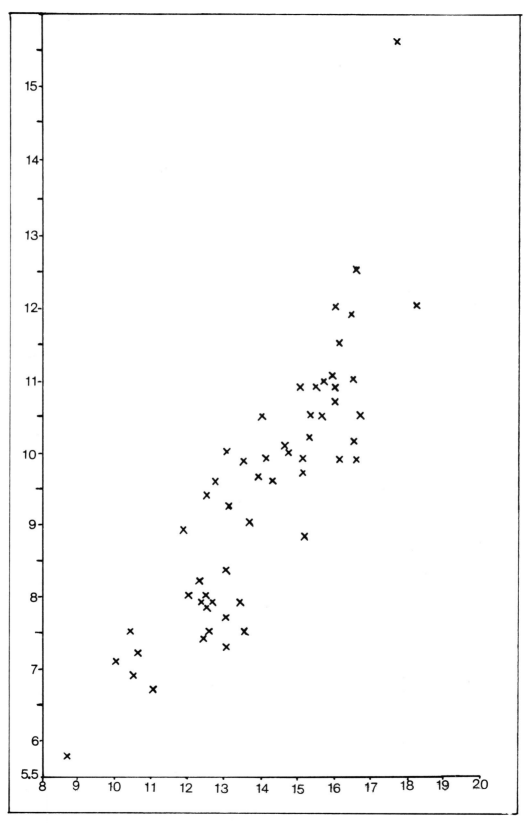

Diagram 2   Relationship of Diameter of Rim to Height of Vessel

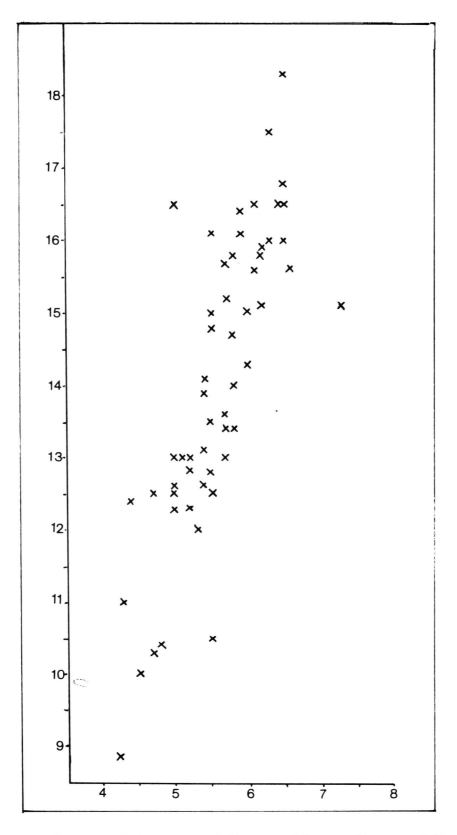

Diagram 3   Relationship of Diameter of Base to Diameter of Rim

INDEX OF COLLECTIONS

This index is comprehensive only for pendent semicircle skyphoi used in the typology but other material is included whenever possible. Geometric pottery from Al Mina which is referred to in the text and footnotes is listed also. Most references are to catalogue numbers, a minority are to page numbers.

DELPHI MUSEUM

ERETRIA MUSEUM

1955.4-22.4	*3*
1955.4-22.5	*4*
1955.4-22.8	*5*
1955.4-22.9	*6*
1955.4-22.10	*7*
1955.4-22.11	*8*
1955.4-22.6	Chapter 2 *Al Mina:* wall fr. = Robertson Chapter 2 *1* Fig.1 e.
1955.4-22.8 (This number has been allocated to two separate fragments. See *5* above).	Chapter 2 *Al Mina*: wall fr. = Robertson Chapter 2 *1* Fig.1 f.
1968.3-25.150	Chapter 8 n.39

LONDON, UNIVERSITY COLLEGE

Inv. 720	*246*

MANISA MUSEUM

Sardis	*198*

MITYLENE MUSEUM

Antissa	*21*

MYKONOS MUSEUM

Inv. 20 (=A1466)	*192*
21 (=A1464)	*190*
22 (=A1467)	*193*
23 (=A1468)	*194*
24 (=A1465)	*191*
25 (=A1463)	*189*
733	*42*
734	*50*
736	*43*
737	*49*
739	*51*

OXFORD, ASHMOLEAN MUSEUM

K1355	*88*
K1356	*89*
K1357	*90*
K1358	*91*
K1359	*92*
K1360	*93*
K2235	*178*
K2237	*179*
K2247	*200*
K3022	*22*

UNIVERSITY OF NEWCASTLE-UPON-TYNE 689 (formerly Wellcome Foundation R1936/1108)

Cyprus	*39*

INDEX OF SKYPHOI

214

Delphi 5909	58	25,79,84, 86,106-8, 112,119-21, 163,199
Delphi 1957	59	25,79,97
Delphi no number	60	27,79,93
Delphi no number	61	27,79,94
Delphi no number	62	27,79-81
Delphi no number	63	28,79,129
Delphi no number	64	28
Delphi no number	—	79
Didyma	65	28
Donousa	66	28
Emporio	67	28,90
Eretria FK E/8 B640	68	29,77-8,80, 104,127
Eretria FK E/8 B650	69	29,77-8, 104,127, 143
Eretria FK E/8 B639	70	29,77-8, 104,127-8, 133
Eretria no number	71	29,77-8, 104,127
Eretria no number	72	29,77-8, 104,127-8, 133
Eretria FK 1643.19	73	29,104,173
Eretria FK 3038.1	74	30,173
Gortyn	75	31,77-8
Hama 7B23	76	31,99-100, 128,148, 194
Hama L941	77	32,99-100, 128,148
Hama 6A290	78	32,99-100, 148
Hama 8A189	79	32,100,148, 194
Iasos	80	33
Ibn Hani	81	33
Ikaria	82	33
Iolcos	83	33
Kalamaria 5710	84	34,78-81, 93-4,119, 121
Kalamaria 4714	85	35,78-80, 99-100, 137,150
Kalapodhi	86	35,99-100
Kapakli 55	—	151
Kapakli 56	87	35,78-81, 90,93,121
Kapakli 57	88	35,78-81, 90,93
Kapakli 58	89	36,78-80, 87,89,106, 121,141

Lefkandi-Xeropolis (Levelling)	*162*	51,97
Lefkandi-Xeropolis (Levelling)	*163*	52,104,142
Lefkandi-Xeropolis (Levelling)	*164*	52,104,142
Lefkandi Br.School no number	*165*	52,77-78,93
Lefkandi Br.School no number	–	77-78
Marmariani 115	*166*	52,78,81, 94-5,119 –21,123-4, 165
Marmariani 116	*167*	52,78,80-1, 94-5,119, 140
Marmariani 117	*168*	53
Marmariani 118	*169*	53,78,81, 86,112
Marmariani 119	*170*	53,78,81, 90,93
Marmariani 120	*171*	54,78,81, 87,89
Marmariani 121	*172*	54,78,81, 84,86,119- 21
Marmariani 122	*173*	54,78,81, 86,107
Marmariani (Copenhagen NM 7025)	*174*	54,93-4, 107,112
Mersin	*175*	54
Methymna	*176*	55,100,141
Naxos	*177*; Addenda *8*	55,193
Nea Ionia, Volos K2235	*178*	55,78,83, 93-4,119 –21,124,141
Nea Ionia, Volos K2237	*179*	56,78,83, 87,89,121
Nineveh	*180*	56
Orchomenos	*181*	56,95
Palekythro	*182*	56,171
Paros	*183*	57
Phaistos	*184*	57
Phocaea	*185*	57
Phthiotic Thebes	*186*	57
Pontecagnano	Addenda *9*	193
Pteleon	*187*	57
Ras el Bassit	*188*	58,
Rheneia Mykonos 25 (= A1463)	*189*	58,78,81 99-100,107
Rheneia Mykonos 21 (= A1464)	*190*	59,78,81, 99-100,107, 119,123
Rheneia Mykonos 24 (= A1465)	*191*	59,78,81, 99-100,107
Rheneia Mykonos 20 (= A1466)	*192*	59,78,81, 99-100,107
Rheneia Mykonos 22 (= A1467)	*193*	59,78,81, 99-100,107
Rheneia Mykonos 23 (= A1468)	*194*	60,78,80-1, 99-100,107
Salamis 106	*195*	60,99-100, 127

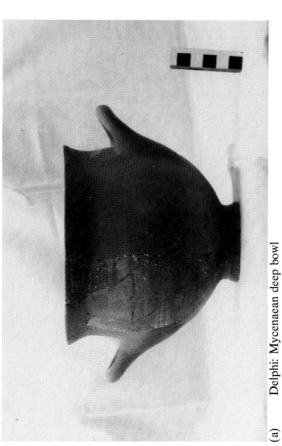

(a)   Delphi: Mycenaean deep bowl

(b)   Tenos Kardiani T.III 3 (96)

(c)   Delphi 5909 (58)

(d)   Athens NM Marmariani 121 (172)

PLATE 1.

(a-b)   Thessaloniki 4647 Chauchitsa (31)

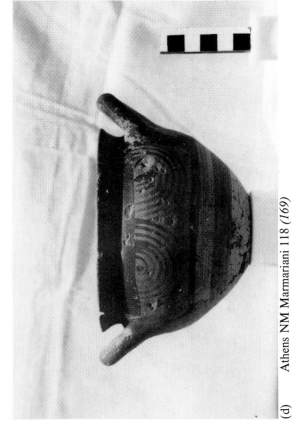

(d)   Athens NM Marmariani 118 (169)

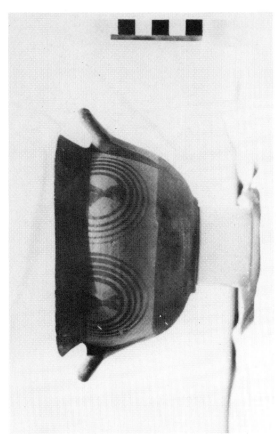

(c)   Athens NM Marmariani 122 (173)

PLATE 2.

(b) Volos K3022 Argyopouli Tirnavou (22)

(d) Athens NM Marmariani 120 (171)

PLATE 3.

(a) Tenos B79 Kardiani (95)

(c) Volos K2247 Sesklo (200)

(a) Volos K1354 Kapakli 56 (87)

(b) Volos K1355 Kapakli 57 (88)

(c) Athens NM Marmariani 119 (170)

(d) Volos K1352 Larisa (106)

PLATE 4.

(a)   Volos K1356 Kapakli 58 (*89*)

(b)   Volos 2237 Nea Ionia (*179*)

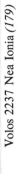

(c)   Volos K2235 Nea Ionia (*178*)

(d)   Volos K1358 Kapakli 60 (*91*)

PLATE 5.

(b) Volos K1359 Kapakli 61 (92)

(d) Volos K1117 Thessaly (224)

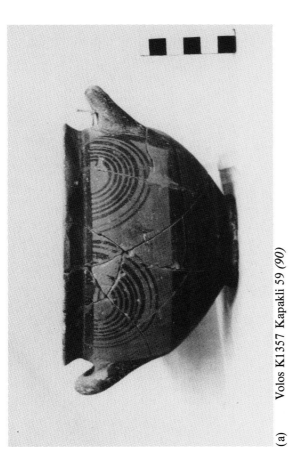

(a) Volos K1357 Kapakli 59 (90)

(c) Volos K1144 Thessaly (223)

PLATE 6.

(b) Athens NM Marmariani 115 (166)

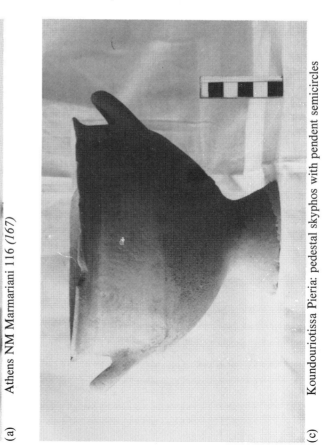

(d) Volos K1360 Kapakli 63 (93)

(a) Athens NM Marmariani 116 (167)

(c) Koundouriotissa Pieria: pedestal skyphos with pendent semicircles

PLATE 7.

(a)   Sydney Nicholson Museum 73.03 (244)

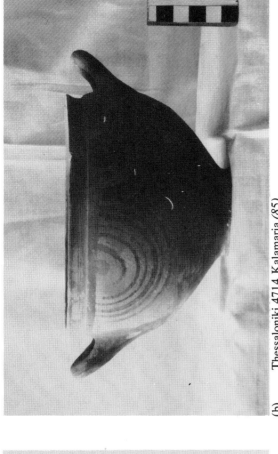

(b)   Thessaloniki 4714 Kalamaria (85)

(c)   Mykonos 755 Delos 16 (54)

(d)   Mykonos 752 Delos 6 (44)

PLATE 8.

PLATE 9.

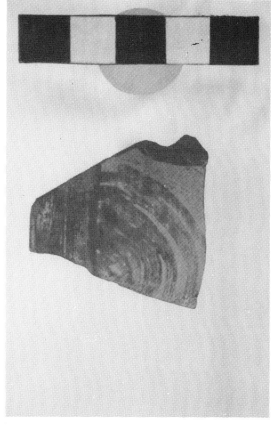

(a) Oxford 1954.271/12 Al Mina (*14a*)

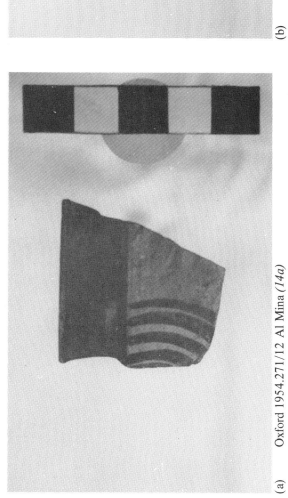

(c) Oxford 1954.271/7 Al Mina: lekanis

(b) Oxford 1954.271/13 Al Mina (*14b*)

(d) Athens, British School, Lefkandi no no. (*165*)

UNIVERSITY OF LONDON

INSTITUTE OF CLASSICAL STUDIES

PUBLICATIONS

BULLETIN NUMBER 34 (1987): ESSAYS ON GREEK DRAMA Ed. B. Gredley.
ISSN 0076-0730. £22.50.

BULLETIN NUMBER 35 (1988). ISSN 0076-0730. £22.50.

CULTS OF BOIOTIA, Fascicle 2 — Herakles to Poseidon By Albert Schachter (1986). Bulletin Supplement Number 38. Fascicle 3 in preparation. Fascicles 1 and 4 available. SBN 900587 41 5. 1 £20, 2 £25, 4 £10.

RESOLUTIONS AND CHRONOLOGY IN EURIPIDES: The Fragmentary Tragedies By Martin Cropp and Gordon Fick (1985). Bulletin Supplement Number 43. SBN 900587 46 6. £15.

PROLEGOMENA TO CLAUDIAN By J. B. Hall (1986). Bulletin Supplement Number 45. SBN 900587 49 0. £30.

GREEK MANUSCRIPTS OF THE ANCIENT WORLD By E. G. Turner. Second edition revised and enlarged , edited by P. J. Parsons (1987). Bulletin Supplement Number 46. SBN 900587 48 2. £30.

GREEK BOOKHANDS OF THE EARLY BYZANTINE PERIOD: AD 300-800 By G. Cavallo and H. Maehler (1987). Bulletin Supplement Number 47. SBN 900587 51 2. £30.

SOPATROS THE RHETOR By Michael Winterbottom and Doreen Innes (1988). Bulletin Supplement Number 48. SBN 900587 54 7. £30.

THE CREATIVE POET: Studies on the Treatment of Myths in Greek Poetry By Jennifer R. March (1987). Bulletin Supplement Number 49. SBN 900587 52 0. £25.

VIR BONUS DISCENDI PERITUS: Studies in Celebration of Otto Skutsch's Eightieth Birthday (1988). Bulletin Supplement Number 51. SBN 900587 55 5. £30.

ROMAN MYTH AND MYTHOGRAPHY By. J. N. Bremmer and N. M. Horsfall (1987). Bulletin Supplement Number 52. SBN 900587 53 9. £20.

GREEK AND LATIN PAPYROLOGY By Italo Gallo, translated by Maria Rosaria Falivene and Jennifer R. March (1986). Bulletin Supplement Number 54, Classical Handbook 1. SBN 900587 50 4. £9.

Supplements in preparation:

MONUMENTS ILLUSTRATING NEW COMEDY Third edition. By A. Seeberg and J. R. Green. Bulletin Supplement 50.

DEATH, WOMEN AND THE SUN By Lucy Goodison. Bulletin Supplement Number 53. SBN 900587 56 3.

THE GREEK RENAISSANCE IN THE ROMAN EMPIRE: PAPERS FROM THE TENTH BRITISH MUSEUM CLASSICAL COLLOQUIUM (2 vols) Edited by Susan Walker and Averil Cameron. Bulletin Supplement Number 55.

PLUTARCH: *LIFE OF KIMON* Edited, with translation and commentary, by A. Blamire. Bulletin Supplement Number 56, Classical Handbook 2. SBN 900587 57 1.

THE HEROES OF ATTICA By Emily Kearns. Bulletin Supplement Number 57.

Full details of these and other Publications are available from:

Institute of Classical Studies
31-34 Gordon Square
London WC1H OPY